CANADIAN STUDIES IN CRIMINOLOGY

Reproducing Order:
A Study of
Police Patrol Work

Richard V. Ericson

Published in association with
the Centre of Criminology,
University of Toronto, by
UNIVERSITY OF TORONTO PRESS
Toronto   Buffalo   London

© University of Toronto Press 1982
Toronto Buffalo London
Printed in Canada
Reprinted 1984, 1988

ISBN 0-8020-5569-9 (cloth)
ISBN 0-8020-6475-2 (paper)

Canadian Cataloguing in Publication Data

Ericson, Richard V., 1948–
    Reproducing order
    (Canadian studies in criminology; 5)
    Bibliography: p.
    Includes index.
    ISBN 0-8020-5569-9 (bound). – ISBN 0-8020-6475-2 (pbk.)
    1. Police patrol – Canada. 2. Police patrol –
    Canada – Case studies.   I. University of Toronto.
    Centre of Criminology.   II. Title.   III. Series.
    HV8080.P2E75   363.2'32   C82-094167-0

To Tony
For his good sense of humour
and his keen sense of order

Contents

Tables

Acknowledgments

The research reported in this book would not have been possible without the co-operation of many organizations and people.

Access to police activity was provided through an agreement with the police commission in the jurisdiction studied. The chief of police deserves special mention for encouraging the project and 'paving the way' through the various levels of the force. I also acknowledge the co-operation of the senior officers who helped us as we embarked upon the fieldwork. I am extremely grateful to the patrol officers who allowed us to observe their activities; more than anyone else, they provided the substance of this book.

Successive directors of the Centre of Criminology, University of Toronto, deserve special mention. Everyone who is now at the centre is indebted to John Edwards for having created an active research environment. Gordon Watson assisted in initiating the research program of which this study is a part and co-ordinated the research in its earlier phases. Anthony Doob, the current director, has been extremely supportive at several key stages in the project, providing strong intellectual and moral support.

Many colleagues participated in the data collection process, including Hans Helder, Dianne Macfarlane, Patrick Mulloy, Carol Pitcher-LaPrairie, Peter Turner, and Livy Visano. In data analysis I was ably assisted by Janet Chan, Bob Gebotys, and Birthe Jorgensen. Lynn Bailey has made a substantial contribution in many ways, including the trying task of keeping all the research documents in order and typing the successive drafts of this manuscript. Marie Pearce and Marbeth Greer have also ably assisted in typing the manuscript.

I am extremely grateful to James Wilkins for access to his research materials on the work of crown attorneys, and to Dianne Macfarlane for access to her interview material with lawyers who became involved in cases described in this book.

Many persons have influenced this book by commenting on earlier drafts. At one or more stages I have benefited from the comments of David Bayley, Anthony Doob, David Downes, James Giffen, John Hagan, Hans Helder, John Hogarth, Peter Manning, the late Pauline Morris, Albert Reiss, Paul Rock, Peter Solomon, and James Wilkins; a representative of the police force studied; and two anonymous reviewers.

In writing a revised version of this manuscript, I have benefited from the scholarly environment that comes with being a visiting fellow at Churchill College, Cambridge, and the Institute of Criminology, University of Cambridge.

I appreciate the editorial direction provided by Virgil Duff and the editing skills of John Parry. I also acknowledge the assistance of Dianna Ericson in preparing the index.

The research for this book was supported by substantial grants from the Donner Foundation, the University of Toronto, and especially the Social Sciences and Humanties Research Council. I wish to express my gratitude to these organizations. This book has been published with the help of grants from the Social Science Federation of Canada, using funds provided by the Social Sciences and Humanities Research Council of Canada, and from the Publications Fund of University of Toronto Press.

To all those who have contributed to my work, thank you. I trust you will conclude it was worth it.

RVE

REPRODUCING ORDER

1

The Police as Reproducers of Order

Policing: Expansive and Expensive

Police forces funded by government are a fact of life. The acceleration of their growth and the dispersal of their activities are now so widespread we tend to forget that the modern policing system has been in existence only 150 years. Before that, policing and crime control were mainly in the hands of the 'private' sector (cf Beattie, 1981).

The new police system was not introduced and accepted overnight. At least in Britain, the new police had to work constantly at establishing their legitimacy. There was a general cultural resistance to plainclothes detectives of any type (Moylan, 1929; Miller, 1979; Ericson, 1981: chapter 1), and uniformed officers only gained acceptance via 'tacit contracts' with local populations whereby they used their discretion in law enforcement in exchange for the co-operation of citizens in matters that served the interests of the police and the state (Cohen, 1979; Ignatieff, 1979). As front-line agents in the 'reproduction of social order,' the police eventually gained acceptance and established systematic patterns of operation on this micro-level of every-day transactions with the citizenry. Indeed, they set out to do this from the beginning, after repeated governmental failures in using military force to handle disorder (Silver, 1967).

The legitimacy of modern policing, and its success at keeping intact the glass menagerie of social order, continue to rely first and foremost on this micro-level. However, as policing has evolved it has also entered into other arenas of 'legitimation work.' In keeping with the general trend in modern organizations, police forces have been made professional and bureaucratic. Criteria of efficiency and effectiveness have evolved, particularly in 'crime' work, and these criteria are used in 'selling' the organization to the community.

As we will consider in more detail, the police have been assigned, and have taken on, an impossible responsibility for controlling crime as the key indicator of their success at reproducing order (Manning, 1971, 1977). Regardless of their success in other respects, they have been successful in using their crime work to increase their resources and the dispersal of their activities. Their 'product' of crime control is conveniently elastic, carries a virtuous ring, and cannot be easily assailed: who can deny a people's desire for peace and security, or at least for a *feeling* of security?

There can be no doubt that recent decades have witnessed a major trans-formation in police organizations in terms of size and resources. In the past three decades in Ontario, for example, the trend has been toward fewer, but larger, more bureaucractic, and more centrally controlled, police forces. In the Toronto area each municipality previously had a separate police force, but these were amalgamated to form the Metropolitan Toronto Police Force in 1957. In the 1970s, several regional municipalities were formed in Ontario, and with them came the amalgamation of many small municipal forces into large, bureaucratic regional forces. Furthermore, many small rural munici-palities disbanded their own police forces in favour of using the large, centralized Ontario Provincial Police force. In Ontario in 1962 there were 278 municipal police forces. By 1975 there were only 128.

This trend has been duplicated in other Canadian provinces, and in Britain. Always the argument is that bigger is better (and maybe cheaper). Moreover, whenever a small municipality clings to at least the feeling of autonomy that comes with maintaining its own police force, it is subject to continuing and various pressures to conform with the trend to larger units (Murphy, 1981). If police officers in these small forces are caught by allega-tions of wrongdoing, the central authorities argue that such things are almost inevitable in forces of this type and that the obvious cure is to take them over as part of a larger regional or provincial policing unit (e.g. 'Tillsonburg Police Probe Ordered,' *Toronto Star*, September 30, 1980). The authorities appar-ently do not stop to think about the fact that large regional, metropolitan, and national police forces have also experienced continuing, sometimes systematic, wrongdoings by their officers.[1]

At the same time that police forces have expanded through amalgama-tion, they have also multiplied their manpower and technological resources. Spending on the police in Canada increased at a level far outstripping the rate of inflation (Solicitor General of Canada, 1979). This increase is greater than that in other segments of the system of crime control, and the recent rate of growth is also greater than in other areas of government 'welfare' spending (Chan and Ericson, 1981). Between 1962 and 1977 the number of police personnel per 1,000 population increased 65 per cent from 1.7 to 2.8 (Stat-istics Canada, *Police Administration Statistics*, 1962 to 1977). While this enormous expansion has been accompanied by greater degrees of specialization in police services, most of this growth has been in patrol policing.[2]

Given this expansion of the police, one would expect to find some basic research on obvious questions: How do the police spend their time? What do they concentrate on and what do they ignore? How do they accomplish their results in dealings with the public? Whose interests are served by these outcomes? What does all of this tell us about the role of the police? What wider functions of the police can be theorized from this?

There is an evolving research tradition that focuses upon these general questions. However, this research is largely American, with a few British studies and virtually no Canadian studies. This book, and the research upon which it is based, are aimed at addressing these questions in the Canadian context. The main vehicle for doing this is the use of data collected on the basis of systematic observation in a large Canadian municipal police force. These data are compared with the existing research literature on the police, and related to wider theoretical issues of concern to 'socio-legal' scholars. Before outlining the research design and presenting the results, I shall raise the theoretical issues and define the concepts which inform them.

The Police, Crime, and Reproducing Order

Conventional wisdom – fuelled by the police themselves along with the media, some academics, and other instruments of social reproduction – equates police work with crime work. In television 'cop shows,' in news reports on individual criminal cases, in police annual reports listing levels of crime and clearance rates, and in the research literature dealing with the effectiveness of police as crime fighters, the image is constantly reinforced that crime is, after all, almost everything the police are about.[3] Of course there is talk about the police as a social-service agency – usually including the well-worn assertion that the police are the only 24-hour-a-day 7-days-a-week social-service agency – but in the minds of police officers, in keeping with the thinking of the public, real police work is crime work.

This view has remarkable currency, given that the police, especially the patrol police, actually spend only a tiny fraction of their time dealing with crime or something that could potentially be made into crime. For example, research by the British Home Office inluded a survey of 12 urban policing areas and found that on average only 6 per cent of a patrol policeman's time was spent on incidents finally defined as 'criminal' (cited by McCabe and Sutcliffe, 1978). Similarly, Reiss (1971: 96) employs data from the Chicago police department to document 'the low productivity of preventive patrol for criminal matters alone, since only about two-tenths of 1 per cent of the time spent on preventive patrol is occupied in handling criminal matters. What is more, only 3 percent of all time spent on patrol involves handling what is officially regarded as a criminal matter.' Various ethnographic studies also document the fact that most patrol-officer contacts with the public do not involve criminal matters (e.g. Cumming et al, 1970; Punch and Naylor, 1973; Cain, 1973; Payne, 1973; Comrie and Kings, 1975; Punch, 1979). Reiss (1971: 73) reports from his Chicago study that 58 per cent of complaints were regarded by the complainants as criminal matters, but only 17 per cent of patrol dispatches to complainants resulted in official processing as criminal incidents.

It is clear that the patrol police do not often have the occasion to designate something as a criminal matter. Indeed, the vast majority of their time is spent alone in their patrol cars without any direct contact with citizens. For example, Pepinsky (1975: 4) reports that more than 85 per cent of police patrol time is spent *not* dealing with citizens.

If, in light of this evidence, one is still committed to a view of the patrol police as crime fighters, one could argue that by their visible presence on the street the patrol police are preventing crime. However, this argument is difficult to sustain. In the Kansas City study by Kelling and associates (1974), it was found that increasing preventive patrol by a factor of two or more over a one-year period had no significant impact upon the incidence of crime (for reviews of this type of research, see Clarke and Heal, 1979; Kelling et al, 1979). Even the most optimistic researchers (Wilson and Boland, 1979) produce results which question the advantage of flooding the streets with large numbers of patrol officers, and of aggressive proactive – i.e. police-initiated – patrol. In their survey of 35 American cities, Wilson and Boland present data to argue that police resources (patrol units on the street), and on-the-street-activity,[4] independently affect the robbery rate after controlling various socio-economic factors. However, the same analysis demonstrates no similar effect for rates of burglary and auto theft.

Furthermore, there is no apparent value in having more patrol cars available for quick response (Pate et al, 1976), except perhaps in a tiny minority of incidents with elements of violence, and as a means of reassuring the citizen with a *feeling* of security. In a recent critique of their own research, Kelling et al (1979) conclude that the introduction and subsequent technological 'refinements' of mobile patrol operations have had no appreciable effect on the incidence of crime (for similar critiques of the role of police technology, see Skolnick, 1966; Rubinstein, 1973; Manning, 1977).

Another factor to consider in deciding whether flooding the streets with patrol officers can stem the tide of crime waves is police recording practices. Given the propensity of bureaucratic police forces to measure the productivity of officers, increasing manpower may increase recording, especially of minor matters (McDonald, 1969, 1976; Chan and Ericson, 1981).

Of course, the primary function of the uniformed police has always been to patrol the petty. Thus in the 1830s, following the establishment of the new police in London, 85 per cent of arrests were for non-indictable offences such as public drunkenness and disturbing the peace (Ignatieff, 1978). Apparently, the more police one has the more petty matters will be pursued, especially if organizational procedures are in place to measure and reward that pursuit.

Evidence from these various sources leads one to conclude that patrol police work is not primarily or essentially about crime prevention or law enforcement. It leads one to question what is the place of the criminal law in the work of patrol officers, and to ask what else is going on as they go about their work. Several researchers on the police, along with other 'socio-legal' scholars and social theorists, have provided some answers to these questions. We shall summarize their views – an apparently shared understanding that the patrol police are essentially a vehicle in the 'reproduction of order.'

'Order' is a multi-faceted word that has at least seven meanings pertinent to our concerns (*Oxford Paperback Dictionary*, 1979: 445): 'a condition in which every part or unit is in its right place or in a normal or efficient state, *in good working order: out of order*; the condition brought about by good and firm government and obedience to the laws, law and order; a system of rules or procedure; a command, an instruction given with authority; a written direction ... giving authority to do something; a rank or class in society, the lower orders; a kind or sort or quality, *showed courage of the highest order.*'

The mandate of police patrol officers is to employ a system of rules and authoritative commands to transform troublesome, fragile situations back into a normal or efficient state whereby the ranks in society are preserved. This is to be done according to means which appear to be of the highest quality and is directed at the appearance of good and firm government.

Of course, it is not the mandate of the police to produce a new order. On the contrary, their everyday actions are directed at reproducing the existing order (the 'normal or efficient state') and the order (system of rules) by which this is accomplished. They are one tool of 'policing' in the wider sense of all governmental efforts aimed at disciplining, refining, and improving the population. As such, most of what they do is part of the social machinery of verifying and reproducing what is routinely assumed to be the case (cf Berger and Luckmann, 1966: chapter 2). Their sense of order and the order they seek to reproduce are that of the status quo.[5]

The order arising out of their action is a reproduction because it is made with reference to the existing order and designed to keep it in its original form. However, the 'seed of change' is contained in every 'interactional sequence' (Giddens, 1976) and the outcome may not quite duplicate what was there before the interaction. Moreover, the term 'reproduction' implies that order is not simply transmitted in an unproblematic manner but is worked at through processes of conflict, negotiation, and subjection.

The police are the most visible front-line agents for ordering the population. They represent the extreme end of the 'carceral continuum' (Foucault,

1977), serving as a model of judicial-legal ideology. To the extent that they are successful in portraying their work as professional according to the principles of formal legal rationality (cf Balbus, 1973) and bureaucratic rationality, the police accomplish legitimacy as agents of the state. They can convince the citizenry that they are being policed as legal subjects instead of 'class' subjects (cf Cohen, 1979: 129–30).

The police have always had an ideological function as well as a repressive function. They have been repeatedly employed as an 'advance guard' of municipal reform, especially for altered uses of social space and time (public order), and protection of property, to ensure free circulation of commodities (including labour power) (ibid: 120). Yet part of their success has been to present their problems as technical, related to the control of crime, rather than as ideological: they have difficulty controlling crime because the laws are inadequate; they do not have the communications system necessary to reduce response time; they do not have sufficient manpower to have a deterrent effect, and so on.

The police actively campaign to have the community believe that things will be more orderly if the police are supplied with better cars, better crime laboratories, better-trained police officers, more enabling laws, and so on. The effort is reflected in extensive public relations, including follow-up interviews with victims of crime to make it appear that something is being done (Greenwood et al, 1975; Sanders, 1977; Ericson, 1981), displays at shopping plazas, lectures to students and to other selected groups in the community, and using press officers who generate contacts with the media and 'feed' them (cf Fishman, 1978, 1980). In these efforts the police are concerned not with the dangerous 'symbolic assailant' as conceived by Skolnick (1966), but rather with the symbolic support of 'respectable' citizens who encourage police efforts directed at anyone but themselves.

In addition to reproducing legal and bureaucratic ideology, the police also impose social discipline in the name of public propriety (Cohen, 1979). They are responsible for establishing a fixed presence in the community for systematic surveillance. They patrol with a suspicious eye for the wrong people in the wrong places at the wrong times, reproducing a 'social penality of time and place' (Foucault, 1977). Far from being unsystematic and arbitrary, this work is based on established rules and produces regular results. The patrol officer is more likely to watch closely and stop on suspicion a young man in his 'shagwagon'[6] than a granny in her stationwagon, because the former is more likely to have contraband and is deemed more in need of being kept in his proper place.

The police have a sense of the order they are there to reproduce. This is reflected in the activities they are taught to pursue, in the techniques they are taught to use in pursuit, and in their own identification with the values of middle-class respectability. In keeping with the entire reproductive apparatus of the state, they are there to ensure that everyone possible appears to be the middle Canadian in theory and the working Canadian in practice. Their sense of order is reflexive: they think that they are doing what the powerful and respectable want at the same time as they see this as something they themselves support, but in a way that sustains their own sense of autonomy and purpose.

As Bittner (e.g. 1967, 1967a, 1970) and Manning (e.g. 1977, 1979, 1980) have argued, this sense of order frames the resources needed to maintain it. That is, in dealing with any particular situation the patrol officer decides what, if anything, is out of order and then employs the various tools at his disposal to reconstruct order. If he is seeking compliance from a citizen, he can rely upon the aura of the general authority of his office; his procedural legal powers to detain, search, and use physical force; his substantive legal powers to charge; and various manipulative strategies that form part of the 'recipe' knowledge of his craft. In short, he 'negotiates order,' variously employing strategies of coercion, manipulation, and negotiation (Strauss, 1978).[7] This work is always carried out with respect to rules, including legal rules, administrative rules, and 'recipe' rules of the occupational culture of line officers. In other words, it is the work of producing and controlling deviance, of using social rules in the construction of social order (cf Douglas, 1971).

This view of how order is constituted is neither 'high sociology' (Rock, 1979) nor empiricist sociology of the 'phenomenological' variety. Rather, it is a 'search ... for a joining of social structural and social interactional considerations but with [an] antideterministic stance still intact' (Strauss, 1978: 16; see also Ranson et al, 1980). Attention is focused upon the strategies of coercion, manipulation, and negotiation, and the patterns these indicate, which allow particular parties to secure their interests and sustain advantages over others. These strategies are conceived as deriving from social structure, and their use in interaction serves to reproduce dialectically social structure. The task of the sociologist using this model is primarily empirical: to examine at close hand the strategic interaction as it is used by one's subjects in the reproduction of social order.[8]

Within this 'transactional' view, the police are conceived as 'enacting' their environment as well as reacting to it (Weick, 1969: 63–4; Manning, 1979: 29). While they are responsive to the community and operate within particular elements of social organization (Black, 1968), they also carve out part of their mandate based on properties of their own organization. On the macro-level, this interplay is indicated by such things as public-relations campaigns, setting up special units (e.g. community-relations officer units; ethnic-relations units), and 'selling' the organization in terms of the community's 'crime problem.' On the micro-level the mutual influences of the community organization and police organization are seen in the level and nature of reactive (citizen-initiated) mobilization and proactive (police-initiated) mobilization and in the specific approach taken by police officers and citizens in various types of troubles they come together to deal with.

In studying the reciprocal influences between community forces and police forces, there is no point in trying to weigh up the forces on each side and making a final decision as to who controls. Apart from the inevitable looseness of any such measurement, by the time such an exercise was completed new forces would come into play requiring remeasurement or, more probably, a new system of measurement. However, one thing is clear. In the past few decades the police, along with other forms of governmental policing, have become a force to be reckoned with. As Banton (1964: 6) has observed, the police have changed their role from being 'professional citizens' who carry out 'obligations which fall upon all citizens,' to 'an official exercising authority and power over citizens.' Much of this authority and power comes from within the bureaucratic organization of policing rather than from the law or other community sources.

Something not so clear is the complex ways the police, and political powers in the community, maintain their legitimacy while going about their everyday work. People do not like to be interfered with, lectured, badgered, and harassed, yet the patrol officer must do these things every day. Perhaps they are able to do this routinely because of the macro-level 'selling job' done by the administration, associations of chiefs of police, police associations, politicians, and the media. 'The more resources allocated to increasing the efficiency of repressive policing, the more manpower has to be poured into 'community relations' to restabilize the public image of the force' (Cohen, 1979: 133).

As stated earlier, a major part of this 'image work' is carried out in terms of the police mandate to control crime. A lot of work is done via the media, and official statistics of crime rates and clearance rates, to support the view that the police are struggling to keep the lid on the massive amounts of deviance in the community. The police are held responsible for crime control, even though the causes of crime (social, economic, cultural, and political) are clearly beyond their control (cf Manning, 1971, 1977, 1980).

This situation is ripe for contradiction. The police have to show that they can keep the lid on crime and generally keep the streets clean, yet not so successfully as to suggest that they do not need more resources to fight crime and other filthy activity. Thus there has to be a lot of the disorder they are selling themselves as being able to reduce in order to justify more resources. More generally, the police are agents of the status quo, of consensus, yet each incident they deal with belies the consensus they symbolize. Some researchers (e.g. Wilson, 1968) have observed that in more heterogeneous communities where conflict is great there is likely to be a trend toward policing that is oriented to law enforcement. The irony is that the less the consensus the more the police are used as symbols to produce the appearance that there is consensus.

The very existence of crime control in a community indicates that other means of control have failed and is testimony to the degree of conflict in the community. Moreover, high levels of crime control mean that the symbolic aspects of the wider institutions of law itself are failing. The more repressive the reaction becomes, the more visible are the main contours of conflict and contradiction. In these circumstances the police are most able to increase their own power, even to the point of having some effect on the legislative process itself (Chambliss and Seidman, 1971: especially 68; see also Hall et al, 1978; Cohen, 1979; Taylor, 1980).

This process has the characteristics of 'deviance amplification' as discussed by 'labelling' theorists (Wilkins, 1964; Schur, 1971; Ericson, 1975; Ditton, 1979). The typical reaction to *indicators* of conflict such as crime is to expand the apparatus of control. This occurs not only in more visible forms such as increased resources for the police, but also in expansion of the welfare state (Chan and Ericson, 1981). One effect is an amplifying spiral of official reactions, including an increased rate of officially designated crime (McDonald, 1976: especially chapter 6).

All of this leads one to suspect that the police and other agencies in the reproductive apparatus are not out to eradicate the phenomena they deal with, but to classify, record, contain, and use them in perpetuity (Foucault, 1977). One must suspect that their mandate to constitute and deal with crime distorts more fundamental processes and that the popular conception of the police as crime fighters must itself be treated as creating a problem for both the police and the community. Crime control is an impossible task for the police alone. They are expected to handle a phenomenon caused by social, political, economic, and cultural forces beyond their control and have to give the *appearance* that things are (more or less) under control. Thus there is bound to be a gulf between the structured rhetoric about the police and crime and the everyday reality of policing. One part of the order the police reproduce is the mystical one of crime control, of 'lawandorder,' but their everyday work is of a different order.[9]

The empirical focus of the research reported in this book is the everyday work of the patrol police and the structures reproduced by their work. These structures have systems of rules which control, guide, and justify their actions. We now turn to a discussion of those rules as they relate to the more general question of police powers (discretion) and how these powers are used in the reproduction of order.

Police Discretion and Uses of Rules

Discretion is the power to decide which rules apply to a given situation and whether or not to apply them. Legal scholars traditionally view discretion in terms of what *official* rules can be held to govern the actions of policemen. These rules include laws and administrative instructions. For example, Pound (1960) sees discretion as an authority conferred by law to make considered judgments under specified conditions; it belongs 'to the twilight zone between law and morals' where the official has the autonomy to make judgments within a framework provided by the law.

Some lawyers and sociologists have defined discretion in terms of whether decisions are, or can be, reviewed according to official rules. Thus Goldstein (1960) is concerned with decisions of 'low visibility' in which the police officer takes no official action – he does not write an official report and does not invoke the criminal process via arrest and charge. Goldstein sees these actions as discretionary because there is no routine opportunity for administrative or judicial review. This is similar to Reiss's (1974: 67) definition of discretionary justice existing 'whenever decisions made in criminal cases are not legally or practically open to re-examination.'

'Low visibility' is just one resource available to police officers to maintain control over their decisions. Moreover, while a specific decision may not be reviewed, or may not even be practically reviewable, legal and administrative rules are nevertheless taken into account in making the decision. These rules remain 'invisible,' but they do have an effect.[10]

The question of effects brings us to the essential aspects of the concept of discretion. Davis (1969: 4) refers to discretion as existing 'whenever the *effective* limits on [the official's] power leave him free to make a choice among possible courses of action or inaction' (emphasis added). The limits are not only the formal expectations of the criminal law and administrative rules, but also expectations from other sources such as the occupational culture of police officers and specific groups in the community. Black (1968: 25) provides a complementary definition of police discretion 'as the autonomy of decision-making that an officer has.'

Obviously the definition of discretion in terms of effective limits and autonomy incorporates a conception of *power*. Power involves the probability that one party in an encounter can effect a course of action and outcome he desires in spite of the contrary wishes and/or actions of the other parties. As such power is a *potential* element in any interaction but it is not necessarily exercised. It is therefore difficult to gauge power empirically, except via an analysis of the power resources of the parties being studied, and through observing instances and rates of compliance. As a potential element power mediates between actors' intentions and the realization of outcomes. In use, power involves the mobilization of resources to effect outcomes which serve particular interests.

Another way of formulating the definitions of discretion provided by Davis and by Black is to say that in situations where others do not have the power to circumscribe the person's action, he himself has power because he can choose a course of action and effect an outcome that reflects that choice. Any analysis of decisions made during a sequence of interactions must take into account the relative power advantages of the participants. Who has the advantage is heavily dependent upon access to and control over resources that can be mobilized to influence others to one's own advantage (Turk, 1976). Thus, a focal point for the analysis of power is the resources available to effect it. 'The use of power in interaction can be understood in terms of resources or facilities which participants bring to and mobilize as elements of its production, thus directing its course' (Giddens, 1976: 112).

One group's acquisition of autonomy may involve another group's loss of autonomy. In what area does a group have the ability to coerce, manipulate, or negotiate the establishment of its own rules which others conform to? Those who have control over the law-making process, other agencies of crime control, police supervisors, and various groups of citizens are all able to use rules limiting the choices of patrol officers, while these officers can in turn use rules from these sources and their own 'recipe' rules to control their working environment.

The use of rules in organizational contexts has been a key topic of enquiry among sociologists studying police work. Part of this enquiry has focused on the discovery of the framework of rules used by police officers to constitute their 'sense of order.'[11] This is necessarily an empirical task. For the sociologist, as for the actors he studies, 'to know a rule is not to be able to provide an abstract formulation of it, but to know how to apply it to novel circumstances, which includes knowing about the *context* of its application' (Giddens, 1976: 124). Rules as stated formally have a fictional character; this can only be understood, and the operating rules gleaned, by examining rules in action (Chambliss and Seidman, 1971). As Manning (1977a: 44) emphasizes, 'since the context of rules, not the rules themselves, nor the rules about the rules (so characteristic of formal organizations), determine the consequential (i.e., actionable) meanings of acts, situated interactions, accounts and shared understandings should be examined.'

Rules serve as tools of power and as justifiers of actions taken. In the case of criminal-law rules, the police have an enabling resource to control what and whom are proceeded against and to legitimate actions taken. The law provides 'cover' in two senses. It provides 'blanket' cover through the wide range of substantive offences available to handle any troublesome situation the officer is likely to confront (Bittner, 1967, 1967a, 1970; Chatterton, 1976). Also, the legal procedures for police actions are so enabling that there are very few instances when what the officer wishes to do cannot be legitimated legally (McBarnet, 1979, 1981).

Beyond this, the police officer has control over the production of 'facts' about a case, and this control of knowledge becomes a very potent form of power. The rules are not only taken into account, but they also form part of the account to legitimate the action taken (Kadish and Kadish, 1973; Sanders, 1977; Ericson, 1981, 1981a). In sum, the normative order of rules made applicable and the meanings applied to a situation are closely related (Giddens, 1976: 109, 110). The powerful nature of rules is not to be gleaned from 'perceptible determination of behaviour,' but rather in how rules 'constrain people to *account* for their rule-invocations, rule violations, and rule applications' (Carlen, 1976, referring to Durkheim, 1964).

The motive for patrol officers' actions comes from particular interests defined within their occupational culture. This includes an array of 'recipe' rules which guide him on how to get the job done in ways that will appear acceptable to the organization, which persons in what situations should be dealt with in particular ways (e.g. who should be 'targeted' for stops on suspicion, who should be charged for specific offence-types, etc.), how to avoid supervisors and various organizational control checks, when it is necessary to produce 'paper' regarding an incident or complaint, and so on. No matter what interests provide the motive, the law can provide the *opportunity* to achieve an outcome reflecting those interests (McBarnet, 1976, 1979, 1981).

The criminal law becomes a 'residual resource' used when other methods of resolving a situation are unavailable or have been tried and are unsuccessful. Similar to the way citizens use the police (cf Black, 1968; Reiss, 1971), police use the law according to what other forms of social control are available and can be used effectively. For the patrol police, this is particularly the case in interpersonal disputes and problems of public order and decorum. When all else fails or is deemed likely to fail, the officer decides he must remove one party in the conflict from the situation, and consequently he arrests someone. A specific infraction with a clearly applicable law does not determine the arrest, but rather the law is used to make the arrest to handle the situation. As Chatterton (1973, 1976) found, charges are sometimes used 'as the legal vehicle for conveying someone to the police station and ... the grounds for the *decision to use it* [are] to be found elsewhere than in the reasons provided to justify its use to the courts.'[12]

The patrol officer's concern for the law as an 'all purpose control device' (Bittner, 1970: 108) bears on how he can make it applicable across a range of situations. From his viewpoint, the broader the applicability the better the law, which may explain why the police resist legal changes which decrease their repertoire (cf Goldstein, 1970: 152). When the law is changed, other laws have to be used to serve the same purpose. For example, Ramsay (1972: 65) refers to liquor-law changes in Saskatchewan which prevented police officers from continuing to charge for intoxication in public places; RCMP members continued to arrest and charge persons intoxicated in public places, substituting the 'causing a disturbance' provision of the Criminal Code.

The procedural criminal law is also enabling for the patrol police.[13] As McBarnet (1976, 1979, 1981) has argued, Packer's (1968) dichotomy between a due-process model of procedural protections for the accused and a crime-control model of expedient law enforcement turns out to be not a dichotomy at all, especially in countries such as England, Scotland, and Canada where the suspect and accused do not have entrenched rights. In the law as written, and the law in action, 'due process if *for* crime control.' That is, the rules of procedure as written and used explicitly serve the expedient ends of law enforcement. Even in the United States, where rights are entrenched, there is frequently no empirical referent in law for ideals such as the rule of law or due process (Black, 1972). Furthermore, empirical studies on the implementation of due-process rules such as *Miranda* v *Arizona* (1966) 384 US 436 US Sup Ct indicate that the rules are routinely sidestepped or incorporated into existing police practices (e.g. Wald et al, 1967; Medalie et al, 1968; Ayres, 1970). As Thurman Arnold (1962), cited by Carlen (1976: 95), states, 'When a great government treats the lowliest of criminals as an equal antagonist ... we have a gesture of recognition to the dignity of the individual which has an extraordinary dramatic appeal. Its claim is to our emotions, rather than on our common sense.' As pragmatic actors whose 'recipe' rules for practice are based on common sense, the police can use the procedural law to achieve the outcomes they deem appropriate.

Criminal-law rules, along with administrative rules and rules within the occupational culture, are also useful to patrol officers in formulating accounts that will justify their actions. Thus, rules are used prospectively in taking action, and retrospectively in showing to interested others (especially supervisory officers and the courts) that the action taken was justifiable and appropriate. Prospectively, one rule of the occupational culture is 'Unless you have a good story, don't do it' (Chatterton, 1979: 94). Justice becomes a matter of justifications, as patrol officers set out to do what they believe is necessary to put things in order. They seek the 'cover' of legitimate justifications and take their decisions with a view to 'covering their ass' vis-à-vis any possible source of objection. Indeed, this is the only form of 'under-cover' work patrol officers routinely undertake! In addition to other forms of patrol work, they patrol the facts of 'what happened,' transforming a conflict with a colourful kaleidoscope of complexities into a black-and-white 'still' of factual-legal discourse.

Manuals provide instruction on how to write reports to impress favourably other actors in the crime-control network (e.g. Inbau and Reid, 1967: 129). Socio-legal research also informs us about techniques of this nature. Sanders (1977) examines the process of report construction, showing how the same facts can be used to legitimate a range of offence types, or no offence at all. Wald and associates (1967: 1554) suggest that the police often take statements from accused persons simply as a basis for convincing the prosecutor that a case exists at all. Skolnick (1966: 133) notes how the rules of criminal discovery in the jurisdiction he studied require the prosecutor to allow the defence lawyer to examine arrest reports, producing a situation where 'the police do not report as the significant events leading to arrest what an unbiased observer viewing the situation would report. Instead they compose a description that satisfies legal requirements without interfering with their own organizational requirements.'

In saying the police officer is able to construct the facts of the case, we are not saying that it is a fabrication, although there are many accounts of police fabrication and perjury (see Buckner, 1970: especially 99–100; Morand, 1976; Morris, 1978). Our point is that the rules become embedded in the formulations used to make the case, so that it is difficult to distinguish between the generation of fact, its provision to senior officers and the court, and the use of rules for its accomplishment (see Sanders, 1977: especially 98–99; and generally, Ditton, 1979). Thus, the way in which factual accounts and rules are intertwined makes it difficult to establish what is a fabrication and what is not.

In summary, rules are a power resource of the patrol officer in accomplishing whatever seems appropriate to the situation. Discretion takes rules into account; it is not necessarily a deviation from or outside legal rules. As we shall see in the next section, these rules have many sources and can serve varied functions. Ours is not a government of law; it is a government of men who *use* law.[14]

The Organizational Forums of Police Work

Patrol officers go about their work sensitive to expectations from the organizations within which they operate, including the community, the law and court organizations, and the police organization. The literature on the police deals with influences from each of these sources, but individual studies tend to emphasize one source to the virtual, and sometimes complete, exclusion of others.

One tradition of enquiry explores the influence of the community. These studies consider the influence on police decisions of citizens dealing with the police (informant, victim, complainant, suspect, accused) and of the circumstances in which they encounter the police (who mobilizes the police, where the encounter takes place, the nature of the matter in dispute). These studies are similar to the multiple-factor approaches used in asking why people commit crimes, but here the question has shifted to why a policeman charges people, records an occurrence, and so on.

Patrol officers typically have little information besides the appearance of an individual and of a situation. They can perhaps learn more from accounts and from documents shown them (e.g. driver's licence), and the CPIC (Canadian Police Information Centre) system. Many encounters involve a 'negotiation of status claims' (Hudson, 1970:190) – officers look for and employ status 'cues' to determine what action they should take; in this sense, 'police activity is as much directed to who a person is as to what he does' (Bittner, 1970:10).[15] The more that other types of information are lacking, the more the officer is likely to forge a stereotypical response based on a 'second code' (MacNaughton-Smith, 1968) of these criteria, which may ultimately be used to define the situation as a legal problem.

The studies of this type are centred upon two central variables of American sociological inquiry, race and socio-economic standing, as these are influenced by and influence other variables, especially demeanour, the nature of the incident (seriousness, evidence available, dispute type), and whether the person is 'out of place.' Some researchers have argued that variables of citizen input make spurious simple relationships between status and role characteristics and police decision-making; to the extent members of racial minorities and those of low socio-economic standing tend to be 'unstable,' less deferential, and to request particular forms of police action, police activity towards them is different from that towards other types of citizens.

Black (1968) demonstrates that in reactively mobilized encounters, the most important determinants (in addition to seriousness of the alleged offence and evidence questions) of police action to record an occurrence or arrest are the preference of the complainant, the social distance between complainant and suspect, and the degree of deference shown by both complainant and suspect. When the complainant's preference for action is unclear the degree of deference shown by the suspect becomes a significant influence. In these situations, blacks tend to be more disrespectful towards the police, thereby increasing the probability of arrest (Black, 1971:1101). 'Negroes, it is clear, have a disproportionate vulnerability to arrest mainly because they are disproportionately disrespectful toward police officers' (Black, 1968:231).

Sykes and Clark (1975) attempt to show that it is because lower-status people have less ability to express deference that they more often end up being officially processed. They confirm Black's findings concerning non-white lower-status citizens, who are more likely to be unilaterally disrespectful to the police than whites and those of higher status. They show also that the police are reciprocally more disrespectful to young, male suspects in order-maintenance situations and least likely to be disrespectful in service calls involving women, senior citizens, and the middle class.

Several other researchers, using a variety of methods, have considered the influence of the offender's deference and demeanour on police action. Sullivan and Siegel (1974:253), in a decision-game study, found that the 'attitude of the offender' was the most important item selected by police-officer subjects in reaching a final decision about whether or not to arrest. Research on police handling of juvenile offenders has also emphasized this aspect (Werthman and Piliavin, 1967; Chan and Doob, 1977). Similarly, it has been shown that traffic-law offenders are more likely to be ticketed if they are 'offensive' that if they are 'respectful' (Gardiner, 1969: 151; Pepinsky, 1975: 41).

There is no consensus among researchers on all facets of police response to citizens' preference and suspects' deference. In the research by Reiss and Black, in 14 per cent of reactive encounters the complainant requested unofficial handling of a felony or misdemeanour, and the police invariably complied (Reiss, 1971: 83). Moreover, Black (1968: 216–17) concludes that 'the police are more likely to arrest a misdemeanor suspect who is disrespectful toward them than a felony suspect who is civil.' In their research, Clark and Sykes (1974: 483n) found that the police almost invariably record, and arrest where possible, in felonies regardless of complainant preference or suspect deference.

Other explanations claim that the poor and blacks are particularly vulnerable when 'out of place,' i.e. in social or geographical contexts in which they do not normally participate (Bayley and Mendelsohn, 1969: 93; Werthman and Piliavin, 1967: 78; Rubinstein, 1973: part II). Others have attempted to demonstrate that the important influences are the occupational and domestic stability of the suspect. For example, Skolnick (1966: 84–5) argues that blacks are more likely to be arrested by warrant officers because they are less likely 'to possess the middle-class virtues of occupational and residential stability' that would lead the officers to believe that fine payments could be met. Green (1970) presents data to demonstrate that blacks are more likely to possess such lower-class characteristics as residential mobility and working at marginal jobs or being unemployed, and that these characteristics rather than race per se account for higher arrest rates. Werthman and Piliavin (1967: 84) point out that citizens with these characteristics are aware of how the police assess them and manipulate their appearances accordingly. For example, some of their subjects who were unmarried wore wedding rings 'in order to bolster their moral status in the eyes of the police.'

The influence of personal characteristics, especially socio-economic status, has also been shown to vary by how the police are mobilized and the nature of the matter in dispute. Black (1968) and Reiss (1971) introduced the distinction between proactive (police-initiated) and reactive (citizen-initiated) mobilizations. Proactive policing is directed at lower-status citizens who present problems of public order, or who are out of place. As John Stuart Mill remarked, one of the benchmarks of civilization is the extent to which the unpleasant or uncivilized aspects of existence are kept away from those who most enjoy the benefits of civilization. Patrol officers have a mandate to reproduce civilization in this form, maintaining the boundaries of deviant ghettos and keeping the streets clean of those who are, at the most, offensive rather than offenders (Scull, 1977; Cohen, 1979).

Proactive policing also occurs in traffic regulation, and here higher-status people have frequent contact with the police. Proactive traffic work has been identified as a major area of conflict between the police and the public, e.g. Royal Commission on the Police, 1962: 114; Willett, 1964; Black, 1968: 14. Higher-status citizens view the police largely as reactive agents responding to their complaints, not as proactive pursuers of minor technical violations (Cressey, 1974: 219). Furthermore, they know patrol officers frequently do not charge for traffic offences. Several writers (ibid: 227; LaFave, 1965: 131–2; Grosman, 1975: 2) have stressed that when the police are known to ignore violations systematically this becomes a public expectation; a hostile reaction can occur when someone is selected out and issued a summons. Enforcement of traffic laws is the one area where technically based full enforcement of observed violations is possible, and yet discretion is very frequently used there. Order is reproduced through *selective* use of the law.

According to Reiss and Black, the vast majority of patrol police mobilizations are reactive (87 per cent in their study). They use this finding in support of their argument that the patrol police are dependent on citizens and operate mainly as servants responsive to public demands.

Citizens mobilize the police ('the law') as a power resource to assist in handling their own troubles and conflicts: 'The empirical reality of law is that it is a set of resources for which people contend and with which they are better able to promote their own ideas and interests against others' (Turk, 1976: abstract of article). Mobilizing the police as the first step in using the law is usually done 'less for a sense of civic duty than from an expectation of personal gain' (Reiss, 1971: 173). The 'middle orders' do not typically initiate direct contact with the police except when they are victims of property crime (Black, 1968: 185). The 'lower orders' frequently use the police for this purpose and also mobilize them to handle interpersonal conflicts because other forms of social control have failed, are unavailable, or are absent. There may be conflict over the rules of a relationship, with at least one party trying to establish order by the threat of using the external formal rules which the police have at their disposal (ibid: 108, 181). Research shows that this type of demand is especially frequent at particular times and in particular places (Cumming et al, 1970: 187) and among the 'lower orders' (Black, 1971, 1972, 1976; Meyer, 1974: 81–2; Bottomley, 1973: 45).

Obviously mobilization, type of dispute, citizen characteristics, and citizen input influence decision-making by patrol officers and I examine these elements in later chapters. However, we must also consider the internal dynamics of the police organization and the legal organization within which the police operate. There are major limitations in studies which concentrate on characteristics of the community.

These studies, following the work of Reiss and Black, tend to overemphasize the reactive role of the police and their apparent dependence on the public. Reiss and Black's findings on reactive policing probably reflect their sampling methods (see chapters 2 and 4), and their model is generally one of 'stimulus-response.' Many encounters, however, are long-lasting and complex, with both sides trying to coerce, manipulate, and/or negotiate an outcome that serves particular interests.

'Crime is, above all, a function of the resources available to know it' (Manning, 1972: 234). The citizen can choose not to inform the police about a particular instance of trouble. If he reports it, he can formulate the trouble in ways he believes will influence police actions in the direction he himself wants. He also has choices about giving police access to information (e.g. school, employment, credit records); the police are dependent upon 'those socially structured features of everyday life which render persons findable' (Bittner, 1967a: 706). He can also influence the patrol officer by appealing police actions through the citizen complaint bureau of the police department or through legal action.[16]

The police officer in turn has several resources at his disposal. These include the law, the 'low visibility' of his actions, and the general aura of his office. Manning (1979: 24–6) suggests the significance of calls for service has been exaggerated in previous research. The officer has discretionary power outside the control of his supervisors to transform the encounter. He can use his organizational resources to convince the citizen that the action he is taking is the most appropriate and legitimate one (for examples, see Ericson, 1981: chapter 5). The officer's efforts are eased by the public-relations work of the force as a whole. 'One of the first explanations for police investment in provision of services only peripherally related to law enforcement is that this gives them knowledge and control in situations that have been previously associated with disruption of law and order' (Clark and Sykes, 1974: 462). If the force in general, or a specific policy, is sold properly it can help to further citizen co-operation in providing information and can ultimately generate more crime and other products for the police to commit to their records.[17]

In sum, the more appropriate model is a transactional one of stimulus-interpretation-response. General patterns may be revealed in quantifying status-role and dispute characteristics, but one must also examine how these patterns, and indeed the decisions themselves, are produced. A blend of quantitative and qualitative analysis is called for, and this is the approach we have taken.

A qualitative analysis allows for a better account of the role of legal and police organizational elements. For example, even a cursory examination of the law reveals that many citizen characteristics treated by researchers as 'extra-legal' are an integral part of the written law. This is clearly the case in police handling of juveniles; showing that charging and cautioning are significantly related to status, stability, and respectability should therefore come as no surprise (e.g. Chan and Doob, 1977). Similarly, specific statutes, such as the Bail Reform Act in Canada, for handling adult offenders, rely explicitly on criteria of stability and respectability such as place of residence and previous criminal record. Furthermore, what happens inside a police organization influences the initiation of encounters with citizens and what happens during those encounters. Available manpower, organizational priorities, production expectations, 'recipe' rules for 'targeting' segments of the population, and many other elements influence transactions and the production of case outcomes. In sum, the patrol officer's sense of order in the community is inextricably bound up with his sense of legal order and police organizational order, and these must be taken into consideration in a full account of police work.

Another aspect of legal organization which patrol officers incorporate into their actions is the organization of the court system, including the roles and rules used by judges, justices of the peace, defence lawyers, and crown attorneys. While the historic constitutional position of the constable is that he is answerable to the law alone, in practice he must justify his actions to other actors whose job it is to use the law. He must establish relationships with the various actors in court and respond to their expectations and rules (some of which may have the force of law), in order to achieve outcomes that serve organizational interests.

The constitutional position of the police has meant that the judiciary has not generally interfered with police discretion to investigate or to invoke the criminal process. For example, in the well-known *Blackburn* cases in Britain – *R. v Metropolitan Police Commissioner ex parte Blackburn* (1968) 1 All ER 763; *R. v Metropolitan Police Commissioner ex parte Blackburn* (1973) 1 All ER 324 – the court of appeals stated the opinion that the courts will only intercede regarding a chief officer's discretion where there is an abdication of responsibility for law enforcement in a particular area of criminal law. For example, if a police force had a policy not to charge for housebreaking or theft where the loss was relatively small, the courts would step in; but there would be no intervention in individual cases, or where the policy covers types of crime such as statutory rape involving couples close in age. In everyday law enforcement it is up to the police themselves to decide what action to take.

In spite of this general distance, there are obviously many ways in which judges can and do influence police actions. They can alter the administrative organization of the court in a way that leads to a change in police practice. For example, Gardiner (1969: 132) describes a situation where night-shift police officers were reluctant to issue traffic summonses because they would have to work irregular hours by appearing in court on the next day shift; a traffic-court judge began to allow deferred appearances in court, and the night-shift officers began to write more traffic tickets. Judges also have

considerable control *within* some areas of the law. The law of confessions in
Canada is made by judges, and decision-making on the admissibility of
confessions in each individual case is largely subjective (Kaufman, 1974).

Judicial practices in sentencing can influence police practices in charging. Some researchers (e.g. Grosman, 1969; Klein, 1976) have pointed out
that the tendency of Canadian judges to give concurrent sentences for multiple convictions gives the police less bargaining power in laying multiple
charges with the intention of later withdrawing some in exchange for a guilty
plea. British research indicates that in jurisdictions where police are reluctant
to caution rather than charge people for minor offences, the courts tend to
give a relatively large number of nominal sentences such as discharges;
conversely, where police cautioning rates are high nominal sentencing rates
are low (Bottomley, 1973: 72; Steer, 1970: 20). The unwillingness of the courts
to grant sentences other than discharges for certain types of offences and
offenders may encourage the police to handle them without charge. The
court can support the local police in the way it deals with certain types of
charges that arise out of conflicts between police and citizens, such as 'assault
police' or 'causing a disturbance' (see Williams, 1974: 186–7). The degree to
which the court upholds these charges, which usually rely solely on police
testimony, may affect the degree to which the police will use formal charges in
these situations as opposed to more summary actions.

Similar to their use of rules coming from other sources, police officers
incorporate the rules of judicial practice into their own practices. They are
very successful at doing this, in some cases continuing or even strengthening
their existing practices while managing a show of conformity with the new
rules. Of course, this is a typical result of attempts to introduce new rules in
any organizational setting.[18]

The police are able to sustain control over the criminal process because of
their 'positional advantage' (Cook, 1977) vis-à-vis the other agents of criminal control. The police have 'low visibility' to these other agents and produce
the information required by these others. The latter are thus heavily dependent and must act on trust without any routine independent checks on how the
police have made their case.

The research literature abounds with examples of these relationships and
speculation on their effects. Blumberg (1970: especially 281) describes how
the police develop exchange relationships with prosecutors and defense counsel, who are co-opted as 'agent mediators' to encourage the accused to enter
guilty pleas. Prosecutors are heavily dependent on the police for evidence and
they reciprocate by accepting police recommendations and practices in a way
that allows the police to influence the decision-making authority of the
prosecutor (Skolnick, 1966: especially 179, 191; Ericson, 1981: chapter 6).
Applications for warrants from justices are routinely granted, usually without question (LaFave, 1965: 34; Ericson, 1981: chapter 6). Similarly, police

information and recommendations are crucial in decisions to grant release from custody and bail conditions (Bottomley, 1973: especially 101-3).

Undoubtedly, the police officer must keep in mind the rules of these others as he goes about preparing his case, operating with a set of 'prefigured justifications' (Dalton, 1959) in the event his actions are challenged. However, because of his skill at doing this and because of the organizational arrangements in court, he is rarely challenged. In the vast majority of cases the accused pleads guilty, and the judge knows little if anything as to why that decision was made, including police influences on it. While there is a formal judicial power to enquire into whether or not the plea of guilty was in order – *Adgey* v *The Queen* (1973) 23 CRNS 278 – this is rarely done (cf Grosman, 1969: 30). In this sense most criminal cases result in a determination of guilt without judicial review and control, and the process takes on many of the features of an inquisitorial system (Heydebrand, 1977). Only those cases going to trial have a public adversarial nature,[19] and this includes *possible* counter-accusations that call police judgments into question. In the small minority of cases that go to trial, the trial can be viewed as an appeal from police decisions about an individual (cf Law Reform Commission of Canada, 1973: 9-10).

Typically, when the police officer decides to invoke the criminal process, he 'not only satisfies probable cause but also concludes after his careful evaluation that *the suspect is guilty and an arrest is therefore just*' (Reiss, 1971: 135; see also Wilson, 1968: 52). In proceeding to court, he is primarily seeking routine confirmation of what he assumes to be the case. If this confirmation is not routinely forthcoming, he may see that the other agents are calling into question his judgmental processes, his legitimacy, and their trust. It may be seen as an attack on his competence and, by implication, on police competence. The possible effects are many, ranging from rethinking the desirability of charging in similar situations to an alteration in strategies of presentation in court while otherwise continuing to do the same thing. As Newman (1966: 196) states, 'Efforts at control are resisted by the police, who do not rethink the propriety of the enforcement program but rather adopt alternative methods of achieving their objectives.'

Overall, the legal organization within the court structure is enabling for the police. 'Social order depends upon the co-operative acts of men in sustaining a particular version of the truth' (Silverman, 1970: 134). The ordering of the criminal process is very much under the influence of the police because their versions of the truth are routinely accepted by the other criminal-control agents, who usually have neither the time nor the resources to consider competing truths. In the vast majority of cases, the effective decision is made by the police, with the co-operation of the prosecutor, free from direct judicial constraint. The message from the literature seems to be that when additional formal rules and opportunities for judicial review are created, the police are still able to construct truth in a way that allows their

version and their desired outcome to be accepted. This has led one commenta-
tor to conclude that a system of judicial control of the police is not practically
possible. 'The absence of sufficient information is one reason why it would be
unrealistic to expect the courts to investigate and control the discretionary
powers of the police in law enforcement, especially those concerned with
prosecutions, through the familiar process of judicial review of administrative action' (Williams, 1974: 164).

One must look *within* the police organization to see how legal rules are placed
in the context of other organizational rules. Additionally, it is necessary to
examine dynamics within the police organization because most police decisions are not directly related to criminal law anyway. As we saw earlier, very
little of the patrol officer's time is spent doing criminal-law investigation or
enforcement. Most of the time is spent waiting or looking for trouble. When
trouble is reported or discovered, the possibility of defining the matter as
criminal may be taken into account, but this is only one among a range of
justifiable choices. A host of decisions about mobilizations and information-
gathering form the bulk of all decisions by patrol officers, and they are
subject to few if any formal rules from outside the police organization. In
sum, a full view of police decision-making requires a look inside the police
organization to see how internal expectations articulate with those from the
outside.

The research record suggests that increasing bureaucratization and professionalization have brought the police organization increased autonomy
from the community (Reith, 1943; Silver, 1967; Bordua, 1968; Fogelson, 1977;
Miller, 1977; Ignatieff, 1979). Studies of attempts at organized community
control of the police and of dealings between police administrations and
police commissions show that the police are able to co-opt community efforts
at control to serve their own organizational interests (e.g. Norris, 1973;
Evans, 1974; Washnis, 1976; Brogden, 1977). In Britain, several researchers
are arguing that the police have become a fundamental force in shaping
community structure, using the media and other sources of power (e.g.
Bunyan, 1976; Hall et al, 1978; Cohen, 1979; Taylor, 1980).

At the level of the individual patrol officer, bureaucratization has meant
distancing from the community. Encounters between citizens and officers
involve *a* policeman, not *the* policeman, with less personalized contact and
the displacement of responsibility to a more anonymous entity. Bureaucratization and professionalization also foster a greater orientation to law enforcement (Wilson, 1968; Murphy, 1981).

In addition to insulating the patrol officer from the community, bureaucratization and professionalization can militate against internal control of
the line officer while giving the appearance of greater control. In an ironic
and contradictory fashion, bureaucratization and professionalization can
have a strong debureaucratizing effect, shifting power into the hands of line

officers as a collective force (Clark and Sykes, 1974: 473). As the size and degree of specialization within the police organization increase, the line officers come to rely on their immediate colleagues, rather than distant superiors, for co-operation (Cain, 1973: 222). Moreover, expansion and specialization lead to increased conflict, with sub-units establishing their own interests, often in direct conflict with those of other sub-units (Banton, 1964: especially 263; Skolnick, 1966). Various means are used to create and perpetuate internal power resources, such as not communicating, or selectively communicating, essential information (Bittner, 1970: 65).

The police organization differs from most other organizations in the extent to which essential decisions and the input of knowledge occur among the lowest-ranking members and filter upwards. In most industrial concerns policies are set by the board and senior executives and are then passed on to managers who oversee its implementation by those working on the line. The line member's task is to carry out what has been delegated to him, although he can of course object that the demands are too stringent or develop other ways of accomplishing the task. In the police organization, the administration can establish general production guidelines, but it is much more heavily dependent on the decisions taken and information produced by line members.

Wilson (1968: 7) points out, 'The police department has the special property ... that within it discretion increases as one moves *down* the hierarchy." This is owing to both the 'low visibility' of these decisions and their 'situated' nature. As Wilson (p 66) goes on to state, due to the fact the administrator 'cannot in advance predict what the circumstances are likely to be or what courses of action are most appropriate – because, in short, he cannot be there himself – he cannot in advance formulate a policy that will 'guide' the patrolman's discretion by, in effect, eliminating it' (see also Bittner, 1974; Punch, 1979). Given the variety of human beings and troubles the patrol officer deals with, it is unlikely that rules could be written short of a compendium on the manners of society (Laurie, 1970: 111).

The police officer's rules for action are the 'recipe' rules learned on the job. Of course, these rules take into account rules from other sources – the community, the criminal law, and the police administration – especially as they are useful in the formulation of accounts for justifying actions taken. However, these 'recipe' rules also cover a range of circumstances and practices not directly addressed within other rule systems. They 'are not the administrative rules, which derive substantially from the criminal code or municipal regulations, but are those "rules of thumb" that mediate between the departmental regulations, legal codes, and the actual events he witnesses on the street' (Manning, 1977: 162–3). They cover a wide range of matters, such as whom to stop on suspicion in what circumstances; when official paper is necessary as opposed to a notebook record or nothing at all; how to prepare official paper; when and how to charge, including charging-up and multiple-charge possibilities; how to deal with lawyers and crown attorneys in the construction of case outcomes; and so on.

Many of the 'recipe' rules are known only among line officers. The rules of the 'law in action' are fully known and thus predictable only to them, and not to police administrators, other criminal-control agents, and the public. Patrol officers control the creation of these rules, their use, and knowledge about them in ways that fundamentally secure their power within the organizational 'order of things.'

The administration attempts to compensate for lack of control by emphasizing bureaucratic and professional standards. As mentioned earlier, this accomplishes the appearance of control, but also strengthens tendencies it was designed to oppose, especially 'occupational individualism and defensive fraternal solidarity' (Bittner, 1970: 67). Administrative control systems provide cover for the control systems within the occupational environment of patrol officers. They '(a) protect against the claim that something was not done; (b) punish persons after the fact; (c) maintain the appearance of evaluation, if not evaluational capacity; (d) maintain autonomy among and between units within the system by leaving the principal integrative bases tacit and unspecified' (Manning, 1979: 26; see also Manning, 1977: chapter 6).

The police administration's efforts at control are multifaceted and include a disciplinary code, direct supervision, measurement of production, and a division of labour in terms of resources.

The appearance of a disciplined and cohesive unit, the embodiment of consensus, is created through the use of military-style dress and procedures. This gives a police patrol operation *some* of the characteristics of 'total institutions' as described by Goffman (1961). Definitions of reality constructed within the organization are intended to exclude conflicting meanings and thereby solidify particular orientations to the range of problems the patrol officer has to deal with. This is accomplished by techniques such as 'identity stripping' in the initial training and socialization phase for new members of the organization, and by an appearances code that includes such things as military-style uniforms and 'parades' before each shift. The result is an image of strict control over symbolically important matters even if they have little to do with the essential work of patrol officers. Unlike in total institutions, however, members are not cut off from routine contact with those outside. On the contrary, the central task of patrol officers is to confront outsiders and to engage directly in conflicts over competing definitions of reality.

The disciplinary code provides an enabling framework for the administration in its efforts to create an appearance of organizational order (for an analysis, see Ericson, 1981a). As Rubinstein (1973: 41) observes, 'The Duty Manual offers almost unlimited opportunities to bring charges against a man.' The rules, subsumed under provincial police acts (e.g. Ontario Police Act RSO 1970) and departmental orders, are written in such broad and general form that they resemble rules for maintaining 'good order and discipline' within prisons (Ericson, 1981a). Every police officer violates them. Some have even noted that rules are contradictory, so that following one necessarily entails violation of others (Ramsay, 1972). The rules place the patrol officer in a state of 'dependent uncertainty' (Cain, 1973: especially 181), because he knows the administration can always 'get' him if he falls from official grace in other matters of importance. Just as patrol officers use enabling criminal-law rules to deal selectively with troublesome citizens, the police administration is able to use Police Act and departmental rules to deal selectively with troublesome officers.

The appearances code has another control function for the administration: to the extent that petty complaints regarding dress, coffee breaks, cheap meals at restaurants, etc, become the focal point of occupational grievances, the administration can play out concessions in these areas and deflect the more fundamental labour-management problems which characterize any bureaucratic working environment. Concerted effort at control from line-officers – even in the apparently strong police-union movement in the United States (Juris and Feuille, 1973; Halpern, 1974) – is deflected into these areas of petty grievance, deflating the opposition of line officers and ultimately co-opting them.

The administration also employs line supervisors (patrol sergeants) to patrol and enforce its conception of internal order (see especially Rubinstein, 1973: chapter 2; Muir, 1977). These supervisors develop procedures covering a variety of matters, from office routine to handling prisoners. They give daily briefings which include directions about what areas of enforcement to concentrate on or ease up on. They spend considerable time patrolling in a platoon area. Their ability to listen in on messages from dispatchers to patrol officers means they can respond to any dispatched call, and this possibility is constantly kept in mind by patrol officers. The patrol sergeant and other higher-ranking officers review any official written reports submitted by patrol officers, and this is also kept in mind in deciding whether and how to construct reports (Reiss, 1971: 124–5).

Part of the 'recipe' knowledge the patrol officer learns is directed at controlling supervisors. This takes the form of an exchange, whereby the officer follows the appearances code and formulates official reports in the appropriate bureaucratic framework in return for leniency in areas which ease the humdrum nature of patrol work. A lot of time and energy is spent on 'easing' work (Cain, 1973; Chatterton, 1979), but the first requirement is to gain the co-operation of the patrol sergeant. This is relatively easy given the importance of the appearances code within large bureaucratic police forces.[20]

Productive appearances are of considerable significance. Measures of productivity serve to inform supervisors what a patrol officer is up to, and they also provide data with which the organization as a whole can 'sell' itself. One obvious form of control is the development of quota requirements for enforcement activity. For example, researchers have documented how patrol-officer involvement in traffic-law enforcement can be influenced by a quota system. Wilson (1968: 97) reports that in Oakland a quota of 2 tickets per traffic division officer per hour was met with an actual rate of 1.97 tickets per traffic division officer per hour over a six-week period selected at random (see also Gardiner, 1969).

Another form of influence is the establishment of policy and attendant rules concerning charging. Senior administrators have attempted to articulate criteria concerning the decision to charge or caution. The rate of cautioning has been shown to be significantly influenced by the preferences, ideological or otherwise, of particular police chiefs (Steer, 1970: 17).

Research has shown that adoption of production criteria fundamentally affects decision-making about arrest and charging. One consequence of measurement in any organization is overproduction in the areas that can be measured and underproduction in the areas more difficult to measure (Etzioni, 1961). For example, detectives concentrate on cases that can be cleared rather than on those which require considerable investigative attention and are unlikely to result in a measureable payoff (Greenwood, 1975; Ericson, 1981). Similarly, patrol officers are more likely to concentrate on measureable areas of proactive enforcement, such as traffic, liquor, and narcotics, rather than on more abstract areas of reproducing order, if they are explicitly rewarded for doing so (cf Fisk, 1974: 25).

The emphasis upon 'clearances' of all sorts rather than just charges can lead to a number of other practices. In his research, Steer (1970: especially 21, 38) found that when adults are formally cautioned, the caution is typically employed as an alternative to no formal action, because of a lack of evidence, rather than as an alternative to prosecution. Indeed, Steer found that many cautions are given for activities that do not legally constitute a crime and could be more suitably written off as unfounded. Cautioning procedures thus help to swell clearance rates and make suspects arrested and investigated with no substantial grounds believe that there were grounds but that the police are exercising leniency.

Police officers with a high volume of cases to work on and perceiving administrative expectations to clear as many as possible may try to obtain a greater number of clearances for each arrest and reduce the overall number of investigations and arrests (Chaiken, 1975: chapter 9). This is frequently accomplished by having the suspect admit to a large number of offences on the promise that he will not be charged for them. Lambert (1970) reports that in a sample of 2,000 recorded property offences in Birmingham, 43 per cent of those cleared were done so by this method. LaFave (1965: 374) records that in Detroit, when talking with an accused, 'the interrogating detectives stress the fact that any additional offences admitted are "free offences" in that there will be no prosecution for them.' Skolnick (1966: 78) cites the case of two accused persons who received lenient sentences in exchange for admitting to over 500 burglaries.

Where police officers perceive extreme organizational pressure for production they may turn to more extreme methods, including excessive use of physical force (cf Whitaker, 1964). However, the research literature shows that such measures are relatively rare because they are not necessary (cf Skolnick, 1966: especially 174; Reiss, 1968: 12; Wald et al, 1967: 1549). The other tactics enumerated above provide enough resources to allow the line officer to proceed by way of the carrot rather than the stick. These procedures become bureaucratically accepted and routinized, allowing predictability and control in a way that other approaches, such as excessive physical force, cannot accomplish.

These practices have important ramifications for the productive efforts of police organizations as a whole. They lead to the production of crime rates in a way that seriously affects their validity as measures of crime control, although they serve the organization's 'crime-fighting' image. Several writers have pointed out that similar processes operate in other organizational contexts (see generally, Ditton, 1977, 1979). For example, Bensman and Gerver's (1963) study of an airplane factory revealed that line workers used an illegal tool that caused long-term hazards to airplane safety. They did so because it helped to meet production quotas; moreover, its use was condoned sub rosa by superiors. There are also many similarities in the work of bailiffs (McMullan, 1980). In sum, members of occupational cultures, in response to bureaucratic demands, can be adaptive and creative in producing their own rules to achieve their own needs. Those in the police organization can circumvent expectations from the wider organization of crime control and indeed alter the nature of both organizations.

Administrative influence affects resource allocation and the division of labour. For example, various types of dispatch systems regarding calls for service have control implications for patrol officers (Cordner, 1979; Manning, 1979; Jorgensen, 1979). In most police organizations, dispatched calls are tape-recorded and also recorded on a card system by the communications officer and dispatch officer. The officer is required to report back to the dispatcher on what happened, although if he is not filing official paper this may be only a brief coded message. Pepinsky (1975, 1976) found that in dispatches where the dispatcher named an offence, especially other than traffic, sex, or assault, the officer filed an official report on the offence as dispatched subject only to routine collaboration by the complainant (see also Jorgensen, 1979). Some police forces have attempted to control further through the instalment of vehicle-locator systems. Moreover, some forces may circumvent collusion among dispatchers and patrol officers by having civilian dispatchers, who do not have the experience of, and affinity with, the occupational culture of patrol officers.

While there appears to be substantial control via the dispatch system, ethnographers (e.g. Rubinstein, 1973; Manning, 1977, 1979) have documented the many means by which patrol officers collectively resist this form of control. Those who book off on a call can remain booked off while they go about their personal business after handling the call. Dispatchers can 'cover' for patrol officers who are 'missing' and the subject of inquiry from supervisors. The majority of calls do not result in official paper, and these can be accounted for in ways the dispatcher is unable to check. Even when official paper is submitted, there is usually no systematic linking of the paper with the original dispatch; moreover, most supervisors know that events become transformed and there is no meaning in a correlation between dispatcher labels and the officer's final accounting. There are strategies for circumventing vehicle-locator systems, e.g. finding spots where the signals are distorted.

Specialized division of labour characterizes urban police forces. An obvious division is between uniformed patrol officers and detectives. For example, in the Metropolitan Toronto Police Department there is an administrative regulation stipulating that uniformed personnel must turn over all arrested suspects to the detective branch for further investigation and charging, except in provincial-statute cases and areas of the Criminal Code dealing with driving and public order (Johnson, 1978). This type of bureaucratic ordering significantly influences what the respective units work at (see Ericson, 1981: especially chapter 3).

Obviously, it is essential to examine the internal order of police organizations because it is there that the sense of order from community and legal organizations is translated into action. A fully social account of patrol-officer discretion must inquire into the sense of order derived from each of the organizational forums within which he operates, and ascertain how this sense of order frames what he does on the job. In this way we shall learn something about the reproduction of order within organizations (cf Ranson et al, 1980) and how this articulates with the reproduction of social order.

Reproducing Order: Some Research Questions

In this chapter we have described and scrutinized the socio-legal literature on the police in order to derive a conception of their work. The position advanced is that the patrol police operate within a framework of rules emanating from the community and legal and police organizations. These rules collectively provide patrol officers with their sense of order, as they work to reproduce this order by taking these rules into account and using them as part of their accounts.

In light of the expansion and expense of police in Canada, it is surprising that there has been little attention by researchers to the police. Moreover, the police are an excellent vehicle for studying topics of significance to social science, including most generally how forms of social control are related to the reproduction of social order. Questions of importance to both academics and public administrators are involved in this area of research.

Some basic questions need to be addressed. As the editor of a recent collection of articles on the British police states, the most basic question is, who controls the police and how is this accomplished? (Holdaway, 1979). How do police officers spend their time? What do exercises of discretion look like? What does this tell us about the role of the police in constituting crime and other objects of their environment? What does it suggest about their wider social, cultural, economic, and political functions? Ultimately, does the view of policing portrayed in research lead us to question the massive build-up of policing and its dispersal as an everyday fact of community life?

Tentative answers to these questions require major research on a continuing basis. In this book I study patrol officers in a large Canadian municipal police force. We used systematic observation, official records, and unstructured interview data to study police patrol work from the viewpoint of the line officers whose work it is. We utilized both quantitative and qualitative data, emphasizing the strengths and limitations of each in providing a rounded view of patrol officers at work.

Accepting the portrayal of previous researchers including Bittner, Chatterton, and Manning, we do not view criminal-law enforcement as the primary work or goal of patrol work, but rather see it as one of many tools used by the patrol officer to order the population. In consequence this is not a study in the tradition of police effectiveness as crime fighters.[21]

Our research is concerned with patrol officers as *actors* who actively shape, and are shaped by, the nature of the work they undertake. We are interested in their use of rules, of the citizens they confront, and of each other. This work is largely within the 'social action' tradition in sociology (cf Blumer, 1969; Strauss, 1978; Rock, 1979a). Man is given the ontological status of producer. The locus of inquiry is interaction, which reveals both the nature of the structures produced by actors and the influence of these structures upon them. As Giddens (1976: 122) points out, 'The proper locus for the study of social reproduction is in the immediate process of the constituting of interaction. On the other hand, just as every sentence in English expresses within itself the totality which is the "language" as a whole, so every interaction bears the imprint of global society; that is why there is a definite point to the analysis of "everyday life" as a phenomenon of the totality.'

In sum, I undertake an organizational analysis within a social-action framework (cf Silverman, 1970; Ranson et al, 1980) in order to contribute both to sociological understanding of organizations and to the substantive area of policing. In terms of socio-legal studies, our work can be placed within the type identified by Cain (1979) as 'the police and deviancy' and more generally within the tradition examining the social construction of work outcomes (theoretically, see Berger and Luckmann, 1966; on the criminal process, see McBarnet, 1981). We examine the patrol officer as he constructs images and facts of 'trouble,' 'deviance,' and 'crime' and the implications of what he does for the mandate of policing, and ultimately for social order.

In chapter 2, I describe the research design and procedure. In chapter 3, I consider the internal occupational environment of patrol work and provide descriptive data on how time is spent and what generally the work looks like. In subsequent chapters, I examine specific decisions of patrol officers and explore the influences, rule usage, and accounts which form these decisions. Chapter 4 focuses on the decisions about mobilization; chapter 5 includes an analysis of decisions vis-à-vis victim-complainants, such as whether to take an official report or other action; and in chapter 6, I study investigative, charging, and conviction decisions relating to suspects and accused persons. In chapter 7, I return to the general issues discussed in this first chapter, examining them in light of my empirical findings and using them to speculate upon trends in policing.

2

Research Strategy

Our primary research task is to examine empirically how patrol officers constitute the world they inhabit through their decision-making processes. This entails extensive and intensive observation of patrol officers in the full round of their work activities.

An approach of this type has been used by a number of researchers studying police work (for an excellent review of police fieldwork studies, see Van Maanen, 1978; for a Canadian field study, see Vincent, 1979). This approach is in keeping with a sociological tradition emphasizing the need to understand organizational life through first-hand contact with the actors who comprise it. As Goffman (1961: ix–x) has counselled, 'Any group of persons – prisoners, primitives, pilots, or patients – develop a life of their own that becomes meaningful, reasonable, and normal once you get close to it, and ... a good way to learn about any of these worlds is to submit oneself in the company of the members to the daily round of petty contingencies to which they are subject.'

This entails proceeding according to the designs of those who are being studied in their natural environment, not only according to the researcher's design. The researcher's task is to glean and confirm social meanings by seeking extensive time in the field, varied status opportunities, varied social contexts, familiarity with language, and intimacy (Bruyn, 1966: 181ff). If one can grasp the meanings, and the processes by which they are constructed, one can understand and explain the reality under investigation using the members' framework as an essential tool. 'Meanings tend to be transbehavioral in the sense that they define, justify, and otherwise refer to behavior and are not simply a description of it. Meanings interpret behavior among participants in a social world (even though they may also describe it)' (Lofland, 1971: 24). By direct dealings with members in their 'daily round,' the researcher can begin to understand the 'recipe' knowledge of those he is studying and thereby the nature of their social relations. Through this process the researcher engages, with his subjects, in 'the social construction of reality' (Berger and Luckmann, 1966).

A major aspect of this approach is the 'discovery' of data and attendant ideas that would otherwise remain hidden (Glaser and Strauss, 1967). This approach is especially needed in any research on police work because of the tendency of the police to keep their criteria of operation at a low level of visibility (see Goldstein, 1960; Rubinstein, 1973: especially 215; Thomas, 1974: especially 148).

While quantitative data are useful, 'statistical portrayals must always be "interpreted", "grounded", and given human meaning in the context of the qualitative – direct face-to-face – "knowing"' (Lofland, 1971: 6). Without observation the researcher is unable to check the verbal and written accounts of members against their deeds. The researcher can then only be an accountant, whose analysis is not significantly related to the reality he is concerned with. He will produce an idealized picture of the world as his subjects want him to see it and not as they do see it. As Berger and Luckmann (1966: 45) state, 'Both misinterpretation and "hypocrisy" are more difficult to sustain in face-to-face interaction than in less "close" forms of social relations' (see also Reiss, 1971a: 29).

Research Procedures

To obtain first-hand observation we had to contact a police force which would permit our inquisitive presence over an extended period. Our decision to approach the police force studied was based upon three criteria. First, this force was known to be projecting a progressive image and therefore would likely be responsive to a request for the type of access we desired. Second, the community concerned was of manageable size in terms of our research interests compared with large metropolitan areas with many more police divisions and many more courts in which to follow cases. Third, the community was accessible to our research project office.

Initial meetings were held with the chief of police and the chairman of the board of police commissioners, who granted general permission to conduct the project. This was followed by meetings with the deputy chief in charge of field operations (uniform patrol) and with the commanders in each of the three patrol divisions. In turn, the research staff were assigned to staff sergeants in each of the three divisions who were to be liaison officers.

The first task for the researchers was to familiarize themselves with the community and the police organization. This was accomplished by several visits to police headquarters where the flow of organizational records, the organization of patrol areas, the dispatch system, the shift system, and measurement of workload were studied. A day was spent with each of the divisional administrators to obtain their view of divisional operations. The researchers then undertook 15 shifts of preliminary observation, including attachments with patrol sergeants who covered all the patrol areas of their platoon and thus were able to provide a general overview of the divisions.

During these preliminary shifts, workload data were collected to ascertain variance in volume of official occurrence report activity and dispatch activity according to shift periods and patrol areas. These data were to be used in developing a sampling procedure that would generate sufficient cases. Research instruments were constructed for activity on the shift, the background of police officers, and police-citizen encounters observed on the shift.

Upon completion of a draft of the research instruments a pilot study was undertaken. Five fieldworkers each engaged in ten patrol shifts according to the volume of activity as indicated by force data on occurrences and dispatch. The pilot work revealed that these data did not predict volume of activity by shift time, or day of the week. Partly on this basis, the decision was made to employ a simple random sample, accounting for patrol areas, days of the week, and shift time (day, afternoon, and midnight shifts). The pilot work also resulted in further revision in the research instruments and sampling procedure. The revised strategy was then implemented for the main fieldwork period, from May through September 1976, involving five fieldworkers in a total of 348 patrol shifts.

Data were collected in six different forms. A *shift sheet* was developed to detail the time and area in which the shift occurred, the volume and nature of activity, and background information on the police officer and his view of the police role.

Incident schedules were designed initially along the lines of those developed by Reiss and Black (cf Black, 1968), with mainly closed-ended items and a separate schedule for reactive and proactive encounters. During the pilot period it was discovered that there was no benefit in separating the proactive and reactive schedules; both types of encounter could be recorded using one schedule, keeping a small section of the schedule for items peculiar to one or the other type. Furthermore, to retain scope for establishing new categories as research continued, a more open-ended schedule was created. In its final form, the schedule included the time and circumstances of the incident; the way in which it came to the patrol officer's attention; the initial response of the officer; the status-role characteristics of citizens, their relationships, and their demands on the police officer; actions taken by the police officer to resolve the matter, including the decision whether to write an occurrence report; questioning of suspects; search of suspects; arrest of suspects; and retrospective accounts by the police officer.

The other data fieldworkers collected were not recorded on established instruments. Fieldworkers were asked to record minor *citizen contacts* where there was a brief encounter with a citizen or citizens such as traffic checks, requests for identification, 'service' work (such as returning lost property), 'assistance' calls, and so on. Fieldworkers were to describe the encounter, how it was initiated, characteristics of the citizens involved, the matter in dispute, and the outcome.

Ignored violations were events which might have caused the officer to intervene but he chose not to do so (e.g. seeing a person go through a red light but not stopping him). For these, fieldworkers were asked for a capsule description of the event as seen by the police officer, including what he was doing when the violation was observed; what he said upon seeing the violation; and how he justified taking no action.

General shift activities were those which did not involve direct contact with citizens. Fieldworkers were asked to record the nature and circumstances of decisions by the police officer to undertake licence plate checks, property checks, alarm checks, special duties (e.g. direct traffic where traffic lights are out; court duty).

Field notes were recorded for areas not otherwise covered by the above forms, such as perceptions of the police administration, other police forces, private policing, the role of the criminal control process, policewomen, higher education, prejudice toward citizens of various status and role characteristics, the research project itself, and formal and informal directives. Fieldworkers were free to explore their own interests, and to record any information that might be relevant to an overall understanding of patrol work.

In collecting data, we tried to be systematic while allowing flexibility for discovery. If one becomes too 'systematic,' there is a tendency to select areas because they can be recorded systematically and are quantifiable rather than because they are meaningful. Reiss (1971a: 6–7) reports that in his police research 'it was difficult to record all of the sequential changes in the behaviour of the officers and citizens. The latter observation led us to select certain common points in *all* transactions for observation and recording so that we could make comparison systematically.' Some of his subsequent analysis reflects this decision, showing little sense, either by the actors themselves or by the researchers, of how police-citizen relationships are constructed. Similar problems are encountered in police-effectiveness research, where the officer is viewed as little more than 'an automated vending machine of service' (Kelling et al, 1979).

The principal investigator and one fieldworker made the initial contacts with the police administrators. A second fieldworker assisted in undertaking the preliminary patrol shifts and developing the research instruments and research procedures. One month prior to the main fieldwork, a further three fieldworkers were hired and involved in the pilot study. Two fieldworkers undertook observations in all three divisions of the force, while the other three were each assigned to one of the three patrol divisions.

The liaison staff sergeants in each division were provided with the shift schedules of each researcher, and it then became the responsibility of each fieldworker to make the entree into the field setting. There was a general order: 'The Chief of Police may from time to time grant permission for selected research personnel to accompany members of the Force during assigned tours of duty' and each officer should familiarize himself with appropriate sections of the Criminal Code related to citizens assisting police officers. The line patrol officers apparently had little other forewarning, information, or instruction from the administration regarding the research. Thus, the research appeared to emanate from the police administration, and each fieldworker had to explain and justify the research to each new patrol officer being observed.

Fieldworkers were equipped with a loose-leaf notebook for jotting down times and activities to refresh their memories when writing up schedules and notes after the shift. These notes were similar to those which the patrol officer kept. All shift activity and incident schedules, as well as citizen contact, ignored violation, general shift activity, and field notes, were recorded by the fieldworkers away from the field setting as soon as possible after each shift.

One month after the conclusion of fieldwork, all occurrence numbers involving incidents observed by fieldworkers were recorded and the supporting documentation checked through the records branch at police headquarters. In addition, all 'primary citizens' involved in incidents were checked on the 'police contact' file of cards at the records branch of the force.

Upon completion of data collection the two fieldworkers who engaged in fieldwork in all patrol areas remained on the project staff to organize the documents and establish categories for coding. At the same time an index for qualitative analysis was prepared.

As stated previously, part of the research effort was directed at assessing the relative strengths and uses of quantitative and qualitative data. How could we combine quantitative variable analysis with analysis of officer-citizen transactions? Selecting decision points out of context and choosing independent variables suggesting a stimulus-response model seemed to belie the nature of social process. Yet observations suggested that certain factors directly observable in citizen encounters were used by patrol officers to produce outcomes. The task was to define these factors and outcomes.

We encountered difficulty in defining particular legal criteria. For example, the definitions of 'arrest' and 'search' are by no means clear from a legal perspective (for more detail see chapter 6, and Ericson, 1981: chapter 6). We also encountered difficulty concerning the measurement of evidence. While some researchers have judged, classified, and quantified evidence (e.g. Hagan and Meyers, 1979), we found it inappropriate to decide whether there was sufficient evidence to make a matter 'criminal.' Many patrol officer actions (e.g. intensive interviewing of a victim; proactive searches of suspects) were geared toward producing a definition that would justify treating a matter as criminal or otherwise for organizational purposes, but this was very different from the fieldworker deciding definitely that a criminal incident had taken place.

The qualitative data presented in chapter 5 concerning the decisions to take an occurrence report and how to label it and write it up illustrate this point. Many encounters had 'criminal' potential depending on how far the patrol officer wished to take his investigations and how he chose to handle the situation. Moreover, as argued in chapters 1, 5, and 6, and elsewhere (Ericson, 1981, 1981a) many encounters involve not a question of 'crime' and 'non-crime,' but whether the police officer finds it necessary to *use* the criminal law to handle trouble. Crime is something the patrol officer 'commits' to official channels as a resource for handling trouble (Ditton, 1979).

In this context, the only evidence-related measures that could be appropriately included in quantitative analysis were those dealing with observable incident characteristics, such as property damage and loss, and personal injury.

The 'formal action' variable for suspects in incidents (see chapter 6) illustrates a key problem in classification: should all investigative arrests, order maintenance arrests, and charges by patrol officers be included, or only particular types of formal actions such as Criminal Code charges? We decided to consider all 'further processing' of suspects by patrol officers and charges under provincial statutes as 'formal action' because they were all official police actions of potential consequence to the recipients. While one might assume that Highway Traffic Act charges, for example, would be of lesser significance than Criminal Code charges, it was difficult to impose such a judgment. As Cressey (1974) argues, many traffic offences are as serious as many criminal offences. Moreover, it is arguable that a person issued a Highway Traffic Act summons in a traffic accident might ultimately suffer greater costs through insurance rate increases than someone charged under the Criminal Code for offenses such as shoplifting or causing a disturbance.

Another task was to decide which variables should be related to decision variables. Among the many measures possible, some were readily excluded because they were not theoretically relevant. We did not include the demographic background and attitude of individual officers because we were concerned with the organizationally structured sources of discretion rather than personal variations in the exercise of that discretion. (For an example of a study emphasizing personal variations in discretion to the exclusion of organizational variations, see Hogarth [1971] on judicial sentencing.) In general we selected for quantitative analysis those features of the encounter and citizen characteristics that were immediately apparent to the patrol officer and could be assessed by him, e.g. mobilization, dispute type, damage and/or loss, injury, and status and behavioural characteristics of the citizens.

We decided to cross-tabulate decision variables with each other and to relate other decisions to each decision in discriminant analyses. In the cross-tabulations, we wanted to indicate the frequency with which one action occurred in conjunction with another. In the discriminant analyses, we wished to determine how one type of decision contributed to the prediction and classification of another decision. This is an important consideration because decision variables could be both 'independent' and 'dependent'; that is, particular decisions could influence other decisions, and there was no particular time-ordering in decisions. For example, a patrol officer's decision to handle a complaint by giving advice rather than recording an occurrence could occur in that order, in reverse, or simultaneously. Similarly, investigative and resolution actions in relation to suspects occurred in a full range of sequences. A suspect stopped for a traffic violation might be subject to a CPIC check during the time the patrol officer was writing out a summons, and if the CPIC check indicated there was an outstanding committal warrant, the suspect would be then subject to the execution of the warrant with or without the original violation being charged. The CPIC check might also suggest grounds for searching the suspect and his vehicle. While decisions of patrol officers may be presented in a particular sequence for analytical purposes, they do not always follow a particular sequence in their actual work.

After the pilot stage of the research we decided to categorize encounters of patrol officers with citizens into two types, namely, citizen contacts and incidents. Citizen contacts were defined as brief encounters involving minor troubles while incidents were more extensive and involved substantial troubles. In practice, then, we divided encounters into the less serious and the more serious.

The main reason for developing this distinction was to reduce the workload of fieldworkers, who discovered during the pilot observations that they could not cope with the paperwork expected along with a full-shift schedule of observations. It was decided that in minor encounters, only the basic details of the matter in dispute, citizen characteristics, and decisions by patrol officer would be recorded. This decision created other problems for our conceptual framework and ideals for analysis.

The categorization proved problematic for two reasons. First of all, the distinction between 'major' and 'minor' incidents was at best vague. What one fieldworker judged to be an incident another one might judge to be a citizen contact. Moreover, we cannot ignore the possibility that it was easier to call something a citizen contact because the written report requirement was much less for this type of encounter. In the same way that patrol officers sometimes 'skated' away from taking occurrence reports (see chapters 3, 5, and 6) our researchers might have avoided the more extensive writing of an incident schedule by calling it a citizen contact.

More fundamentally, there was a tendency to call something an incident if what started out as a brief 'routine' contact produced information that transformed the matter into a more major involvement. For example, if a 'routine' stop of a youth on suspicion resulted in a search in which marijuana was found, the matter was an 'incident'; if nothing was found, it would probably be judged a citizen contact unless there were other extensive investigations. The effect of this on our analysis is obvious. The 'incident' and citizens involved therein were 'loaded' in the direction of official action and 'successful' investigative actions, while citizen contacts were 'loaded' in the direction of unofficial action (except traffic summonses) and 'unsuccessful' investigative actions. While our definition accorded with whether or not the patrol officer regarded the encounter as 'major' or 'minor,' his determination of 'major' or 'minor' was often influenced by whether he happened to uncover information or evidence that could transform the encounter.

In retrospect, we realize that it would have been better to have viewed all encounters uniformly and to have had one schedule apply to them all. Depending on what the officer bothered to seek information about and what information he obtained, all encounters had the *potential* to become increasingly substantial and serious. However, the differences in the quality and type of data collected for citizen contacts and incidents meant that we had to treat them separately for purposes of analysis.

In sum, we produced a series of cross-tabulations on variables deemed uniformly applicable to citizens of particular types in particlar types of encounters. In general, these variables were based in what was immediately apparent to patrol officers as they were dealing with citizens. These variables informed us on an individual basis about what patrol officer actions were associated with what types of mobilization, dispute, citizen characteristics, and other major forms of actions by patrol officers.

We also employed stepwise discriminant analysis, which weights and combines independent measures in a way that forces two or more groups to be as distinct as possible so that one can predict on what criteria the groups are distinguishable (see generally, Morrison, 1969; Tatsuaka, 1971). This method was chosen over the more widely used regression analysis because there was no clear time-order or causal order in variables. As Greenberg (1979: 165–7) states, in discriminant analysis the emphasis is on the prediction of group membership without regard to the time-order or casual structure of the variables. Moreover, these aspects along with a nominal measure of the 'decision' variables mean that there are fewer restrictive assumptions necessary when employing discriminant analysis in comparison with other techniques, such as path analysis (ibid). In using discriminant analysis, we wished to further our classification of what elements most strongly predicted whether or not a particular action was taken by a patrol officer.

Research Setting

The research was conducted in a regional municipality in the province of Ontario, Canada. This regional municipality consisted of several small towns, townships, and villages. Prior to amalgamation under a regional government two years prior to the research, each of these smaller units had its own local police force or was policed by the Ontario Provincial Police. The local forces were replaced by a regional police force, which was created along with the more general regionalization of municipal government. The provision of regional services at the time of the research did not extend to any rural territory, so that the area covered by the police force studied was 267 square miles; the remaining 221 square miles of the region (with 3 per cent of the population) were policed by the provincial force.

Since the Second World War, the region has been transformed from rural and semi-rural to suburban and urban. This was largely a result of the rapid expansion of the adjacent metropolitan area, which was bulging beyond its boundaries and creating a need for decentralization of industry as well as land suitable for affordable housing. By 1971 only 2 per cent of the region's population could be characterized as farm population, compared with 6 per cent in 1961, and there were 475 fewer farms in 1971 than in 1961. It is estimated that in the mid-1970s 85 to 90 per cent of the rural land was owned by investors, developers, and speculators. The region is now diverse, ranging from upper-middle-class residential areas to high-rise apartment buildings and government-supported low-rental accommodation; from large-scale heavy industry to hundreds of small firms employing less than 25 persons; from a major airport to small pockets of rural territory.

Between 1961 and 1976 the region population increased an average of 8.4 per cent annually, compared with a rate of 1.9 per cent for the province and 1.6 per cent for the country as a whole.

The income level for residents of the region has tended to be higher than that for the province and the country. In 1971, the average male income in one town in the region was $9,550 while the average for Ontario was $7,250 and for Canada, $6,538. In June 1976, the average annual earnings of industrial workers residing in another town in the region were $12,000. The number of able-bodied persons seeking government assistance for unemployment in this town was approximately 200 in 1976 compared with 259 in 1973.

It should be noted that the labour force in the region is highly mobile. In general, middle- and upper-class managerial and professional workers commute to their place of employment outside the region but seem to prefer the residential suburbs that characterize the community. However, there is an abundance of industrial labour jobs which attract many people who reside outside the region. In early 1976, 58 per cent of the labour force were residents of the region, and 57 per cent of the resident labour force were employed in the region.

It is difficult to ascertain the ethnic composition of the population at the time of the research fieldwork. The latest available data are contained in the 1971 *Census of Canada*, in which it is indicated that 69.1 per cent were of British origin, 5.5 per cent German, 4.7 per cent Italian, 3.3 per cent French, with the remaining 17.4 per cent being small percentages of all other ethnic backgrounds. These data do not differentiate in terms of citizenship or date of immigration and of course include those whose families have lived in Canada over several generations.

The police force consisted of several units reporting directly to the chief alone, including accounting, intelligence, a special airport squad with other police forces, staff officer functions (citizen complaints, community relations and crime prevention, planning and research, safety, and traffic co-ordination), and duty inspectors. Under the deputy in charge of administrative operations were, among other matters, training, recruitment, records, communications, and provincial court bureaus. Under the staff support (criminal investigation) deputy were the divisional detective criminal investigation units, youth bureau, and special services (homicide, fraud, morality, auto, specialized criminal investigation, and, later, the polygraph unit). Under the deputy in charge of field operations were the three divisional patrol offices, as well as special units (e.g. marine, canine, accident investigation, tactical, and rescue).

As of December 1976, the force had 653 members according to the rank structure enumerated in Table 2.1. This number represents an overall 16.8 per cent increase in staff compared with the situation two years previous (after the first year of operation) including an increase of 16.9 per cent in police personnel and 21.8 per cent in civilian personnel.

The budget for police operations is the largest single expense of the regional government. For the year ending December 1975, the total gross expenditure of the top-tier regional government was \$44,583,029, of which \$12,788,180 or approximately 28.7 per cent went into operating the police force.

In return for the tax dollars residents receive a service that is, to say the least, difficult to measure. The only data readily available is that contained in the annual reports. These reports indicate that over the first three years of operation there had been some overall increase in volume of activity, as indicated in Table 2.2.

Included among the official occurrence reports are incidents judged by force members to have constituted criminal offences. In 1974, these numbered 26,688, of which 47.6 per cent were classified as 'break, enter and theft' and a further 20.6 per cent were classified as 'other Criminal Code,' including

TABLE 2.1

Rank structure and membership

Rank	Number
Chief	1
Deputy chief	3
Staff superintendent	1
Superintendent	2
Staff inspector	3
Inspector	14
Staff sergeant	23
Detective sergeant	14
Sergeant	50
Detective	39
Constable	396
Cadet	12
Civilian	95
Total	653

Source: *Police Force Annual Report*, 1976

thefts. There were 2 'murders,' 3 'attempted murders,' 54 'robberies,' and 9 'rape' offences.

In 1975, the total volume of police-reported 'crime' rose to 30,939, an increase of 15.9 per cent over 1974. In 1975, 44.9 per cent of all police-reported criminal offences were 'break, enter and theft,' a further 20.5 per cent were 'other Criminal Code' including thefts, and there were 4 'murder,' 1 'manslaughter,' 13 'attempted murder,' 58 'robbery,' and 11 'rape' offences. In 1976, total volume of police-reported crime rose to 31,589, an increase of 2.1 per cent over 1975 and 18.4 per cent over 1974. In 1976, 45.9 per cent of all police-reported criminal offences were classified as 'break, enter and theft,' a further 22.3 per cent were 'other Criminal Code' including thefts, and there were 7 'murder,' 2 'attempt murder,' 60 'robbery,' and 11 'rape' offences.

During the three-year period (1974–76) from its inception, the police force reported an overall clearance rate of 54 per cent. The range is from a rate of 31.2 per cent for 'break, enter and theft' and 42 per cent for 'other Criminal Code' including thefts, to 64.4 per cent for 'robbery,' 74.2 per cent for 'rape,' 100 per cent for 'attempt murder,' and 100 per cent for 'murder.'

The judicial district was 1 of 46 judicial jurisdictions in the province. The judicial district covered the same territory as the regional municipality.

There were three types of courts in the district. The provincial court handled the vast majority of cases, operating on a year-round basis. There were two provincial court buildings. The largest and most active contained three courtrooms at the beginning of the fieldwork and later added two more. Four were reserved for criminal cases and one for traffic cases. The smaller provincial courthouse had two courtrooms for minor criminal offences (e.g.

TABLE 2.2

Percentage change in volume of activity 1974–76

Nature of activity	1974 number	Percentage change		
		1975 compared to 1974	1976 compared to 1975	1976 compared to 1974
Telephone calls directed to communications centre	142,608	+21.7	+ 3.4	+25.8
Official occurrence reports	38,840	+24.8	+ 2.6	+28.0
Motor vehicle collision reports	10,904	–2.6	–4.7	–7.3
Other reactive responses without official reports	42,257	+ 8.4	+10.8	+20.2

Source: *Police Force Annual Report*, 1976

theft under $200), assignment, Criminal Code driving offences, and traffic cases.

These courtrooms were presided over by five provincial court judges (four at the beginning of the research). These judges were appointed by the provincial government and had jurisdiction over all offences created by provincial legislation as well as all but a few offences created by federal legislation. In the province as a whole, over 90 per cent of all trials held for indictable offences are conducted in this court (Ontario Ministry of the Attorney-General, 1975: 15). The traffic offences were normally presided over by a justice of the peace, as were some bail hearings. The provincial court judges presided at bail hearings, at preliminary hearings of criminal cases to be tried in the higher courts, and at the hearings of criminal cases.

The county court was located in a separate building, where there were four criminal courtrooms presided over by four county court judges. These judges also dealt with civil matters, and the number of county courtrooms involving criminal trials at any one time depended on the volume of criminal cases that reached this level. An accused who has been charged with an indictable offence which is not defined as being in the absolute jurisdiction of a provincial court judge can elect to be tried by a county court judge sitting alone (County Court Judges' Criminal Court) or by a county court judge sitting with a jury (The Court of General Sessions of the Peace).

The Supreme Court of Ontario held two sessions each year, one in the autumn and one in the spring, in the county courthouse. Judges of the Supreme Court, travelling on circuit, have jurisdiction to try any indictable offence, but normally only try serious offences such as murder, criminal negligence, and rape.

There were eight justices of the peace in the district. One was the court administrator for the larger provincial court and several presided over municipal by-law cases, traffic cases, and bail hearings. In addition, justices of the peace consider and sign applications for search and arrest warrants by the police and applications for charging by way of private information by citizens and decide whether and under what conditions an accused should be released pending an appearance in court.

There was one crown attorney who was generally charged with the responsibility of criminal prosecution. He was backed by 8 full-time assistant crown attorneys, 12 part-time assistant crown attorneys drawn largely from the practicing criminal bar in the area, and 1 assistant crown attorney on a limited-term contract. In addition there were 2 'lay prosecutors' as well as police 'court officers' who handled prosecutions in minor provincial offence cases involving traffic and liquor violations.

In terms of total volume of criminal cases, this judicial district ranked third among the 46 jurisdictions in Ontario in 1975 and in 1976. In 1975, there were 10,906 Criminal Code charges laid, and in 1976 this increased by 8.9 per cent to 11,881 (*Police Force Annual Report*, 1976).

Research Execution

The first and most fundamental problem in generating data through field research is to gain acceptance from and access to research subjects. Without this, the most elaborate and sophisticated research scheme will fail to produce worthwhile results. We achieved a great deal of co-operation, but not without problems, and in some areas not without loss to the ideals of the research as originally conceived. There were many obstacles placed in the way of fieldworkers in their search for information. Usually these obstacles were erected for clearly understandable reasons.

A key power available to the police is the control of information. Researchers attempting to gain access to this information and to use it for purposes largely unknown to the patrol officer are bound to face problems. Many researchers have stressed that police officers are secretive even among themselves. For example, Rubinstein (1973: 215) observes that the patrol officer 'fortifies his control [over fellow officers] by denying them the information he accumulates and sharing it with them only when he feels it is to his benefit.' It is likely that the patrol officer is even more guarded when dealing with an inquisitive outsider.

In order to help readers appreciate what we have produced and to guide those considering similar projects, I will list the problems we encountered, discuss how we attempted to resolve them, and count up the gains and losses that ensued.

As outlined previously, line officers were left guessing as to who the researchers 'really' were and who they represented. The fieldworkers outlined the nature of the research (including the focus upon decision-making) to each patrol officer at the beginning of each shift. However, weeks after the commencement of the research some patrol officers still seemed confused about the identity of the researchers and their purpose in conducting observations. During the course of fieldwork, patrol officers stated a wide range of views on who they thought the researchers were, including: 'government workers,' agents of the Ontario Police Commission, university-based police science experts, students writing a thesis, 'civil libertarians,' instructors there to teach patrol officers the finer points of police work, researchers inquiring into deviant work habits of patrol officers, assessors of daily performance, and agents of the force administration reporting to the administration about working conditions 'on the line.' While fieldworkers made efforts to dispel misconceptions, some distorted views or ignorance about the project persisted.

A prevalent view was that the researchers were working for the force administration in order to provide them with information about how officers were behaving 'on the street.' This view was repeated in varying ways by a number of patrol officers to different fieldworkers. A patrol officer, talking three months after the beginning of fieldwork, stated that patrol officers had still not been told anything by the administration about the purposes of the research. He used the research as an example of 'secrecy' which the administration practiced in relation to line officers. The patrol officer questioned the fieldworker: 'This is our job – how would you like it if people were assessing your performance daily?' He added that his concern was not only with the researchers but with 'students,' 'lawyers,' 'members of the press,' and all other 'civilians' who are allowed to observe police activities because the administration deems it acceptable.

Other officers refused to accept the fieldworkers' explanation that the study was not concerned with them as individuals. Their response was to argue that if the study was quantitative, then the researchers would rely on official reports and documents without directly observing patrol officers. These officers argued that what *should be* 'public' is what is officially documented for police organizational purposes. An inquiry into what was not regarded by patrol officers as officially reportable was no one's legitimate business; rather, it was illegitimate in the sense of 'obviously' being aimed at uncovering practices that would be publicly reported in a way that ultimately conflicted with the interests of patrol officers.

As we convey in subsequent chapters, patrol officers do not view the world in consensus terms; to them, human beings act in terms of particular interests, whether their own or those of particular groups they represent. Therefore, patrol officers were initially unwilling to accept replies from fieldworkers that the research was 'value neutral,' unconcerned with their deviant practices, etc. Indeed, persistent attempts by fieldworkers to convey a neutral position were probably less helpful than a detailed account of the issues the research was concerned with.

We did not keep a systematic tally of how many patrol officers expressed these concerns. One fieldworker frequently mentioned negative reactions, while two rarely mentioned these matters. Perhaps some fieldworkers were more adept than others at explaining and legitimating the research to patrol officers and gaining their acceptance. Nevertheless, these sentiments were expressed often enough to different researchers to suggest these matters were of continuing concern.

This situation raises an ethical problem: patrol officers may not have felt their participation was voluntary. The administration 'volunteered' access to patrol officers, who may have felt constrained to co-operate because they feared refusal might be viewed unfavourably.

Only five patrol officers explicitly refused to co-operate, resulting in assignment of patrol officers by the patrol sergeant. These refusals were made in relation to four different fieldworkers. In each case the patrol sergeant arranged the reassignment. One patrol officer refused the observer, but was then asked by the patrol sergeant to co-operate and subsequently complied. Of course, reassignments after refusals may also have occurred before the arrival of fieldworkers for a shift and thus remained unknown to them.

A few patrol officers who did comply later told the fieldworkers that they were doing so only because they felt they had no choice. One officer said he felt compelled to co-operate because of orders from the patrol sergeant and expressed his view that the researchers were 'spies' for the administration. Another was supposed to have the observer in his car and refused on the grounds that he did not want a woman with him on a midnight shift. The patrol officer who was substituted told the fieldworker that he would not refuse to co-operate because he was still on probationary status.

While the vast majority of patrol officers did not refuse to have an observer go along with them, some indicated that the researchers could never grasp the reality of policing because patrol officers would not act normally in their presence. This was expressed in various ways, e.g. that fieldworkers 'cramped the style' of patrol officers, that fieldworkers only saw what the officers wanted them to see, that officers approached encounters in a different manner when fieldworkers were present in order to 'cover their own ass' and to avoid having to rely upon the fieldworkers as court witnesses, and that the officers were less likely to engage in proactive activity, such as stopping cars on suspicion for routine checks.

It was, of course, extremely difficult for the fieldworkers to ascertain the impact of their presence on the 'normal' activity of patrol officers. On some shifts it was apparent that the type of activity engaged in and avoidance of certain activity were influenced by the presence of a fieldworker. For example, on one shift the fieldworker noted that the patrol sergeant reassigned a patrol officer to the patrol area preselected for observation. This patrol officer was scheduled to appear in court during the shift and also chose to take the annual proficiency test in pistol shooting during the course of the shift. As a result, only one and one-half hours of the shift was spent on mobile patrol. On another shift the dispatcher asked the patrol officer if he had an observer in his car, and when the patrol officer replied that he did, the dispatcher decided not to send the officer to guard the scene of a homicide that had just been reported.

One item on the 'incident schedule' asked the fieldworkers to report whether they believed their presence seemed to influence the officer's actions in any way. In 37 of 507 incidents the fieldworkers felt their presence was of 'some influence,' and in a further 11 incidents they felt there was 'obvious influence.'

The nature of fieldworker influence can be categorized into situations 1) where the patrol officers apparently approached the matter in a different way by the mere fact of the fieldworker's presence and 2) where the patrol officers attempted to use fieldworkers as an additional resource to handle the dispute.

Fieldworkers believed that in some circumstances patrol officers took a less aggressive approach with suspects because of their presence. For example, a suspect was arrested at a hotel bar for 'causing a disturbance' while drunk. The suspect was well known to the officers who arrested him, and they engaged in verbal attacks on each other during the drive back to the station. Upon arrival at the station the patrol officers drove into the garage near the cell area, and as they removed the suspect from the car they punched him several times. Later, the patrol officer told the fieldworker that if there had been 'fewer witnesses' the accused would have been 'softened up' considerably more, rather than just 'tuned.'

Patrol officers also admitted to fieldworkers that their presence led them to more detailed attention to complaints. For example, a patrol officer was hailed by a citizen who proceeded to show the officer two bicycle wheels he discovered on a road construction area. The patrol officer took the wheels as 'found property' and wrote up property tags, a found property report, and a found property occurrence report. He later commented that if the fieldworker had not been present, he would have 'tossed' the items somewhere else as a means of avoiding the paperwork. We have no way of knowing (other than through patrol officer accounts) what would have happened if fieldworkers were not present.

There was no systematic pattern to the use by patrol officers of fieldworkers to assist them, except that they usually sought assistance only when they were dealing with suspects or accused persons.

One fieldworker was six feet five inches tall and weighed 240 pounds. He reported three occasions on which he was presented to a suspect as an ally of the patrol officer who would be used to effect compliance if the suspect did not co-operate. Other fieldworkers were presented to suspects as police officers, serving to demonstrate an additional show of force and to destroy any possibility that the suspect would see the fieldworker as a third party he might consult regarding his rights. For example, a patrol officer stopped a young male pedestrian and questioned him about drugs. He then searched the youth, taking a package of tobacco cigarettes and tearing them up one by one. He told the youth that the fieldworker was a detective who would not put up with any 'bullshit.' When he discovered that the youth was from another province, the patrol officer told him that he could be arrested in Ontario on 'mere suspicion' of being a drug user. All of these strategies, including the identification of the fieldworker as a detective, were part of the patrol officer's intimidating display of authority against the suspect. The suspect eventually agreed to find out names of drug users in the area.

Fieldworkers were used in other ways to aid the patrol officer's investigative efforts, including running CPIC checks while the officer questioned and searched suspects, covering the patrol officer's back while he searched inside a vehicle, locating victims and witnesses and taking information from them, and posing as a school official as a pretext by which the patrol officer could gain entry to the suspects' residence.

In other situations, patrol officers had fieldworkers assist them in potentially dangerous situations, e.g. standing by to use the radio as a 'dangerous' suspect was approached at gunpoint, calling for back-up assistance after suspects threatened an officer, and being handed a nightstick and flashlight to use as weapons in dealing with several 'brawlers' at the scene of a hotel bar fight. Fieldworkers were also called upon to guard prisoners in particular circumstances, e.g. a female fieldworker was asked to escort a female prisoner to the toilet.

Fieldworkers occasionally participated in official accounts of how officers had dealt with suspects, e.g. signing as a witness to a written statement given by an accused person, and giving a statement as a witness concerning the arrest of two people where police brutality was being alleged. In these cases, fieldworkers were used as an additional resource. The dilemma was both ethical and practical. Should they allow themselves to be used in a way that might eventually be worked against the interests of the suspects or other parties involved? Would their refusal to co-operate with an officer offend him, thus affecting his willingness, and that of others, to allow access to events on future shifts?

In a few isolated situations, fieldworkers were perhaps legally bound to assist by the provisions for civilian aid requested by police officers in section 118(b) of the Criminal Code. In other situations fieldworkers gave tacit co-operation simply by remaining silent, e.g. not reporting to outsiders instances of apparent excessive use of force or not countering the officer's identification of the fieldworker as a police officer. It was a difficult matter of being too detached or too involved. Either course had potential ramifications for future co-operation and for the ethics of the research.

Overall, the fieldworkers displayed agility in this balancing act, avoiding confrontations with patrol officers while keeping to a minimum direct participation which would affect investigations and raise ethical problems. This is one reason why fieldworkers were able to secure trust and acceptance to the point where access was routinely granted.

The researchers experienced various signs of acceptance and attendant entree into additional contexts in which data could be obtained. Just past the midpoint of the fieldwork period, a patrol officer informed the researcher that the patrol officers had initially been opposed to the project because they thought the administration was 'shoving a bunch of bleeding heart liberals down our throats.' This officer claimed that he and his colleagues had tested the fieldworkers to ascertain if they were 'reporting back to the brass.' He stated that the researchers had passed the test and were receiving cooperation because they had not turned out to be 'civil rights assholes and anti-police.'

The rapport established was certainly not that of an equal colleague. Rather, it was that of any new member of the police organization: once they were viewed as not being in opposition to police interests, fieldworkers could be initiated into the ways of the police culture. As one patrol officer expressed it, the fieldworkers were similar to cadets and rookies, who in his view did not become 'one of us' until they had proven themselves over 'years.' Since fieldworkers did not have 'years' to accomplish the task, they could never be more than initiates.

Patrol officers who had fieldworkers ride with them transmitted acceptance to other patrol officers who had not been subject to observation and who remained wary. For example, a patrol officer began a shift by telling the fieldworker in no uncertain terms that he was against the research. However, at a meeting with another patrol officer later in the shift he apparently changed his attitude and told his colleague that the fieldworker was not a threat. After the fieldworker was introduced, the second patrol officer said, 'Oh, I better watch what I say,' to which the patrol officer replied, 'No, he's cool, you can say whatever you want.' The officers then engaged in an open critical discussion of the force.

This openness with fieldworkers was particularly noticeable during the seeming endless hours spent in the privacy of the patrol car with no shift activity. In these circumstances, patrol officers sometimes 'poured out' their grievances and frustrations about the job, using fieldworkers as sounding boards. Patrol officers sometimes admitted that they would not talk to their own colleagues about certain concerns they were expressing to fieldworkers, for fear that they would be viewed unfavourably. In this way, fieldworkers were sometimes able to glean information that was not shared even among the otherwise apparently cohesive group of patrol officers.

This tendency to be open in private conversation often contrasted with the situation at the station during parade or at lunch, when patrol officers would try to distance themselves from the research and the researchers as a means of displaying an affinity with their colleagues. Patrol officers would be friendly with fieldworkers and talk freely about their work while in the patrol car and then do an about-face when in the presence of other officers to indicate that they were treating fieldworkers as outsiders and not 'one of us.'

Another sign of acceptance was that fieldworkers rode with patrol officers who clearly deviated from the expectations of the police culture. The fact that these persons were not reassigned or otherwise kept from exposure to fieldworkers indicated that there was no active attempt to have fieldworkers assigned to preselected 'ideal' officers. Furthermore, while some patrol sergeants expressed the view that fieldworkers should only be assigned to more experienced officers, the fieldworkers regularly observed officers who were not of first-class constable rank and those who were on probationary status. Among the patrol officers observed 23.6 per cent had one year or less of experience and 71.4 per cent had three years or less of experience in the force or its prior municipal counterparts.

As the fieldwork evolved, some patrol officers began questioning why they had not been subject to observation and expressed a keen desire to participate in the study. For them, it became a matter of feeling 'left out' of what had become defined as something worthwhile – another indication that the research was being more favourably viewed by patrol officers.

The only situation that fieldworkers were systematically excluded from was the in-station interrogation of suspects. The administration decided at the beginning of the research that fieldworkers would not as a rule be allowed into these situations, because they might then have to be subpoenaed as witnesses in court (see Ericson, 1981). Also, patrol officers frequently turned over arrested suspects to other uniformed officers or detectives and were not themselves involved in the interrogation process (see chapter 6); they returned to their patrol area and/or wrote official reports on their segment of the occurrence.

In this chapter I have tried to help the reader to appreciate the strengths and limitations of how our research work was accomplished. We now turn to an analysis of the accomplishments of patrol officers in their role as reproducers of order, beginning with an examination of their occupational environment and work routines.

3

The Occupational Environment

A focal concern of patrol officers is orders received from the force administration and mediation of these orders within the occupational culture of line officers. Idealistic recruits soon learn that the 'crime-busting' image of police work in television serials and news accounts bears little relation to the work they actually do and that a different orientation is required. This orientation is derived from officers who are similarly situated and is common to line workers in any bureaucratic organization. The questions collectively asked include: how can we deflect controls over our work? how can we make it look as if our work is being done adequately, or even *credit*ably, while engaging in 'easing' behaviour (Cain, 1973) and gaining 'perks' which make the work routines more tolerable? In sum, there is a realization that patrol work is not dramatically different from other types of work (Reiss, 1971).

In this chapter we first document the work routines of patrol officers. We then consider bureaucratic controls, usually filtered through the patrol sergeant, and consider the effects of these controls on patrol work. Finally, we examine adaptations by the patrol officers to make the working environment more tolerable.

Work Routines

The vast majority of the patrol officer's time is spent not working on crime-related troubles. In fact, a substantial part of the time is spent driving around without any specific duty or direct contact with citizens. In a review of American research, Cordner (1979) reports that 40 to 50 per cent of a patrol officer's time is taken up on dispatched calls and that a substantial amount of the remaining time is devoted to administrative duties. Moreover, the gaps left by the lack of reactive work are not usually filled with a high volume of proactive work. Webster (1970) reports that less than 10 per cent of

TABLE 3.1

Uniformed patrol shift activity

Activity	N (348 shifts)	Mean (348 shifts)	Number of shifts on which activity undertaken	Percentage of 348 shifts on which activity undertaken	Mean for shifts on which activity undertaken
Citizen contacts	816	2.34	262	75.3	3.11
Incidents	507	1.46	257	73.9	1.97
Industrial property checks	427	1.23	163	46.8	2.62
Special duties	236	0.68	104	29.9	2.27
Occurrence reports	371	1.07	225	64.7	1.65

a patrol officer's time was taken up by proactive work in the California jurisdiction he examined. We quantified a number of shift activities and the time spent on some of them and our findings are in keeping with these and other British and American studies.

In Table 3.1 we quantify the main activities that occurred during the 348 shifts of observation. 'Citizen contacts' involve direct face-to-face encounters between officers and citizens where the encounter is brief and the dispute a minor one, e.g. routine stops and checks of motor vehicles and their occupants where no major investigation and no charges other than traffic summonses arise; dealing with found property; dealing with neighbour complaints of a trivial nature; checking the occupants of parked vehicles; checking hitchhikers, or youths in parks; asking 'disorderlies' to move on; and responding to a complaint that is immediately judged to be 'unfounded.' In absolute numbers these are the most frequent activities engaged in, but they do not occur at all on one-quarter of the shifts and occur on average only slightly more than twice per shift. In the 747 citizen contacts for which time was recorded, 85.3 per cent took 15 minutes or less and 98.2 per cent took 30 minutes or less. The mean time is 16.6 minutes and the median 15 minutes.

The other category of citizen encounters, termed 'incidents,' number 507 over the 348 shifts of observation. Incidents are defined as more lengthy and complex encounters than citizen contacts, possibly involving the patrol officer in taking information for an occurrence report; conducting some investigation such as searches or talking with alleged or possible suspects; issuing a summons or appearance notice to a culprit; arresting and/or charging and/or releasing someone; and so on. While incidents average three for every two patrol shifts, there are none at all on just over one-quarter of the shifts. In the 504 incidents for which time was recorded, 57.3 per cent took less than 30 minutes and 83.3 per cent were completed within one hour. The range is from 2 minutes to seven hours and 35 minutes, with an average time of 42.2 minutes and a median of 28 minutes. Thus, even though they are less numerous than citizen contacts, incidents involve considerably more police time and effort than citizen contacts, and they are certainly a more major component of patrol activity than citizen contacts.

If we consider the average of 2.34 citizen contacts per shift with a median duration of 15 minutes, and the average of 1.46 incidents per shift with a median duration of 28 minutes, we see an approximate median of 76 minutes per shift spent on direct encounters with citizens. If we add to this figure 60 minutes for lunch and an estimated 40 minutes travelling time for return trips between the divisional stations and the patrol area, we find approximately five hours per shift of general patrol, writing reports, preparing notebooks, checking property, or undertaking special duties. Most of this time is spent on general patrol, and more than one-half of the working time is spent patrolling in a way that makes the officer visible to citizens but not in direct interaction with them. Despite the considerable amount of time in which the officer could be pursuing proactive work, there are on average only 1.8 proactive stops per shift.[1]

We did not make provision to record time for the other three major shift activities in Table 3.1. These additional activities include 'industrial property checks,' which are typically dispatches to specific business premises as a result of an alarm call sent in through a private security company, or checks ordered by superiors as a result of such things as recent break-and-enters in an area or a report of suspicious persons or circumstances in an area. This activity occurs on slightly less than one-half of the shifts; overall the average is approximately five such calls for every four shifts, but during the 163 shifts on which this activity was undertaken the average is five such calls for every 2 shifts.[2]

'Special duties' include a wide variety of other activities, such as residential property checks, general surveillance, and attendance at court. These average two for every three shifts overall, but over two for each shift on the 104 shifts on which such activity took place. It is noteworthy that activities in these categories – especially surveillance and court duty – can take a substantial part of a shift or all of it, and in turn can reduce what is produced in the other categories.

The writing of 'occurrence reports' is one consequence of encounters with citizens, or occasionally, if something unusual (e.g. a sign of entry) is found during a property check. This activity results when the officer decides a written account of a matter, and the action he took, is necessary. It occurs on average once per shift, although on one-third of the shifts none was taken.

The level of activity on a shift varied by the volume and type of reactive calls the patrol officer received and by his own initiative in undertaking proactive stops. The number of encounters with citizens on a shift varied from none to ten or more. When the number of encounters was high, it reflected an officer's initiative to undertake proactive work.

Bureaucratic Controls and Routine Work

While patrol officers obviously have some control over how much they do and how they go about doing it, their autonomy is restricted by bureaucratic controls. From the beginning of the modern police, administrators have continually searched for methods of controlling line officers.[3] Administrative rules have multiplied, and new technological innovations have been heralded both as an improved means of dealing with 'criminals' and as a better control over how police officers go about catching them.

THE PATROL SERGEANT

The internal control system is filtered through the patrol sergeant who, as the first-line supervisor, functions as an adviser, evaluator, and disciplinarian (cf Muir, 1977). As an adviser, he maintains the division of labour regarding criminal investigation between the patrol branch and detectives, oversees some investigations, and supervises report writing. As an evaluator, he is a source of opinion on job performance and ensures an acceptable level of work among officers on his platoon both individually and collectively. As a disciplinarian he uses the rules of the Police Act and administrative orders to make his officers appear efficient, effective, and otherwise orderly. Of course, these three roles overlap in everyday work.

The patrol sergeant has the opportunity and occasion for direct observation of patrol officers. He spends considerable time on general patrol in the divisional area where his officers are operating, and he sometimes responds to encounters involving patrol officers, either on his own initiative or at the request of an officer. In the 1,323 police-citizen encounters recorded by our researchers, 74 (5.6 per cent) involved the presence of a patrol sergeant. The patrol sergeant is more likely to be involved in incidents (47 of 507 or 9.3 per cent) than citizen contacts (27 of 816 or 3.3 per cent), probably because incidents are more likely to be reactive and thus known to him through the radio dispatch system and also because they typically involve more complex and lengthy disputes in which the patrol officer is likely to request assistance. In addition, there is the general influence that comes from the officer knowing the sergeant can appear at a citizen encounter the patrol officer is involved in or during times of 'easing' behaviour.

A major component of the patrol sergeant's advisory role is the division of labour regarding investigations. Criminal Code offences, with some exceptions (e.g. some minor thefts, driving offences, public order offences), are generally turned over to detectives for investigation. From an administrative viewpoint, this division of labour functions to keep the patrol officer on the street for preventive policing and makes him available for reactive calls. It also ensures that more experienced officers are preparing the case against the suspect. Experience is important in allowing the detective or senior uniformed officer to select the best charge and construct the evidence accordingly. It is also important in terms of the trust which is so necessary among police officers in constructing a case for court appearances (see chapter 6).[4]

Among the 170 suspects patrol officers encountered in incidents and subjected to 'further processing' (mainly arrest and/or charge; see chapter 6), 56 per cent were processed as a result of a decision taken by a patrol officer acting on his own. For a further 16 per cent the decision was taken by the patrol officer in conjunction with other line officers and/or detectives; for 8 per cent in conjunction with patrol sergeants; and for 9 per cent in conjunction with private security officers. For a further 11 per cent, we could not ascertain whether the decision was taken alone or with others. Furthermore, if patrol officers took suspects to the divisional station for further processing, they frequently gave over part or all of the investigation to other police officers. Of the 83 suspects taken to the station, 56 were interrogated – 25 by the patrol officer, 8 by other patrol officers, 10 by superior officers from the uniformed branch, and 13 by detectives.

In general, patrol officers are left to handle minor offences. Major offences, or situations calling for intensive interrogation of the suspect regarding other criminal activity, are turned over to others. For example, a patrol officer arrested a suspect running away from the scene of a reported residential break-and-enter. This person was apprehended in possession of a .22 calibre rifle and taken back to the divisional station where he admitted to a series of offences during the same night. However, rather than have the patrol officer complete the interrogation and processing of the suspect, the staff sergeant ordered that the suspect be held in the cells overnight until the detectives coming in at 8 am could deal with him. The staff sergeant justified this to the arresting officers by saying 'the D's aren't busy anyway,' and adding that the detectives would probably be able to generate additional charges from the suspect.

Our observations in general investigation detective offices (Ericson, 1981) revealed several instances of friction along these lines between patrol officers and detectives. For example, a patrol officer entered a detective office along with two detectives and a youth he had arrested after an extensive chase. The detectives immediately took the youth into the interrogation room and made no attenpt whatsoever to involve the officer or even to contact him about the progress they were making. The officer, in front of other detectives in the general office, released a verbal barrage that clearly indicated the nature of the sentiments we are discussing: 'Those guys [the investigating detectives] piss me off. I busted my ass over the last three days looking for this guy. Look at my boots, they were clean this morning. Crossing fields, looking for this prick, and what happens? I get him while those guys [detectives] are just sitting on their thumbs, and then they don't even say thank you, they don't even ask for my name. No wonder no one [in the uniformed branch] wants to come into the D office.'

Occasionally patrol officers are involved in interrogating suspects and otherwise pursuing an investigation alongside detectives. However, our detective study suggests that this is typically undertaken only when there are not enough detectives available or when one member of a two-person detective team is unavailable and the patrol officer is needed as a witness. For example, an interrogation of two co-suspects regarding a series of break-and-enter offences initially included the arresting patrol officer because the junior detective team member was involved elsewhere on special assigment. However, as soon as this detective returned to the office he joined his partner in the interrogation room; the patrol officer was excluded and did not have any further involvement. This was the case even though the junior member had no knowledge of the investigation before his return to the divisional station.

Detectives sometimes appear at the scene of a reported offence in progress, or, at the questioning of victims, complainants, and witnesses shortly after a reported incident (see also Ericson, 1981). This usually occurs in more serious offences, especially violent ones, although it also occurs when the detectives are driving and hear dispatched calls that sound interesting or potentially important. What is particularly annoying to patrol officers in these circumstances is that detectives often undertake preliminary assessment of the matter and then turn it over to patrol officers to do the 'dirty work.' For example, two detectives responded to a call dispatched to patrol officers regarding a 'break and entry in progress' at a school administration building. One of the detectives entered the building and emerged with a suspect who turned out to be an inarticulate mongoloid individual. The detectives searched his wallet in an attempt to ascertain his home address, but could not find it. The detectives turned the culprit over to the patrol officers who had subsequently arrived, saying 'He's all yours.' Situations of this nature reinforce the patrol officer's subservient position as a 'dirty worker.'[5]

Supervisory advice extends to areas other than the use of the criminal law and the criminal process. Paperwork is generally subject to the scrutiny, and correction, of supervisory officers. For example, a patrol officer spent two hours at the divisional station preparing a report on a serious personal injury accident he had been dispatched to attend. At the station a patrol sergeant, staff sergeant, and duty inspector each repeatedly gave their advice on how to construct the report. This greatly annoyed the patrol officer, who was an experienced first-class constable, and he later demonstrated his frustration to the researcher by verbally attacking 'the administration' for treating him as a 'rookie'; he then launched a general tirade against the 'petty rules,' especially the appearances code.

The patrol sergeant evaluates capabilities and translates production expectations from higher levels to patrol officers and vice versa. Evaluation sometimes conflicts with the advisory role. Patrol officers may be reluctant to seek advice because they think they will be seen as unable to make important judgments themselves. In particular, probationary constables want to show they can take action on their own and yet are fearful of making a mistake. This dilemma is compounded by a tacit rule within the occupational culture that one should not involve colleagues in matters that could be handled by a single officer. When the patrol officer feels he needs advice or help, he frequently chooses one of his colleagues rather than the patrol sergeant.

An extreme form of this dilemma was indicated by actions of a patrol officer who responded to a residential break-and-enter call. The incident was reported by the neighbour of the apparent victim, who was away on vacation. Upon arrival the officer checked the garage and noticed signs of entry there. He then noticed that lights in the house which had been on when he first arrived had since been turned off. The officer decided to seek assistance. He perhaps feared confronting a suspect and, more significantly, taking an action (e.g. an entry) that might be judged wrongful by superiors. He sought help from a colleague, but not through the usual routine of using the radio to call for a back-up. Instead, he drove to another patrol area to find the patrol officer there, a person he trusted would be discreet in collaborating in his rather unusual approach. Upon return to the residence no suspect was present.

The sergeants 'patrol' the production of 'activity facts' to ensure that their platoon is seen as in order by the administration.[6] The activity sheet system requires the patrol officer to report at the end of each month the number of 'tics' he has in each of several areas of activity, e.g. occurrence reports; traffic, liquor, and narcotics summonses; Criminal Code arrests. It is not officially regarded as a quota system because expectations are discussed and fulfilled at the platoon level. The 'level of production' is typically the monthly average produced by all members of a platoon, a system which can lead to controls over 'rate-busting' colleagues.[7]

Production expectations can conflict with the curtailment of investigative autonomy of patrol officers. Probationary officers, who are most concerned about productivity, are left to pursue the few things that are possible to proactively generate, namely traffic, liquor, and narcotics violations.[8] During one shift an officer being observed constantly referred to his monthly activity sheet and the upcoming assessment of his status. He felt he could produce more 'brownie points' by proactive rather than reactive work and said he longed for the day when his probation ended so that he could 'relax' somewhat. Another probationary officer was told by a patrol sergeant to increase his Criminal Code charges. This officer was also quite concerned about his status and felt the only way he could obtain more Criminal Code charges was to search for impaired drivers, since the discovery of other Criminal Code offences was largely beyond his control.

More experienced officers tend to be concerned about other credits. If they seek promotion, especially to the detective branch, they remain concerned about their level of law enforcement activity. Patrol officers also seek to build up productivity credits to use in arguments when their supervisors find they have violated force regulations.

The combination of little investigative autonomy and production quotas also entails competitiveness for credit among patrol officers. This can take the form of responding to dispatched calls in a way that obtains credit over and against someone else. After a call dispatched to another car regarding a domestic dispute that also involved a potential 'Mental Health Act' case, a patrol officer offered back-up to prevent officers from another division taking it over and obtaining credit. One officer may take all the credit for charges in an investigation conducted with others. A patrol officer who caught four suspects stealing from cars in an apartment parking garage obtained credit for 48 charges while the officer who assisted him received no credit.

The activity sheet becomes an end in itself (cf Skolnick, 1966, and Mann and Lee, 1979: especially chapter 4). One officer said he had stopped worrying about right and wrong and now only worries about 'tics.' Officers frequently gauge their response to calls or assignments by reference to the activity credit they obtain for it. Upon being dispatched to a supermarket regarding a shoplifter being detained by a store employee, an officer's comment was, 'Here's one free tic for probably $1.49.' One patrol officer was assigned two committal warrants to be executed to persons in the local jail; his fellow officers said this was a 'gift' from the sergeant – he would obtain two 'tic' credits for it.

The division of labour regarding criminal investigation and production expectations force patrol officers to produce occurrence reports and detectives to clear them by investigation. Perceived pressure for occurrence production can result in things being recorded that otherwise would not be. Patrol officers record occurrences rather than investigate them; a larger volume of occurrences lowers the overall clearance rate. Thus, the production pressure can militate against the clearance rate of detectives. Patrol officers detract from the productive appearances of detectives in the same way that detective control over investigations detracts from the arrest and charge production of patrol officers (cf McCabe and Sutcliffe, 1978).

The sergeant has at his disposal a set of enabling rules under the Police Act, RSO 1970, and attendant administrative orders about conduct and discipline. These rules are of the 'Ten Commandments' variety (Kelling et al, 1979: 17), telling the patrol officer what he should not do in such general terms that he is very likely to be found an offender if the administrative need arises (cf Ericson, 1981a).[9]

While the patrol sergeant has considerable discretion in using these rules, especially to induce conformity in areas that count administratively, patrol officers expect that in routine circumstances these rules will not be used. Of course, as with subordinates in most organizations, patrol officers can embarrass their superiors by collectively reducing their activity level, revealing their indiscretions, etc (Rubinstein, 1973: 43, 49). Enforcement is withheld in exchange for co-operation in making it appear that other rules are in force.

As Manning (1977a) has argued, supervisory power can often be enhanced by keeping rules at a tacit, less visible, informal level. This allows supervisors to manipulate the structure to serve their own interests whenever exigencies call for it. Moreover, when subordinates have control over a crucial area of operation, they can supply the valued commodity in exchange for non-invocation of particular administrative rules. A patrol officer is as likely to seek circumvention of administrative rules by giving information his superiors want as the patrol officer's 'informant' is to look for leniency regarding criminal laws the policeman might invoke. The likelihood that the superior will 'blow the whistle' is remote. When the whistle is blown, it is more a 'status-enforcing ritual' to reassert a 'semblance of power' than a means of altering existing relationships (ibid).

In these conditions, officers see enforcement as arbitrary and can readily point to examples of arbitrariness. One of the most frequently cited examples is 'neglect of duty' charges for sleeping during a shift. When it comes to light enforcement varies: sometimes it is ignored, sometimes a 'conduct sheet' is submitted by the patrol sergeant, and sometimes this leads to a formal charge and punishment. One patrol officer who had recently received a commendation for apprehending break-and-entry suspects was not charged after he was found sleeping on duty; another, who had no commendation, was charged for the same activity. The latter complained of unfair treatment in comparison with his colleague who 'got off.'

Some patrol sergeants, especially those identified as being from 'the old school,' are believed to follow the patterns of reciprocity as described above. Others, especially those with aspirations for promotion, go by the book. The more the sergeant enforces the more he is seen as being on 'the other side.' Some officers believed that enforcement was on the increase, undermining the expectation that the sergeant should be an ally. A nine-year veteran charged with sleeping on duty referred to the 'old days'; now 'when the chips are down, you're completely by yourself; not even the fuckin' patrol sergeant will help you out.'

The patrol sergeant is seen as hypocritical for enforcing rules which he violated regularly as a patrol officer. The patrol officers feel he should understand deviance and the reasons for it, but refuses to do so because he has 'changed face' toward administrative interests.

DEPENDENT UNCERTAINTY AND BOREDOM

These arrangements and the feelings they create are a prime source of the 'dependent uncertainty' of the patrol officer's working conditions. They can make him hypocritical when he comes to enforce the criminal law, for he knows that he is selectively making an example of someone just as he has been (or might be). Just as he gets his own work done by the 'ways and means act' within the occupational culture, so he is subject to the 'ways and means act' which supervisors implement to keep him in working order (cf Ericson, 1981a).

The patrol officer is particularly susceptible to punishment if the force needs a scapegoat in response to complaints from the community. Police administrations, like all bureaucracies, typically follow the 'rotten apple' theory rather than calling their own structure into question.[10] Since the boundaries of deviance are flexible and relative (see Erikson, 1966), one can always find some who are starting to 'go off' to show that the rest are still usable.

The underlying sentiment left by this situation is a feeling of being caught in a 'vice' between the police administration and the public. The administration is viewed as malleable in the face of demands from particular segments of the community and as often yielding to those demands at the expense of officers' interests. Line officers see that they are pawns in manoeuvres between the administration and the community and take the actions least likely to result in complaints. *The* rule of the patrol officer is 'cover your ass.'

Thus, one reason for distance from the police administration is its perceived political relationship to the community (see Grosman, 1975). Some officers take this as the inevitable order of things: 'It's obvious that our interests are different.' Others identify the police administration with the community élite, arguing that its interests are taken into account over, and often against, the interests of line officers.[11]

Patrol officers are critical of the 'public relations' emphasis of the force. A perpetual barrage of media accounts, shopping plaza displays, and equipment purchases was aimed at creating a professional, progressive image. Patrol officers know, as do researchers (Kelling et al, 1979), that technological innovations have not solved and cannot solve the 'crime problems' of a community. Yet the display is deemed necessary to maintain the legitimacy of the police.

'Public relations' can be seen as image creation, a compensating gloss for many routine actions that necessarily belie it. As two officers pointed out separately, it is difficult to sustain the image while handling traffic enforcement or interpersonal disputes where one side must be taken to accomplish a resolution. There is also a contradiction inherent in administrative expectations for production in proactive enforcement dealing with vehicular traffic, liquor, and drugs, while at the same time maintaining an emphasis on public relations.

Public relations has to be taken into account in deciding what actions to take. One officer said he was 'prostituting' his discretion in the interests of public relations. Line officers believe the administration sometimes fails to support them in disputes with the public for reasons they see as illegitimate. This obviously reproduces the order dependency and affects morale.

A sense of dependency is a dominant feature of the 'shop talk' which permeates the locker room, lunch room, and meeting places on the street. Patrol officers perhaps feel like the automatons their technological trappings make them out to be. Some may argue that the feeling of powerlessness serves as a check on the officer's extensive powers. Some officers, however, argue that it creates a greater personal need to exercise power as a means of achieving some sense of personal worth.

In sum, each bureaucratic 'advancement' by the administration makes patrol work more routine. The patrol officer spends most of his time waiting and watching through the lens of windows in a marked car that distances its occupant from those outside. His relationship to the organization he represents is also distant; he is merely a reporter or 'accountant.' He frequently responds to someone else's definition of trouble; he tries to diffuse that definition and take no further action, or use it to justify the action he takes; and if further action is taken, it is frequently done by others (supervisors or detectives). A patrol officer said boredom is the hardest part of the job, 'Lost person reports, writing up small PD accidents, etcetera, make you just a secretary. You're just a secretary when you do those jobs.'

The physical organization of mobile patrol contributes to the routine and boring nature of the work. There was a practice of rotating officers to different patrol areas after each shift cycle, and they could not become familiar with the citizens in any patrol area (for a description of the opposite policy and its implications, see Wilson [1968] and Rubinstein [1973]). At the time of the research there was only one foot beat patrol in the jurisdiction. One officer said he once made an effort to alter his role. He and a colleague initiated with their staff sergeant a foot patrol system around a concentrated area of major commercial establishments. While they had to justify it in terms of crime prevention, this system gave them a chance to become familiar with the area and its citizens. However, the system was terminated in a week by the divisonal superintendant.

Even when patrol officers are reactively mobilized (an average of twice per shift), they generally treat the matter as routine or even boring. Upon receipt of calls all but 15.6 per cent were viewed as unexciting, and on the way this figure dropped to 11 per cent. After the incident, only 6.4 per cent were characterized as 'exciting' (see Table 3.2; see also Reiss, 1971).

Officers realize their work is the ordering of relationships among people who call upon them to handle their trouble, stopping people on suspicion to keep them in order, and proactively enforcing infractions under regulatory statutes. The patrol officers we observed had great difficulty in answering a survey question on how they see their role. Among the 348 respondents, 38 per cent did not define any particular role in their work, while 12 per cent said their role is primarily public relations (social service) work, and 9 per cent defined it mainly in terms of traffic law enforcement. Only 41 per cent said their prime role is law enforcement under the Criminal Code.

Responses

In order to sustain a sense of personal worth and to make their working conditions tolerable, officers turn to their collective power. They respond to the pressures, conflicts, and contradictions of bureaucractic controls by devising strategies which make their job more rewarding and sometimes allow them to encounter the controls. These reactions are common to workers in all bureaucratic organizations, although there are variations according to the opportunities available (see, for example, Taylor and Walton, 1971; Bryant, 1974; Ditton, 1977; and in the police case, Cox et al, 1977; and Reed et al, 1977). The patrol officers we observed did not respond by seeking financial rewards through graft, bribery, and extortion, although these are common responses in other police forces (see United States National Crime Commission, 1967; Rubinstein, 1973: ch 9; Quebec Police Commission, 1977) and among other enforcement agents (in the case of bailiffs, see McMullan, 1980). Their responses include 1) collectively developing a form of discourse among themselves which helps them to define their identity by attacking those they do not identify with; 2) sharing ways of what they term 'skating' around work, i.e. doing as little as possible in the easiest way possible while still maintaining sufficient 'cover' to avoid repercussions from superiors; and 3) institutionalizing 'covering' or 'easing' (Cain, 1973) practices which save them from administration attacks. These responses can be interpreted as part of a perpetual search for autonomy among those at the lower end of the organization's scheme of things (Goffman, 1961).

These responses are based on assumptions and attendant rules of the occupational culture (e.g. Manning, 1971, 1977; Muir, 1977). There is initial suspicion of most people and things outside the culture; policemen know best about crime and criminals, and about 'human nature' in general, and

TABLE 3.2

Patrol officers' characterization of reactive incident calls upon receipt, prior to arrival, and after the encounter

Characterization	N	%
Upon receipt		
Exciting	65	15.6
Boring	44	10.5
Routine / none indicated	309	73.9
Totals	418	100.0
Prior to arrival		
Exciting	45	10.8
Boring	37	8.9
Routine / none indicated	336	80.3
Totals	418	100.0
After the encounter		
Exciting	27	6.4
Boring	62	14.8
Routine / none indicated	329	78.8
Totals	418	100.0

therefore make the best judgments. The primary means of knowing is experience: learning on the job rather than at the academy; using 'recipe' rules rather than abstract rules. There is a belief that this knowledge and practice require protection by secrecy and the manipulation of appearances at several levels. Thus, there is a sensitivity to providing 'covers' both within the organization, and between the organization and the outside world. Covers are created for easing behaviour, for the control of production vis-à-vis expectations, and more generally for avoiding the revelation of something that might affect another officer's career. Covers are also developed for producing organizational records of events and actions. As Manning (1979a: 25) states, in general terms 'Officers work to do two things: to accomplish work within the premises of the work as they understand them, and to create, if necessary, the proper official paper which will represent events within the official, sanctioned format for such events as they are administratively understood.'

One way the patrol officer seeks to find a 'consistent and satisfactory basis for his self conception' (Wilson, 1968: 138) is to attack verbally various types of people and organizational arrangements. The talk is directed against some expectations of the administration, and groups within the community are categorized in political terms and approved of or criticized on that basis. There is also criticism of certain types of law, the court process, and the corrections process. Patrol officers create a collective identity, a sense of autonomy, and a degree of personal distance from organizational arrangements by constantly reminding each other what they are against.

Verbal attacks are frequently directed toward fellow officers who have 'minority characteristics' that are encouraged by the administration but are viewed as deviant by the dominant patrol officers. Two examples are officers with higher education and policewomen. The administration is seen to be actively encouraging these persons to join the force, but they are viewed by some as deviant within the patrol office culture. Some try to play down their 'scapegoat' characteristics. Some policewomen try to become 'one of the men.' Some officers with higher education play it down and are particularly likely to extol the ideals of 'real police work' as a means of indicating a 'correct' relationship to their colleagues.

In the eyes of many, formal education is an example of the public relations gloss which provides a protective coating against outside elements. Arguments are made that formal education is not useful on the job because it does not relate to the 'real tools' of police work, namely 'common sense' or 'street sense.' At the same time, education is seen as a key to promotion because of the administration's emphasis on it; this belief appears especially prevalent among those who do not have higher education. Consequently, many undertake part-time courses at community colleges or universities, but distance themselves from their activity by saying that it is strictly utilitarian, aimed at promotion rather than of any intrinsic value. Thus, as with the administration's production expectations, there is considerable conformity to administrative expectations combined with a personal and collective distancing from the activity, expressed through verbal attacks on its intrinsic value.

Policewomen are another target of 'scapegoating.' As one male officer perceptively commented, policewomen become easy targets for those experiencing the dependent uncertainty generated by the administration. Similar to those with higher education, policewomen are 'new' and 'different,' creating an unpredictability that yields the predictable allegations that they do not have the ability to be good 'street' patrol officers and that they receive preferential treatment by the police administration.

There is a pervasive belief that policewomen tend to be less proactive, and this is supported in statements by some policewomen. The explanations given fit within the typical sexist mould, e.g. policewomen do not have the physical presence to intimidate citizens or the physical strength to enforce compliance in situations of escalating conflict. There is also a belief that a policewoman more often needs another officer to 'backup' a call because she is unable to handle it on her own.[12]

It is perhaps because of these perceived problems that policewomen are sometimes transferred from patrol work and given specialized tasks in such units as the youth bureau or at headquarters. This only 'adds fuel to the fire,' however, because male officers frequently use such transfers to support their argument that the administration gives preferential treatment to policewomen. Several male patrol officers complained to superior officers about preferential treatment that seemed to be accorded a policewoman on their platoon by their patrol sergeant. The administrative response to this complaint was to transfer several of the male officers to other platoons and to add two more policewomen to this platoon. This served to reinvigorate the cycle of 'rumblings' among line officers against policewomen and the administration in general.

Patrol officers type community groups and members according to both 'political characteristics' and 'minority characteristics' (see note 11), particularly on the basis of whether or not they support or oppose interests the officers feel they represent. If groups are placed in the antagonistic category, then talk about them becomes negative and they become scapegoats.

Patrol officers divide the community by whether groups or individuals are 'for' or 'against' the police. If they are for the police they are 'conservatives'; if they are against the police they are 'liberals.' Thus, talk about community processes affecting the police – such as legal change, and calls for law enforcement 'crack-downs' in particular areas or in relation to particular laws – are initially judged in terms of whether they reflect supportive conservative or antagonistic liberal sentiments. If deemed liberal, then the talk takes the form of referring to 'bleeding hearts,' 'do gooders,' 'self-interested politicians'. So strong is the peer pressure to support a conservative position that some with more liberal sentiments keep them to themselves and steer conversation away from topics which might lead them to reveal their sentiments.

This categorization typically has little to do with the position of these groups in the community's power structure. Thus, more powerful politicians who support the interests of certain minority interest groups are likely to be labelled as liberal. Lower-status citizens who support the virtues of middle-class 'respectability' are taken to symbolize the community interests the patrol officer sees himself as representing.

This identification with middle-class respectability makes some officers react negatively to any groups whom they cannot place within it. Thus, in discussion among themselves, there is derision of certain racial and ethnic minorities, as well as citizens at the bottom end of society's 'scheme of things' who do not appear to be seeking upward mobility in a way that would indicate an identification with the values of middle-class respectability. Included in this latter group are persons identified by patrol officers as 'Coasters' (people from the Maritime region of Canada) and 'pukers' (apparently hedonistic young people whose activity, dress, and demeanour indicate a departure from middle-class respectability).[13] There is constant talk about these types being 'the scum of the earth,' 'the source of all police problems,' and so on. For example, an officer came into the lunchroom stating, 'I got my spook for the day,' followed by a statement that he almost ran over a 'fucking Paki' who was hitchhiking (actually the hitchhiker was Chinese). This type of talk is common.

Patrol officers also talk negatively about law and other segments of the criminal process – in situations in which they feel constrained to act in one way and in conversation, especially about cases they have been involved in or major incidents involving other officers in the force that become generally known about.

Patrol officers talk about four aspects of criminal law: who has the power to change laws through the legislative process, the harshness of the penalty structure, enforceability, and procedural restrictions.

Police officers continually complain that politicians, representing minority interests opposed to those whom patrol officers feel they represent, have control over the legal apparatus and use it to their benefit. 'Liberal' politicians erode the potency of 'lawandorder' which the police feel they represent on behalf of the 'silent majority.' This erosion is believed to result from legal changes, or failure to undertake legal changes, that make punishment too lenient, enforcement too difficult, or place procedural restrictions on police actions.

Talk about leniency centres on capital punishment. During the course of our fieldwork, the Canadian House of Commons voted to abolish the death penalty for killings of any type. This resulted in a range of tirades against politicians, the government, and 'liberal' influences of all types and produced suggestions that the police would be more likely to 'take the law into their own hands.' The issue is also used to support the belief that politicians do not act in accordance with the will of the majority. A typical comment is that because the clear majority of Canadians favour capital punishment, abolition represents a 'blow to democracy.'

Patrol officers are primarily concerned with the pragmatic utility of a particular law. They favour it if it proves handy in dealing with a particular situation and oppose it when it interferes with the way they want to go about their work. An example is the Bail Reform Act.

Patrol officers regularly complain about how they 'have to' release an accused person even though they know that he is unlikely to appear in court on the scheduled date and is likely to commit another offence. For example, an officer returned to the divisional station a prisoner who had been arrested by another police force on a warrant issued by the force studied for failing to appear in court on an impaired driving charge. After processing the accused, another 'promise to appear' release was made, this time through the justice of the peace. The officer was very annoyed at this and commented that it would probably be another six months before the accused was apprehended again.

While this is typical talk, it does not always reflect action. For example, among five persons arrested for a series of break-ins at retail establishments, one was released after charge even though he had an extensive criminal record and had only been released from prison three weeks prior to the current arrest. There was considerable talk about this 'criminal' being allowed to return to the streets *because of* the lenient provisions of the Bail Reform Act. However, the detective who charged him readily declared to a researcher involved in the detective study (Ericson, 1981) that he had the accused released in exchange for an agreement to provide information on the criminal activities of others.

This example shows how negative talk emerges whenever an example can be found, even if the subject of the talk has also aided police work. It is a reassuring 'display' of the officers' own interests as workers, rather than an indication that they always oppose what they are deriding.

In criticism of the courts, judges are the main target, especially for their bail decisions and sentencing practices. Sometimes in dramatic cases a judge is selected for criticism. One judge was singled out and condemned for a sentence he gave to a member of the force, as well as other incidents. Comparisons were made with the 'lenient' sentences he routinely gave 'civilians' for offences such as break-and-enter. Each time he made a pronouncement which was heard by officers, or received publicity, the negative comments flouished.

Once again, the theme is non-support of officers' interests, including threats to autonomy. Patrol officers routinely see judicial decisions as going against their own decisions. As one stated, 'Police officers involve themselves so seldom with criminals that when in fact an arrest is made they are damn sure the offender is guilty.'[14] Moreover, in their eyes their decision to lay a charge or charges deserves to be supported by judges by punishment that establishes the authority of the law-enforcement machinery. This pertains even to minor offences. One officer said he issues 'speeding tickets' only when he feels the citizen deserves it, and he reduces the charge in the process. He becomes annoyed when the charge is further reduced in court.

Patrol officers also criticize the way sentences are carried out: prisoners receive too many benefits during incarceration and too lenient release provisions. A youth was arrested while fleeing from the scene of a series of residential break-and-enter offences. The information that began filtering among patrol officers included the 'fact' that he was a parolee. One victim in this case, a member of the provincial legislature, was told by the officer interviewing him that the suspect was a recently paroled ex-convict. In fact, the suspect was a youth of 17 who had no previous criminal convictions.

In summary, patrol officers use ritualized talk against the police administration, community segments, and the legal process to shape their own identity and sense of autonomy. This pervasive activity is immediately apparent to initiates, including new recruits and research observers. It can easily be taken to indicate a severe problem of morale and an almost pathological cynicism (see Niederhoffer, 1969). However, it is perhaps better viewed as a human response to the circumstances within which patrol officers find themselves and find their selves. Much of it takes the form of stereotypical 'banter' and even joking which, if absent, would be a sign of problems (see Rubinstein, 1973: 444–45). It also shows that patrol officers cannot take the world for granted and must quickly learn the problematic quality of 'the truth.' They have an occupational need to disregard claims made by others and to construct their own 'truth' to allow them to accomplish their work. The verbal expression of these needs makes patrol officers appear very cynical and callous. They realize that while to *feel* secure one must take things for granted, to *be* secure one must never take things for granted. The occupational culture provides security in this verbal form.

The occupational culture also fosters more tangible means of gaining some autonomy and control over work. The level of activity on any particular shift is adjustable, and patrol officers share many devices for avoiding work without detection by supervisors. 'Hiding spots' are designated in each patrol area; these also serve as meeting places for officers in cars from two or more patrol areas. For example, two patrol officers spent the final two hours of a 3 to 11 pm shift listening to a hockey game on a transistor radio, moving their location four times to avoid detection. These designated places are also used to rest or sleep, activities most likely to occur on midnight shifts.[15]

Other breaks are obtained through techniques of dealing with the dispatcher. After calling the dispatcher for permission to leave the patrol car to undertake an investigation, the officer wanting a break does not call back to the dispatcher that he is clear until he has taken a break. An officer wanting extended time to engage in non-police activity develops excuses such as a claim that the radio system in the car is not operating properly.

There are various strategies for increasing the amount of work. Patrol officers spend a lot of time on monotonous general patrol void of direct contact with other. They 'make work' by increasing their proactive activity or by responding to calls dispatched to officers in other patrol areas.

As one officer expressed it, sometimes you have to make your own action, 'to hustle or you'll go out of your mind.' This action often involves stopping vehicles, which officers sometimes claim they do only because it is 'something to do.' Indeed, some officers 'save' their proactive work for the midnight shift, which otherwise is the most boring. One officer made nine proactive stops in the first four hours of a midnight shift with few reactive calls, as a way of keeping busy. This same officer on a day shift appeared indifferent to proactive work.

Administrative pressure to undertake proactive work is often an inducement to do so. Thus, what relieves boredom is also a possible source of production credit, and vice versa. During a reactively 'slow' day shift, a patrol officer checked six different parks on three separate occasions each, as well as parked vehicles elsewhere, looking for liquor and narcotics violators. While recording the park checks in his notebook, the officer stated that the checks were as much a means of 'looking busy' as of actually being busy.

The inactive patrol officer can respond to dispatched calls in other patrol areas. A few officers do this on a systematic basis, taking every opportunity to inform the dispatcher that they are willing to back-up if required or simply drive over to the situation unannounced. Most officers do this if there is a potentially dramatic or exciting incident, such as a fight. For example, two cars were dispatched to a reported fight at a club, and four additional cars responded. A fist fight between two youths in a tavern adjacent to a divisional station occurred just as the change from afternoon to midnight shift was taking place; the divisional office was emptied of patrol officers from two platoons as well as detectives.

Moreover, the chance to become involved in an investigation yields an enthusiastic response. An officer investigating a complaint about a theft used information provided by a policewoman, who lived in the same apartment building as the suspects, to ascertain that the suspects used marijuana. He convinced his sergeant to obtain a search warrant on this basis, and he obtained the warrant. The sergeant and five officers executed the warrant without the presence of the occupants, seizing a few grams of marijuana after a thorough 40-minute search.

Some officers realize that in their search for an interesting involvement they overreact. One officer described overreaction as a tendency to create a new scene rather than to patch up an old one. This response is brought on by both the number of policemen responding and the nature of the response. On these occasions, officers may produce disorder rather than reproduce order. Others explain overreaction as a response not simply to boredom, but also to production demands. For example, an officer reasoned that because there are too many patrol officers, there are too few opportunities for dramatic involvements that might produce charges and result in credit. Therefore officers seek any opportunity to become involved in anything that might 'count.'

'Easing' practices are established by agreements among patrol officers. Officers enforce these rules just as vehemently as they enforce the criminal law. Indeed, their enforcement of these rules affects their enforcement of the criminal law.

These rules 'cover' activities which might affect their collective interests. Far from the dramatization of police undercover work on television, the undercover work of patrol officers is to learn and use 'covers' to justify activities which make their work tolerable. In doing their work under 'cover,' they expect collaboration from other line officers, including communication bureau officers and detectives.

Patrol officers and dispatchers develop a number of cues to each other which provide suitable covers (cf Rubinstein, 1973; Manning, 1977, 1979; Jorgensen, 1979). For example, even though a long period of being booked off may signify that an officer is in trouble, the dispatcher may assume from the location and circumstances he is taking some time for himself. Officers not anxious to respond to a call use cues to avoid it. One officer was driving back to the divisional station at the end of the shift and was dispatched to a 'noise complaint.' He became annoyed at the dispatcher for giving him such a trivial call at the end of the shift. He asked the dispatcher to repeat the call, giving him the division station gas pumps as his location. The dispatcher quickly interpreted the officer's tactic and dispatched another officer instead.

As we saw earlier, there are conflicts between patrol officers and detectives caused by the division of labour in criminal investigation. However, these conflicts do not prevent detectives from collaborating with patrol officers in 'covering' activities. A detective might not interfere with charges laid by a patrol officer if it might reflect upon the officer's competence. This behaviour reflects a general rule that one should avoid doing anything that reflects unfavourably upon a colleague's work (see Rubinstein, 1973: 149). For example, detectives learned that members of the patrol branch had arrested and charged a man the previous night for 'assault occasioning bodily harm' and 'weapons dangerous.' He had been found 'struggling' on top of a teenage girl in a schoolyard. The detectives consulted with a detective sergeant, who argued that more serious charges (e.g. 'attempt rape,' 'wounding') should be laid. The sergeant was very annoyed that the accused was released on a 'promise to appear' notice; he argued that he should have been held in custody overnight for questioning by detectives the following morning. The two detectives refused to follow their sergeant's suggestion and took no other action on the matter, commenting to each other that it would create conflict with the patrol branch if they did alter the charges (cf Ericson, 1981).

Although they may be of higher rank (full detectives are sergeants), detectives and dispatchers collaborate with patrol officers to build up the mutual trust and solidarity necessary for a predictable working environment. However, collaboration among patrol officers, or between patrol officers and line officers of other types, is not guaranteed in every case. An officer who repeatedly 'blows' the cover will be left on his own to fall victim to the 'rotten apple' theory of administrative punishment. Line officers realize that a member who persistently reveals the deviance which everyone enjoys may eventually cause a full-blown investigation based upon the 'contamination' theory.[16]

Rules also cover the more systematic and pervasive administrative incursions contained in production quotas. While each patrol officer is expected to 'pull his own weight,' he must not 'rate-bust.' Some leeway is given to 'rookies' on probationary status who must produce well in order to obtain their permanent status. However, more experienced officers are typed as 'organization men' or 'movers' (seeking upward mobility) if they overproduce and drive the platoon's production norms upward. Control can take the form of ridicule and exclusion, although it is sometimes more direct. An officer widely known and ridiculed as a rate-buster recalled a veteran of the force sternly telling him to curtail his proactive vigour, adding that it was 'making the older fellows uncomfortable.'

Many studies have revealed the autonomy available to line officers because of the nature of their work and the structural arrangements required to produce it (e.g. Rubinstein, 1973; Manning, 1977; Jermier and Berkes, 1979; Punch, 1979). Patrol officers usually work away from the watchful eyes of supervisors. They have a degree of solidarity, cemented by their own rules. They can control supervisors as long as they agree to co-operate with the 'supervisory ritual' (Manning, 1979). Many essential tasks defy tight controls because officers frequently deal with ambiguous and varied situations that can be interpreted in several ways.

Patrol officers enter into their dealings with the citizenry equipped with, controlled by, and sensitive to the occupational forces outlined in this chapter. There is a perpetual interchange of efforts at control among the architects (administrators) of the bureaucracy, the engineers (supervisors) who are required to shape its appearance, and the workers (patrol officers) who man it. Further examples of these dynamics, as they articulate with community and legal organizational elements, will be presented in the following chapters as we examine the decisions officers face in their dealings with the community.

4

Mobilization

The disorder encountered by patrol officers, and their efforts at reproducing order, result from whatever they, and/or the citizens who mobilize them, initially define as police business. A distinction exists in the academic literature between citizen-initiated *reactive* mobilization and police-initiated *proactive* mobilization. Reactive mobilization generally results either from 'spontaneous requests' by individual citizens for police assistance in handling their troubles, or from 'planned requests' by a community group who demand a pattern of service that will serve the group's particular interests (Kelling et al, 1979: 3). Proactive mobilization generally results from 'spontaneous decisions' by individual patrol officers to stop citizens for investigative checks; these decisions sometimes reflect administrative and/or supervisory decisions to pursue particular types of people and the trouble associated with them.

The simple dichotomy between reactive and proactive mobilization is problematic. An immediate decision may be traceable to other decisions, such as supervisory or administrative directives, which in turn may reflect more general complaints from citizens. Citizens may decide to mobilize the police reactively as a result of proactive publicity campaigns by the police aimed at encouraging citizen co-operation in providing information, using the police to handle particular types of trouble, etc. These broader considerations can help explain mobilization; nevertheless, they tend to blur the distinction between proactive and reactive and suggest the symbolic nature of police forces and community forces. As we present our data in this chapter we delineate these complications and refine the use of the proactive-reactive concept.

Research on the mobilization of patrol officers emphasizes that the vast majority of contacts between officers and citizens come about as a result of citizen's requests for police presence. For example, Black (1968: 125) and

Reiss (1971: 11) record that in their study of patrol work in Washington, Boston, and Chicago, 87 per cent of mobilizations were reactive. Webster's (1970) study of police 'task and time' reports that less than 20 per cent of the work done by patrol officers is self-initiated, while Cordner's (1979) summary of the dispatch study literature reveals that 40 to 50 per cent of the patrol officer's time is spent on reactive call duties and most of the remaining time is spent on driving and on administrative duties. Findings of this type have led commentators on the role of the police to conclude 'that most police work is *reactive*, that is to say the police wait for the input of information from the public before acting,' and that 'it is the general public who decide what level of law enforcement they want from the police' (Morris, 1978: 10–11). This in turn has resulted in speculation that the basis of, and bias in, 'crime' discovery lies with the citizen, not the police (Bottomley and Coleman, 1979, 1980), and in attendant survey research concerning criminal victimization and reporting patterns (Sparks et al, 1977). In general, these researchers and commentators convey an image of the police as servants responsive to citizen demands.

Our observations yield a contrary view. In the 1,323 encounters between officers and citizens recorded in our study, 47.4 per cent came about as a result of proactive mobilization and 52.6 per cent came about as a result of reactive mobilization (Table 4.1). On the surface, our data reveal that patrol officers are much more assertive in producing encounters with citizens than the figures provided by Reiss, Black, and others would lead us to believe. Obviously we need much more detail of differences in the nature and circumstances of proactively and reactively initiated encounters in our sample. We provide this detail in the following sections of the present chapter, and use it in our analysis in subsequent chapters.

We can introduce two possible explanations for the difference between our finding and that of Reiss and Black. First, it may be an artefact of sampling. Reiss and Black used a non-random sample of officers operating in areas with high levels of reported crime over weekend evening shifts in Boston, Washington, and Chicago during the early 1960s. It should not be surprising to find that the volume of reactive mobilization was particularly high in these locations during these periods. Through our simple random sample of all patrol areas over all shift periods and days of the week, we provide the full spectrum of reaction possibilities. Moreover, our data were collected more than a decade later and in a very different social and cultural context.[1]

Second, Reiss and Black include in their figures reactive calls that did not result in encounters with citizens, while our data pertain to mobilizations producing police-citizen interaction. Thirty per cent of the reactive mobilizations in their study did not result in encounters; these included alarm calls and parking problems (Reiss, 1971: 13; Black, 1968: 46). If these are excluded their

TABLE 4.1

Types of mobilization and types of citizen encounters

| | Types of citizen encounters | | | | | |
| | Citizen contacts | | Incidents | | Totals | |
	N	%	N	%	N	%
Proactive	538	65.9	89	17.6	627	47.4
Reactive	278	34.1	418	82.4	696	52.6
Totals	816	100.0	507	100.0	1,323	100.0

df = 1; $p < 0.01$; $\chi^2 = 293.5$

figures for reactive mobilizations resulting in citizen encounters would be approximately 78 per cent, leaving 22 per cent proactive on the assumption that nearly all of their proactive mobilizations resulted in citizen encounters. Even with this adjustment, however, their data still indicate a much higher degree of reactive mobilization than of police-initiated mobilization resulting in citizen encounters.

Another preliminary observation can be made about our finding. In chapter 2, we found it impossible to categorize encounters into those involving 'crime' and those involving 'non-crime' troubles because of our view that 'crime' is constituted by the patrol officer as one possible means of handling an encounter. However, our categorization of minor encounters (citizen contacts) and major encounters (incidents) allows us to determine whether minor matters as opposed to major matters are more likely to be mobilized in a particular way. In our sample, two-thirds of citizen contacts were proactive, while only 17.6 per cent of incidents were proactive. In other words, proactive encounters typically involved brief contacts that did not develop into major incidents. As documented in the next section and subsequent chapters, proactive contacts usually involved stops for traffic violations and/or stops on suspicion which infrequently produced something that could be made into a 'criminal' matter.

While the officers we studied were working alone in one-officer patrol cars, they were sometimes mobilized along with other patrol officers, asked for the mobilization of other officers, or took the initiative to join other patrol officers in an encounter. This 'back-up' assists fellow officers and controls them, because officers can scrutinize each other.

As recorded in Table 4.2, the presence of other officers in citizen contacts, especially those proactively mobilized, is infrequent, leaving the officer to make his decisions away from the direct scrutiny of his colleagues. The presence of other officers is three times more likely in incidents than in citizen contacts, reflecting the more substantial scale of incident encounters. In particular, other officers are much more likely to be involved in proactive incidents than in proactive citizen contacts; perhaps if proactive stops do

TABLE 4.2

Type of encounter, mobilization, and the presence of other police officers

Type of encounter and mobilization	N	Percentage of encounters involving*		
		additional police officers of any type	supervisory officers	patrol officer assisting another patrol officer
Citizen contacts				
Proactive	538	3.7	0.7	0.4
Reactive	278	22.3	8.3	19.8
Incidents				
Proactive	89	24.7	9.1	6.7
Reactive	418	31.3	9.4	14.4
Citizen contacts and incidents combined				
Proactive	627	6.7	1.9	1.3
Reactive	696	27.7	8.9	16.5

* The categories are not mutually exclusive.

evolve into major incidents, conflict is likely and the assistance of other officers is deemed more necessary.[2] Overall, when the patrol officer decides to initiate an encounter on his own he is much more likely also to engage in it and complete it on his own. When the initiation is reactive, there is a greater likelihood that other officers and/or supervisors will enter into the encounter and influence its course: reactive encounters are more likely to involve major incidents, and reactive calls can be heard by other officers who may respond whether or not they are requested to do so.

The request for back-up usually occurs in four types of circumstance: a potentially dangerous situation, a potentially dangerous person, a large number of people, and situations where the officer wants advice or wishes to protect himself by having another officer concur with his decision.

An example of a potentially dangerous situation occurred when a patrol officer was cruising past a warehouse that was supposed to be closed and noticed that a rear door was open. Before entering the premises, he called the dispatcher to receive assistance and waited for another patrol officer to arrive.

Potentially dangerous persons are often identified by the dispatcher in the initial dispatch, either as a result of information from the complainant or based on the dispatcher's prior knowledge of the person. In these situations, the dispatcher typically sends other mobile units, and in turn the first officer on the scene usually calls back to the dispatcher to give his exact location and to request more help. This occurred, for example, when the dispatcher initially gave an 'all cars' alert to find a vehicle being driven by a man described by the dispatcher as having a record for violence and having just been seen swinging a hatchet at some young persons; the officer first spotting the vehicle was to contact the patrol sergeant immediately. Upon seeing the vehicle, the officer called the dispatcher to give his location and received back-up assistance from three other patrol officers and a patrol sergeant.

Back-up assistance is also routinely called for when a patrol officer is faced with taking action against a large number of people. An officer was dispatched to a scene where 'a female is having trouble with four males.' Upon arrival in the parking lot of the apartment building area, the officer spotted seven youths, two of whom ran away as the car approached. The officer became suspicious that they might have marijuana and decided to question and search the five remaining persons. Before he departed from the car for the encounter the officer called the dispatcher for back-up assistance.

A patrol officer, especially if he is inexperienced or unsure of himself, sometimes seeks back-up presence for advice and/or to 'cover' his actions from possible allegations of improper conduct, by displacing responsibility for decisions to another officer. For example, a motorist stopped for driving too fast was checked on CPIC, which revealed that a person of the same name was wanted by another police force for 'false pretences.' The officer decided to call for the assistance of a more experienced officer to question the suspect and to ascertain whether he was the wanted individual. The evaluator role of the patrol sergeant usually means that he is not called for advice in these situations unless the matter potentially involves a major criminal investigation.

Patrol officers sometimes respond on their own intiative to calls dispatched to others, either asking the dispatcher for clearance to do so or simply proceeding unannounced. Patrol officers sometimes also stop when they observe a fellow officer in an encounter with a citizen (see Table 4.2). Many of the reasons we have considered for back-up requests also apply to these back-ups on the officer's own initiative. Patrol officers are particularly likely to respond in this way if the matter involves a crime in progress, a reported wanted suspect, a large number of citizens, or an officer who is having difficulty handling citizens. These back-ups can entail what some might judge to be an overreaction, especially in hindsight.

A reported crime in progress typically brings several cars to a scene because it is seen as potentially exciting and unpredictable. A dispatched 'theft in progress' concerning a youth seen by a private security officer on a construction site turned out be to unfounded. The youth was a worker on the site who decided to stay there overnight. Nevertheless, hearing only the initial dispatch, four additional officers responded to this incident. A report of a person matching the description of a wanted suspect frequently brings a similar response.

Dispatched reactive calls that indicate a large number of citizens are likely to lead a number of officers to respond. For example, an officer was dispatched as a back-up for an 'NCA party' ('drug party'). A third officer eventually arrived. A married couple were alone in their apartment smoking marijuana. At 3:30 am on another shift, 15 officers, including a duty inspector and 2 patrol sergeants, responded to a dispatched call concerning a fight at a party in a private residence.

Many of these back-up responses are in situations where there is potential for officers to experience difficulty in handling citizens, including the possibility of violent conflict. When there is any indication that an officer is experiencing difficulty, there is a spontaneous response of many officers. For example, a patrol officer was dispatched to back-up a detective who had called for assistance. He was being taunted by three youths from inside their townhouse, while he was outside trying to assist a man in a drunken condition. When three officers arrived, the detective proceeded to the townhouse to deal with the youths and eventually arrested one of them. In the mean time, an additional five officers arrived to back-up. On another shift, a patrol officer called for back-up assistance, but she did not specify the nature of the encounter, which involved an impaired driver who was somewhat obstreperous. The quality of the radio transmission was not clear, and sounds similar to screams could be head in the background as the request was being made. Eight patrol cars responded, producing a rather sobering effect on the impaired driver.

Proactive Mobilization

The research literature has repeatedly pointed out that there is little scope for the discovery of crime by the police themselves (e.g. Skogan, 1976; Bottomley and Coleman, 1979). The police are heavily dependent on citizens to report possible criminal occurrences, and most official reports of crime arise out of reactive encounters. Nevertheless, as recorded in Table 4.1, the officers we observed did initiate almost as many encounters with citizens as were initiated through the dispatch process. We shall consider what precipitates proactive mobilizations, the nature of the troubles involved, and where the encounters take place.[3]

The territory of the patrol officer is the streets of *his* patrol area (see Rubinstein, 1973: especially chapter 4). When he is not reactively called upon to handle troubles defined by others, he often goes looking for things and people out of order within his territory. He sees his mandate as maintaining order on the streets and reproducing it when something or someone is found out of order. He knows he is equipped with the legal authority (see chapter 6), as well as the symbolic authority of his office (Manning, 1977), to do this work.

In order to document the *public* nature of the officer's proactive work, and the nature of the trouble which leads him to do the work, we categorized all mobilizations in terms of the nature of the disputes and the setting of the disputes (Table 4.3; compare with Table 4.4).

The 816 citizen contacts were categorized into four basic types of dispute which apparently led the patrol officer to initiate the encounter with the citizen(s). 'Suspicious persons/circumstances' involve the patrol officer inferring that some undetermined trouble might unfold if he investigates a person or set of circumstances. For example, patrol officers frequently stop young men of lower socio-economic standing ('pukers') in the belief that these persons are the most likely candidates for a variety of violations under the Criminal Code, Liquor Licence Act of Ontairo, and the Narcotics Control Act. In 'possible criminal' matters the officer has grounds to suspect that a criminal violation might be occurring or might be produced upon investigation. For example, the officer follows a car and decides to stop it when he sees an occupant throw an object from the window which he believes to be marijuana. 'Traffic' includes any matter involving violations under the Highway Traffic Act or driving offences under the Criminal Code. 'Assistance/service' includes encounters initially defined by the officer as matters where a citizen is in need of help other than to resolve a dispute. For example, a motorist is given a lift after being found stranded with a broken-down car. In the 816 citizen contacts, the contacts were proactive for 75.4 per cent of all suspicious persons/circumstances situations, 28.7 per cent of all possible criminal disputes, 83 per cent of all traffic matters, and 17 per cent of all 'assistance/service' involvements.

The 507 incidents were each categorized as involving disputes concerning either property, automobiles, interpersonal matters, or other matters. 'Property' disputes include any possible Criminal Code occurrence where allegations of property loss or damage are assessed by the patrol officer. 'Automobile' incidents include any dispute involving an automobile, such as a possible offence under the driving-related provisions of the Criminal Code or, the Highway Traffic Act, or automobile accidents with or without traffic violations. 'Interpersonal' incidents involve non-property conflicts between two or more persons, usually including allegations of assault or sexual violation. 'Other' incidents include all other matters, such as liquor violations, narcotics violations, and sections of the Criminal Code not classifiable as property, interpersonal, or driving offences. The encounters were proactive for 4.4 per cent of all property disputes, 33.6 per cent of all automobile-related matters, 3.5 per cent of all interpersonal disputes, and 29.2 per cent of all other types.

Both citizen contacts and incidents were categorized by main location of the encounter. Among the 1,323 encounters, 25 per cent took place in a residence, 48.4 per cent in a public street area, and 26.6 per cent in other public places. A 'residence' includes any private habitation and surrounding private property, whether apartment, condominium, or single-family dwelling. A

TABLE 4.3
Nature and setting of disputes in reactive mobilization

Setting of dispute	Citizen contacts*						Incidents†					
	Suspicous persons/ circum- stances (%)	Possible criminal (%)	Traffic (%)	Assist- ance/ service (%)	Total N	Total (%)	Prop- erty (%)	Auto- mobile (%)	Inter- personal (%)	Other (%)	Total N	Total (%)
Residence	5.7	11.1	1.4	15.8	19	3.5	16.7	0.0	25.0	2.4	3	3.4
Street	62.4	59.3	90.6	52.6	432	80.3	0.0	89.2	25.0	45.2	53	59.6
Other public places	31.9	29.6	8.0	31.6	87	16.2	83.3	10.8	50.0	52.4	33	37.1
Column percentage	100.0	100.0	100.0	100.0	538	100.0	100.0	100.0	100.0	100.0	89	100.0
Total N	141	27	351	19			6	37	4	42		
Row percentage	26.2	5.0	65.2	3.5	100.0		6.7	41.6	4.5	47.2	100.0	

* df = 6; $p < 0.01$; χ^2 = 74.27
† df = 6; $p < 0.01$; χ^2 = 34.52

TABLE 4.4

Nature and setting of disputes in proactive mobilization

	Citizen contacts*						Incidents†					
					Total						Total	
Setting of dispute	Suspicious persons/ circumstances (%)	Possible criminal (%)	Traffic (%)	Assistance/ service (%)	N	(%)	Property (%)	Automobile (%)	Inter-personal (%)	Other (%)	N	(%)
Residence	50.0	46.3	15.3	38.7	101	36.3	40.2	16.4	67.6	66.7	208	49.8
Street	15.2	4.5	63.9	33.3	87	31.3	6.8	64.4	1.8	9.8	68	16.3
Other public places	34.8	49.3	20.8	28.0	90	32.4	53.0	19.2	30.6	23.5	142	34.0
Column percentage	100.0	100.0	100.0	100.0		100.0	100.0	100.0	100.0	100.0		100.0
Total N	46	67	72	93	278		132	73	111	102	418	
Row percentage	16.5	24.1	25.9	33.5		100.0	31.6	17.5	26.6	24.4		100.0

* df = 6; $p < 0.01$; $\chi^2 = 66.38$
† df = 6; $p < 0.01$; $\chi^2 = 182.16$

'public street' area includes streets, sidewalks, highways, and public parking areas. 'Other public places' includes shopping areas, public areas of private businesses or government offices, and places of public recreation. Only 6.7 per cent of all mobilizations in relation to private residences were proactive; 75.8 per cent of all mobilizations on public streets were proactive; and 34.1 per cent of all mobilizations in other public places were proactive. This confirms the view that proactive policing primarily involves 'ordering the street.'

In Table 4.3 we consider the relation among the nature of disputes, the setting of disputes, and whether the matter was a citizen contact or an incident, for the 627 proactive encounters. This table reveals a number of significant features of proactive work, as well as some findings which we can elaborate upon only when we consider the same relationships for reactive work (see Table 4.4).

From Table 4.3 we learn that most proactive mobilizations relate to matters visible to patrol officers in public-street settings. The sizeable majority of these in turn are constituted by a combination of 'traffic' related citizen contacts (especially routine stops after the officer decides there may have been a violation of the Highway Traffic Act) and 'automobile' related incidents, which consist largely of either proactive stops where driving-related criminal violations are uncovered (e.g. impaired drivers) or reportable accidents the officers discover before the accidents are called into the police communications bureau by the citizens involved.

By way of contrast, relatively little proactive work is undertaken in other public places, and still less in private residential spaces. The proactive work in other public places largely involves checks in parks, or other known 'hangouts' such as take-out fast food chains or shopping plaza malls, where the main target is youths who are potential candidates for violations of the Liquor Licence Act and Narcotics Control Act.

The finding that proactive work is rare in private residential space should not be surprising, given the greatly reduced visibility of citizen activity in these areas (see Stinchcombe, 1963). What may be surprising is that there were even 22 proactively mobilized encounters in private areas. A number of these occurred in visible areas such as the above-ground or underground parking areas of apartment or condominium complexes. Others occurred when the officer pursued a vehicle that was not stopped until it had pulled into the driveway of a residence. In one of the three *incidents* in this grouping, the officer was leaving one apartment residence after a reactive call when he was accosted by youths outside another apartment. The youths began swearing at the officer and taunting him, and he then undertook to question them and check their identities.

Apart from traffic, the other major type of proactive citizen contact encounter is 'suspicious person/circumstances.' These encounters most frequently take place on the street and typically involve stops of vehicles on suspicion, enabling the patrol officer to check the driver's documents, undertake a CPIC check, and/or search the person or vehicle for liquor, narcotics, or stolen property violations. They occur less frequently in other public places, but here too they are usually in checks of youths for liquor and narcotics violations.

Assistance or service is very rarely a part of the proactive effort of patrol officers. It is relatively rare that an officer sees a situation he can enter solely to give assistance; the bulk of his time is spent in patrol on public streets. Because of the changing role of the officer that has resulted from bureaucratization, most assistance/service encounters come about only through reactive mobilization.

Proactive incidents are most likely to involve automobile-related disputes or matters we have labelled 'other.' Proactive automobile incidents typically involve impaired drivers and/or accidents. Proactive 'other' incident disputes are often the equivalent of citizen-contact 'suspicious person/ circumstance' disputes, except that they bring some 'payoff' for the officer including criminal charges. For example, 'other' incidents include searches of vehicles and persons that produce narcotics and liquor violations, as well as CPIC 'hits' that reveal the person stopped is wanted on a committal warrant. Also included are more lengthy 'assistance' matters, for example dealing with a retarded adult in difficulty after he was first observed near a shopping plaza.

Given that 61.9 per cent of all proactive encounters were either traffic-related citizen contacts or automobile-related incidents, we must re-examine the overall figure of 47.4 per cent for proactive encounters. How does mobilization come about for mainstream criminal disputes? If we include only the 'suspicious person/circumstance' and 'possible criminal' citizen contacts and the 'property,' 'interpersonal' and 'other' incidents, we have only 220 of 1,323 (16.6 per cent) mobilizations proactive with the potential for some criminal production. However, this figure is also misleading because it excludes Criminal Code driving offences such as impaired driving, and also the many traffic stops that include a CPIC check of the driver and/or a search of the vehicle with the aim of producing possible criminal matters. Traffic violations – such as having a plate light out, failing to stop for a traffic light, failing to signal, erratic driving, etc – form the main excuse by which an officer justifies to the citizen a stop that is essentially to check out the person because he has otherwise aroused the officer's suspicion.[4]

In summary, the officers we studied were almost as often proactive as reactive, and part of this activity was aimed at uncovering information that on the odd occasion could produce a criminal charge. Given the amount of time they were not involved in reactive encounters they could have been much more proactive than they were (see chapter 3, note 1). To understand further the level and nature of proactive work, it is necessary to examine controls over this type of activity and the framework of cues available to officers that enables them to undertake it.

CONTROLS ON PROACTIVE WORK

Patrol officers have considerable autonomy in undertaking some aspects of proactive work. They have a great deal of autonomy concerning when and where they undertake proactive activity, some autonomy concerning the volume, but little autonomy as to what violations they can pursue.

Proactive work aimed at law enforcement is essentially limited to stopping vehicles for observed violations of the Highway Traffic Act, stopping vehicles and pedestrians in the hope that an information search might reveal sufficient evidence to generate a charge under the Criminal Code (e.g. possession of stolen property; impaired driving), the Narcotics Control Act (e.g. possession of marijuana), or the Liquor Licence Act (e.g. a minor consuming liquor). As we learn later in this chapter and in chapter 6, proactive work is more commonly aimed at ordering the streets by the assertion of police authority against those who are at the most offensive rather than offenders.

While proactive production is limited to these areas, officers can usually ignore proactive work or actively pursue it on any particular shift. Moreover, within the limited range of activities that can be pursued, they can choose to specialize. For example, some concentrate on 'pukers' who are deemed likely candidates for liquor and narcotics violations. Others specialize in seeking out particular types of traffic offences; for example, observing a stop sign where violations are known to be frequent or patrolling truck routes in order to stop trucks for overweight loads. Some undertake random stops in search of impaired-driving charges to increase their productivity in Criminal Code offences.

Proactive work is frequently treated as a residual activity – what the officer does when he has nothing else to occupy him. For example, an officer set up radar for a 30-minute period during the shift, in between coffee breaks and sporadic reactive calls.

Proactive work can be ignored completely over entire shifts or at particular times during a shift. Ignoring proactive work involves two separate possibilities. The officer can simply not undertake general stops on suspicion. Furthermore, when a suspicious matter or traffic violation is observed, he can choose to ignore it. During the course of the 348 shifts observers recorded 60 'ignored violations,' defined as matters apparently observed by the officer that could have been subject to investigation and enforcement but were not. There was at least one ignored violation on 42 different shifts, and the vast majority of the violations were connected with traffic matters. The officers frequently justified not taking action by referring to excusable conditions: for example, that it was too late in the shift, that another matter was more pressing, or that it would be unjust to enforce because a stop sign that had not been observed by a motorist was not in place long enough. During one shift there were 4 ignored violations of the Highway Traffic Act; the officer said it was not the 'quota' time of the month for him.

As we saw in chapter 3, organizational influences exist to control proactive production. In particular, the monthly activity sheet that each patrol officer has to submit influences the total monthly volume of his proactive work even if he is free to adjust the level on any particular shift. Patrol officers and their superiors know that the volume of what they record as violations in regulatory areas (traffic, liquor, narcotics) is largely up to them. The volume is used in assessment by supervisors and 'made' by patrol officers.[5]

Probationary officers in particular believe that the monthly activity 'tics' received for proactive work are viewed more favourably by the administration than reactive 'tics.' Overall, those on probation are much more concerned about their proactive production than others are. On one Sunday-evening shift the patrol officer justified his low level of proactive work by stating that he was about to pass probation and therefore did not have to be as concerned any more. Those in the higher constable classifications who seek promotion and special assignments are also concerned with undertaking a lot of proactive work. Their operating philosophy is that the more proactive stops on suspicion, the better the chances for an investigative payoff. On several different shifts first-class constables seeking assignment to the detective office and/or promotion to sergeant were observed making repeated random stops in the hope that their 'lottery' approach might result in some investigative payoff.[6]

Everyone is concerned with the monthly production expectations for the platoon. Officers may decide they have to increase their proactive work in order to meet expectations. On one shift the officer issued 40 parking tags, commenting to the fieldworker that he did this once a month 'for the cheat sheet.' On another shift, he expressed his need for 'blueies' (traffic summonses) and later stopped a car for speeding. 'Quota-filling' techniques also include seeking out 'easy' Highway Traffic Act violations – by looking for overweight trucks or parking at intersections where infractions are known to be frequent. Liquor and narcotics violations are also pursued on the same basis. For example, an officer spent 12 to 1 am checking numerous vehicles and their occupants for these violations, with the expressed purpose of 'looking good' on the monthly report.

The level and nature of proactive work is also influenced by specific directives from patrol sergeants. These directives include 1) those aimed at all patrol officers and pertaining to special groups of suspicious persons, 2) those aimed at all patrol officers and relating to changes in the level of proactive stops and enforcement activity, and 3) those aimed at individual patrol officers and referring to a particular officer's level of proactive stop and enforcement activity.

In the parade period before each shift, the patrol officers on a platoon are given instructions by their sergeant and read new directives and memos from the administration. On occasion, memos relate to special groups or organizations within the community, and the officers are asked to be proactively vigilant towards members of these groups. For example, a patrol sergeant read a memo and then gave his own instructions concerning members of a suspicious political group. According to the memo, this group held that various 'big shots' were responsible for acts of international terrorism. The memo had the group aligned with an identified left-wing radical group, other leftist groups, as well as a right-wing racist group.[7] The patrol sergeant read on that someone had shown a great deal of interest in the structure of the police force, especially the staffing at headquarters, on a recent trip to headquarters. Officers were told to be on the lookout for these types and to report immediately anything suspicious as there was some feeling these radicals may be out to 'get' the police. Following his reading of the memo, the patrol sergeant indicated how members of this group might be identified and then added: 'If you see one go up and talk to them, but be real friendly because once you get them talking they never shut up. They're really crazy. Then maybe you can get them on a MHA [under the Mental Health Act].'

General instructions include broad statements: a patrol sergeant said that officers should reduce proactive stops aimed at producing traffic, liquor, and narcotics violations if they are likely to be viewed as harassment. Other instructions are more focused, e.g. establishing a particular expectation, such as five parking tags per midnight shift, or asking for more enforcement of particular matters such as stopping 'unsafe vehicles,' and issuing CV3 (vehicle inspection) forms. It is important to note that some of these instructions originate in complaints from citizens, so that some alternatives in proactive activity could ultimately be traceable to reactive calls. For example, parking complaints from citizens eventually yielded an instruction to increase proactive traffic enforcement in a particular area.

Instructions to individual officers usually state that the officer is underproducing in a particular area of proactive enforcement. One was told to produce more impaired-driving charges, and another was told after his anual assessement that he was not producing enough narcotics charges.

PROACTIVE CUES

Patrol officers themselves develop their own criteria for deciding what is worthy of proactive activity. Most of these are developed collectively as 'shared-recipe' knowledge about whom to stop for what purpose in particular circumstances. In general, patrol officers develop and use cues concerning 1) individuals out of place, 2) individuals in particular places, 3) individuals of particular types regardless of place, and 4) unusual circumstances regarding property.[8]

'Individuals out of place' are engaged in activities at a time and/or in circumstances deemed not normal. Examples included youths who were not well dressed (what an officer defined as 'cruds') and who were driving an expensive Cadillac, a man at 4 am in a commuter train station with no scheduled train due for several hours, an old man in 'derelict' condition walking in a wealthy residential area, and a group of men sitting in a car outside a bank.

A person is more likely to be defined as out of place if in the area of a recently reported offence or an area where offences are frequent. A person who is initially acting in a suspicious manner and then does something else as the police car approaches is also likely to be subject to a proactive stop. Typical examples include a driver sitting in the parking lot of an apartment building at 1:50 am who drove away with haste as the patrol car approached, and a car that slowed and drove close to the curb, providing a cue as a possible impaired driver.

'Individuals in particular places' are certain types of people found in places defined by patrol officers as known deviant contexts – mostly public places where youths congregate. Typical locations include parking lots outside fast-food-chains, shopping plazas, entertainment spots such as discotheques, and public parks. Proactive stops are aimed at dispersing congregations of youths and checking for liquor and narcotics violations.

Checks with other expressed motives include going to secluded areas of parks or secondary roads searching for 'parkers' (amorous couples parked in vehicles). Officers say the purpose is to ensure the woman is there voluntarily. Given conventional wisdom and legal wisdom, there is never similar questioning of the man. Checks are also made of persons in or around private property, such as the meeting houses of motorcycle groups.

'Individuals of particular types regardless of place' covers citizens typed as being particularly troublesome. The categories are usually very broad, e.g. 'pukers' and 'assholes' (see Van Maanen, 1978a). Routine stops of these are frequent. For example, a patrol officer spotted a 'puker' walking along a residential street in mid-afternoon and decided to stop him for questioning and a frisk search.

Another targeted group is 'bikers,' defined as persons whose appearance identifies them with a motorcycle 'gang.' These people are regularly stopped for investigative checks which serve more to remind them of their place in the face of police authority than to produce the possibility of law violations.[9] For example, exclaiming 'I hate bikers,' a patrol officer stopped a motorcyclist to question him and check him on CPIC. On another shift, the officer stated that a biker he spotted should be stopped, and he proceeded to do so. The encounter lasted 17 minutes, most of which was spent waiting for the results of a CPIC check, which revealed the biker was in the 'observation' category. The officer sent the biker on his way and then wrote up a contact card for police records, thereby reproducing the justification for 'observation' of this citizen on a continuing basis.

Proactive stops are also undertaken in relation to known 'troublemakers' or persons known to have criminal records. These are sometimes a favourite target of a particular officer or they may be known about through information circulating among officers. For example, an officer stopped a car driven by an individual with whom he had previous contacts. A CPIC check revealed this person might have a handgun, but the officer did not inquire further, explaining that he had put this information on the CPIC system in the first place. On another shift, a citizen described by the officer as a known 'child molester' was stopped in a parking lot near a carnival site and subjected to 20 minutes of questioning and a search.

Sometimes proactive work in relation to persons with a known record takes on an instrumental character aimed at matters not immediately apparent through the 'dispute' label attached to them. For example, an officer decided to spend part of an otherwise slow shift parked near the home of a well-known person who had a record for driving while suspended and narcotics violations. The officer hoped to catch him for driving while suspended; there was a car sitting in the driveway. Eventually he came out, drove the car about 20 yards, and was stopped by the officer. The officer called for a back-up officer, and the two began negotiating with the suspect, who offered them among other things the names of narcotics dealers in exchange for not charging him on this driving matter. He was apparently willing to deal because he anticipated a heavy penalty for yet another driving-while-suspended conviction. The officers eventually arrested him and turned him over to a detective, who continued the negotiations and ultimately released him without charge after apparently benefitting from his police-produced status as an informant.

'In unusual circumstances regarding property' the cue is provided by the condition of a particular piece of property. For example, an officer noticed window air conditioners out of position in a paint shop located in an industrial park area; after some investigation, this led to two 'attempt theft' occurrence reports. On another shift he described and used a technique that he felt yielded a higher probability of catching a driver with outstanding warrants. He looked for old cars with damage to the front end assuming the driver may have been in an accident where he was the culprit and therefore issued a summons. The person who cannot afford to pay for car repairs might also not be able to pay a fine and is more likely to have an outstanding warrant on him.

In this section I have outlined the nature and circumstances of proactive encounters and the indicators used by patrol officers to initiate this type of encounter. We can further understand the distinctive aspects of proactive mobilization by contrasting it with reactive mobilization.

Reactive Mobilization

Among all the technological changes that have influenced police patrol work, the most significant is probably the radio system. When it was introduced, it was heralded by many as the long-awaited technological breakthrough that would allow the police to dampen, if not extinguish, crime.[10] Of course, as we discussed in chapter 1, neither the radio system nor any other technological innovation has had a demonstrable effect on the level of crime. However, it has had a definite effect on the organization of patrol work, enabling mobile officers to receive requests for their presence on a perpetual basis. This in turn has affected the way people mobilize the police (in general, see Sparks et al, 1977: especially chapter 5); it has probably also affected their willingness to call the police (because of their availability) and the types of things they call them for.

In this section we examine the nature of reactive police work in a department which employs a sophisticated radio system (see Jorgensen, 1979). We describe the nature and setting of reactive encounters according to the criteria outlined above for proactive encounters. We then consider the relationship of the dispatcher and the patrol officer and the control used within it. Finally, we consider the manner in which patrol officers respond to calls for their presence. Throughout we make comparison with proactive mobilization.

Among the 816 citizen contacts, there was reactive mobilization for 24.6 per cent of all suspicious persons/circumstances situations, 71.3 per cent of possible criminal disputes, 17 per cent of traffic matters, and 83 per cent of assistance service improvements. In the 507 incidents, the incident was reactive for 95.6 per cent of property disputes, 66.4 per cent of automobile-related matters, 96.5 per cent of interpersonal disputes, and 70.8 per cent for 'other' types of dispute. Within the 1,323 encounters, 93.3 per cent that took place in a residence, 24.2 per cent that took place on the street, and 65.9 per cent that took place in other public places were reactive.

In Table 4.4 we consider the nature of the disputes, the setting of disputes, and whether the matter was a citizen contact or incident, for the 696 reactive encounters. One of the most evident differences from proactive work (Table 4.3) is the lesser degree of street settings. While 80.3 per cent of proactive citizen contacts occurred in street settings, only 31.3 per cent of reactive contacts were in the street; and, while 59.6 per cent of proactive incidents transpired on the street, only 16.3 per cent of reactive incidents were similarly located. Reactive work primarily involves reproducing the order of citizens in semi-private and private spaces, while proactive work involves reproduction of public order.

If reactive mobilizations do occur in street settings, they are most likely to involve 'traffic' related citizen contacts or 'automobile' related incidents. 'Traffic' citizen contacts typically include calls regarding traffic accidents where the damage is assessed to be unreportable,[11] or other minor citizen complaints regarding traffic violations, e.g. youths speeding or 'squealing tires' in a residential area. Reactive 'automobile' incidents typically involve traffic accidents, where the damage is assessed as reportable and where Highway Traffic Act summonses are typically issued to one offending party for a violation such as an 'improper lane change' or 'failure to yield.' Less common are incidents such as a patrol officer being dispatched to look for and stop an allegedly impaired driver reported by an anonymous caller.

Many reactive automobile incidents result in occurrence or accident reports, as well as Highway Traffic Act or Criminal Code charges. Thus, citizens initiate a significant amount of traffic law enforcement, especially where an accident entails laying blame for the purpose of resolving a property dispute. While the bulk of traffic enforcement is proactive, this reactive component should not be ignored. Indeed, in more serious matters involving apparent traffic violations, including those which cause a serious accident, mobilization is twice as likely to be reactive as proactive. While the police play an active role in charging in these situations (see chapter 6), their opportunity to get a charge is facilitated by citizen-initiated mobilization.[12]

'Assistance/service' reactive mobilizations are evenly distributed among the three types of settings. Excluding these and traffic-automobile disputes, we find that the remaining categories of disputes are fairly evenly split between private residential settings or public areas other than streets. The only major differences are for 'interpersonal' or 'other' disputes; these are much more likely to occur in residential settings. Some of the 'other' incidents include assistance/service calls major enough to be categorized as incidents. We can conclude that reactive work concerning personal troubles is most likely to emanate from conflicts at home.

Most citizen-initiated mobilizations occur through telephone calls to the police communications bureau, where the complaint is lodged and the communications officer decides whether or not to record it and send it to the dispatch officer for dispatch to a patrol officer.[13] In our sample, 95.2 per cent of all reactive incidents came about this way. The remaining 4.3 per cent, as well as a small but undetermined proportion of citizen contacts, were initiated 'on view.' The police were 'flagged down' by a citizen while driving, approached by a citizen while stationary, or approached by a citizen in or around the police station.

For citizen contacts, 'on-view' mobilizations are particularly likely to involve assistance/service matters. For example, an officer was hailed by a passing motorist who asked for the location of the nearest hospital as his son in the car was ill; the officer provided an escort to the hospital. At times these requests are less dramatic, as when an elderly gentleman approached the stationary patrol car and asked the officer for advice regarding a 'loose gadget' in his toilet tank. The officer said he had no specialized knowledge but suggested that the municipal by-law officers would welcome a 'careless plumbing' complaint.

In many situations the complainant sees a patrol car before having a chance to call police communications, or before dispatch is possible. A citizen saw a body floating at the edge of a lake and reported it to a passing officer immediately after he had telephoned for the police.

Citizens may use 'on-view' mobilization because they do not have access to a telephone to call police. For example, an officer involved in a proactive encounter with a youth was approached by a man who explained that his girlfriend was on the telephone with an obscene caller. The officer terminated the proactive inquiry and proceeded to assist the complainant.

'On-view' mobilizations are a means by which the citizen can have a potentially serious complaint dealt with and yet avoid having it officially logged on a complaint card in the police communications bureau. For example, a patrol officer was sitting in the parking lot of a shopping plaza when he was approached by a man who claimed to own a small trucking company. The man was worried that his new driver may have stolen his truck and its load since he had not arrived on schedule and had telephoned with a 'strange' excuse. The officer checked the make of the driver's car, which was on the lot of the man's company, and gave the man the car owner's name and address from a vehicle registration check. It coincided with the information the truck owner had, satisfying his worries that the driver may have duped him and that the car might be stolen and the address false. This confirmation put the man greatly at ease since he surmised that the driver wouldn't leave his actual address and his new car were he planning to steal a truck. This man was able to make a serious allegation, and have an investigative check undertaken, without any official logging of the matter with the police department.

THE ROLE OF THE DISPATCHER

As we saw in chapter 3, the dispatch system is a source of organizational control over patrol officers. In the police force we studied, there was a written procedural directive that 'as per regulations, all persons will act on any directive emanating from the Communications Centre, as though the Chief of Police was giving the order, personally.' All complaint cards recorded by the communications officer and sent to the dispatcher must record the action taken by the patrol officer, including the occurrence number if an official report is taken. All incoming calls are tape recorded and can be traced and played back by supervisors if the need arises. The *potential* for direct control is always there because any dispatch can be heard by other officers and supervisors, who can choose to respond to give guidance and/or make judgments about the patrol officer's work. A prevalent view among patrol officers is that whenever the matter is potentially serious and important, and thus potentially interesting, the dispatcher is likely to intrude by causing the mobilization of other officers and requesting detailed feedback on what happens in the encounter. One patrol officer put it succinctly: 'Discretion doesn't exist with serious offences since the fuckin' dispatcher controls your life.'

Some researchers have argued that the control of the dispatcher is very powerful indeed. For example, Pepinsky (1975, 1976) provides data which convey an image of the patrol officer as an automaton who is routinely responsive to, and made responsible through, the dispatcher. In his study in Minneapolis, Pepinsky (1976: 35) found that from 'a total of 373 calls in the sample, the patrolman received 207 calls in which the dispatcher named no offence [and] ... they reported offences in only four of these.' When an offence was mentioned in the dispatch, the officer almost as routinely took an official report on the offence, especially if it was a property offence (Pepinsky, 1976: 40; 1975: 33).

Pepinsky (1976: 33) further argues that the patrol officer does not circumvent much of his control by doing proactive work, because that rarely involves matters substantial enough to be reportable. In Black's (1968) work 24 per cent of reported offences were proactively initiated, and in Pepinsky's study only 1 of 87 offence reports other than traffic summonses arose out of proactive encounters. Thus, the argument goes, matters significant enough to warrant a written account are much more likely to be reactive and therefore subject to control by the dispatcher.

There are four major problems with arguments that the patrol officer dances according to strings pulled by the dispatcher. First, it is incorrect to assume that if a matter is not officially recorded, it is therefore insubstantial and unimportant. As is documented in chapter 5, many substantial complaints are handled without official reports, while many trivial complaints are recorded. As is documented in chapter 6, many proactive stops involving detention of citizens for extensive investigative checks are important actions within the public-order mandate of patrol policing even if they do not end up on the record.

Second, even when matters are recorded in occurrence reports, what is recorded and the label given to the occurrence are variable. As I show in detail in chapter 5, even property offences can be given a range of interpretations and labels. A complainant's allegation of break, enter, and theft may be judged no crime; lost property; trespass; theft; break and enter; break, enter, and theft; an attempt; and so on. Given the pervasive and persuasive authority of patrol officers in the eye of the public, their judgments in these matters are not often resisted.

Third, even if one uses reportable matters as an indicator, our own research does not support Pepinsky's findings. In Jorgensen's (1979) study of the communications bureau in the police force we studied, only 36.7 per cent of dispatches resulted in occurrence reports. Thus, almost two-thirds of dispatches did not result in official accounts. Moreover, of the 210 dispatches, only 129 resulted in some additional communication between the dispatcher and patrol officer after the dispatch and prior to reporting back 'in service,' and only 102 (48.6 per cent) involved giving the dispatcher information about the situation encountered.

Furthermore, in our research, proactive incidents were almost as likely to involve official reporting as were reactive incidents. 50.0 per cent (20) of victim-complainants (see chapter 5) involved in proactive incidents had official reports taken on their complaints, while 52.1 per cent (407) of those in reactive incidents had reports. 57.4 per cent (129) of suspects (see chapter 6) in proactive incidents were subject to 'official action' by patrol officers, while 53.6 per cent (263) of those in reactive incidents were treated thus.

Fourth, as I mentioned in chapter 3, patrol officers have techniques and devices to circumvent the control of the dispatcher. This has been documented by other researchers (e.g. Breck, 1977; Larson et al, 1978), who show that the response time of the patrol officer is not altered by the priorities set by dispatchers. This is the case even if a vehicle-locator system is used to monitor the officer's performance (cf Manning, 1977).[14] As Manning (1979, 1980) emphasizes, this finding is not surprising because the patrol officer bases immediacy more on the *context* of the call than on the official priority system.

We often saw patrol officers alter the dispatcher's priorities and instructions by delaying his response, not responding at all, or responding even when not called upon to do so. Delayed response is usually not difficult to effect because the dispatcher rarely knows the exact location of a patrol officer when he is initially dispatched. If questioned about a delayed response, the officer can 'cover' by saying he has a considerable distance to travel to the encounter, blame traffic conditions, or even say he is otherwise proactively engaged.

Delayed responses are in any case infrequent, and the delays rarely amount to more than a few minutes. They most often occur with disputes that the officer does not wish to become involved in. Thus, the officer can purposely delay arriving at the scene of the encounter in the hope that the trouble will be over, or in the hope that a back-up officer will arrive first and handle the matter. For example, a 'complaint of disorderlies' call was dispatched to an officer but he did not respond for five minutes, during which time he remained parked and finished drinking a coffee. He justified this to the researcher by stating, 'Usually in this kind of call, the disorderlies leave as soon as the complainant calls the police.' Domestic-dispute calls are also subject to delays for similar reasons.

Occasionally, patrol officers prejudge a dispatched call to be unimportant and therefore delay their response. For example, an officer did not immediately respond to a dispatched 'Theft – JDA' (theft by a juvenile) because he anticipated that the encounter would only involve taking an occurrence report, and he wanted to finish writing up his notebook. A 'threatening' call was dispatched to a patrol officer who 'knew the address' well enough to feel safe in finishing his coffee with an airport security officer before proceeding.

Total non-response (except in the form of delayed response aimed at having a back-up officer take over) is rare, although we did witness several examples. On one occasion, a patrol officer called into the dispatcher to say that he had discovered someone who had been shot. The dispatcher immediately dispatched other cars to the scene, including the patrol officer being observed. However, this officer did not respond, even though he was only dealing with a parking complaint and was near the scene. He covered this by not originally clearing with the dispatcher regarding the parking complaint. The dispatcher was then left to assume that the patrol officer was away from his car dealing with the parking complaint.[15]

At 2 am on another shift, an officer was dispatched to assist two patrol officers regarding 'prowlers' at a school. The officer '10-4d' the message to indicate he had received it and continued to sit drinking coffee. He told the researcher that the patrol officer in charge had a reputation for getting excited about petty matters and that this situation would probably be routine or unfounded. About 10 minutes later, the patrol officer in charge used the radio to tell the other units they could clear the school area; the officer being observed then '10-4d' again to indicate to the dispatcher that he had been involved all along.

Patrol officers also circumvent dispatcher control by responding to calls not dispatched to them and not informing the dispatcher about their actions.[16] We have already seen this type of action in the analysis of back-up reactions. These reactions occasionally occur in what the officer defines as an emergency. Most often, however, they occur because the officer is curious, or in search of some excitement, having nothing better to do at the time. As Pepinsky (1975: 25) expresses it, 'Though in some areas of large cities police can be overloaded with responding to calls (e.g. Reiss, 1971: 78–79), a more common problem for patrolmen is compensating for the poverty of calls they receive.'

We can further examine counter-controls over dispatchers by describing response time, the manner of response, and how the dispatcher's definition of the situation apparently influences the patrol officer's initial response and his response upon reaching the scene of the encounter.

For reactive incidents we recorded the response time and manner of response. The mean response time was 6 minutes, the median 5 minutes, with a range of 1 to 60 minutes, for 392 known responses. Within these 392 responses, slightly more than two-thirds took 5 minutes or less, and only 10 per cent took more than 10 minutes. The manner of the 411 known reactive responses was most often categorized as 'routine,' i.e. the officers proceeded immediately after receiving the call, stayed within speed limits, and did not use the siren or flasher. This type of response occurred in 53 per cent of all recorded responses. In 11 per cent the officers drove over the speed limit. In 27 per cent they drove at speeds far enough beyond the speed limit to constitute violations of the Highway Traffic Act under normal circumstances.[17] Roughly 5 per cent of the responses were recorded by the observers as delayed, either because the officers did not initially proceed to the scene even though they were not otherwise occupied, or because they dallied en route. An additional 4 per cent were categorized as 'other' responses, including some delayed responses where the officers were temporarily occupied at the time of receiving the dispatch. We of course are not including dispatches received but somehow circumvented, or dispatches to industrial property checks or alarms which produced no encounters and no official reports.

The type of response where the officer proceeds at high speed, sometimes using a flasher and/or siren, is most likely to occur for an ongoing dispute, e.g. a crime in progress or an accident involving personal injury. Thus, a reported 'theft in progress' behind a plaza lumber store was dispatched to one officer, and the officer being observed offered to back up and received permission to do so. He drove to the scene at high speeds using the flasher at intersections. A dispatch regarding a 'noisy party – beer bottles being thrown from 17th or 19th floors [of an apartment building]' was proceeded to at high speed, partly because of the potential seriousness of the matter as dispatched and also because the officer had been to the setting of this incident on a similar complaint earlier in the shift and thus had additional background information to judge its seriousness.

Occasionally dramatic responses occur even though the matter looks anything but dramatic. One patrol officer had a reputation for driving at excessive speeds and said he had just been subject to official action regarding his driving. On the shift, he received a dispatch regarding a 'mischief' complaint to an address that he knew well from previous complaints. One neighbour was continually complaining that the other was ruining his lawn by allowing excess water to run from one yard to the other. The officer exclaimed 'We finally got a call – let's boot it' and proceeded to drive at speeds of up to 65 mph in a 30 mph residential zone. Responses of this nature are easy to cover for because dispatch messages are usually imprecise enough to allow the officer interpretive latitude. He can usually say he thought it would involve more than it turned out to involve.

Reduced time of response does not increase the chances of catching suspects. As Kelling et al (1979: 11–12) state, 'The linkage between response time and its assumed outputs has been fairly well undermined.' One reason for this is 'that citizens often wait so long before reporting a crime that a hurried police response is fruitless' (ibid: 24). Patrol officers are aware of these facts and respond routinely to most calls. When they do respond swiftly, it does not often reflect a belief that serious 'crime-busting' has at last come their way, and that the speedier the response, the bigger the payoff. Rather, variable responses mirror the *contextual* nature of patrol officers' judgments, as well as their level of desire for an exciting drive and for the work that awaits them at the encounter.

While there are many ways in which patrol officers can develop independence from dispatchers, they are also dependent upon them. Most fundamentally, they must trust the dispatchers, what they say in their messages, and how they say it.[18] Patrol officers tend to expect the worst. In their communications with each other and with other criminal control agents, they create the worst possible image as the safest basis for proceeding and as a means of leaving open options. The definition can always be altered downwards once there is an opportunity to assess the matter at first hand and to weigh the available alternatives. This includes everything from dispatch messages to constructing charges and descriptions of the 'facts' to pass on to police superiors and the crown attorney.

Troubles between parties known to each other are often interpreted in the worst possible way at the communication officer and dispatch stages Jorgensen (1979). For example, an older sister's complaint that her 17-year-old brother was causing her difficulty by allowing his friends to 'have sex,' drink, and possibly use other drugs in the house was dispatched not as a 'domestic' or 'family dispute' but as, 'unwanted guests refusing to leave. BLLA. BNCA. [Breach of Liquor Licence Act and breach of Narcotics Control Act]. Several possible offences going on there. You'd best stand by and I'll get you a back-up. Don't attend the call without him.'

The patrol officer expects the communications officer to elicit any signs of serious trouble and to have these passed on by the dispatcher. These signs obviously influence the response. For example, a dispatcher reported 'a large group of disorderlies at the ── Hotel,' and he sent the patrol officer being observed as a primary responding car. The patrol officer proceeded at a fast pace, when another statement was made by the dispatcher: 'It comes across now as a large fight.' The officer increased his speed and used his flasher constantly. Patrol officers also employ indirect signs to gauge their response. For example, the seriousness of a call is partially judged by whether the dispatcher sends a back-up car.

The dispatcher's message also influences the patrol officer's actions upon arrival at the scene of the encounter. For the 418 reactive *incidents*, the researchers judged the encounter and the message to be more or less as depicted by the dispatcher in 60.3 per cent, similar but less serious in 20.1 per cent, similar but more serious in 14.1 per cent, and different in some other way in 5.5 per cent.

Most matters less serious than the dispatch indicates, or otherwise different, are probably so because of the way the citizen states the complaint to the communications officer and/or because of the 'worst possible image' rule noted above. For example, a dispatch regarding 'disorderlies in ── Park, three drunk men causing a disturbance' turned out to be a dispute between a citizen and a park attendant over where the citizen could park his van. A dispatch to a shopping plaza to see two youths regarding a theft was judged by the patrol officer to be wrongly reported. The youths had run out of money and they wanted a lift home. The officer could not give them a lift because they lived too far out of the patrol area, but he did give them a dollar for bus fare.

Sometimes citizens may have no independent way of discovering the meaning of an event observed from a distance and therefore report the most serious possibility, and this is reflected in the dispatch. For example, a reported 'break and enter in progress' at a gas station with 'three youths still inside' was judged by the patrol officer to be 'unfounded' as the youths were employees closing down the station for the night.

During the course of our observations, two reactive dispatches describing the culprits as armed and possibly dangerous also involved a message that bore little relation to the reality of the matter that was ultimately produced. On one occasion, a patrol officer backed up on a call regarding a person observed syphoning gas and 'possibly armed with a gun.' The officer drew his gun and thoroughly checked the area but no suspect was located and there was no indication that the alleged matter had taken place. In the previously described incident (pp 76–7) concerning a man armed with a hatchet, the dispatched message was '10–70 re violent male/white 37 years old, blue eyes, 5' 10" 170 lbs., driving [car licence number and description] seen with a hatchet swinging at a youth. Has previous history of violence. Exercise extreme caution. He is assaultive.' Upon spotting the car, the patrol officer pulled it over and drew his gun on the driver. The matter was judged to be a domestic dispute, with the original complaint and description of the suspect apparently being amplified by the suspect's wife.

The dependence of the patrol officer on the communication officer and dispatcher's interpretations of the citizen's telephone account is also illustrated through situations where the encounter turns out to be much more serious than initially described. For example, a patrol officer was dispatched to 'the first house south of [address] re youths in the back yard. Complainant does not wish to see an officer.' The officer proceeded to the scene in a routine manner and commented to the researcher that it was probably just a noise complaint. However, upon arrival he noticed signs of entry into the house. With back-up assistance the officer eventually entered the house and subsequently arrested three suspects for break, enter, and theft. Rare circumstances such as this of course serve to justify the 'you should expect anything' approach of patrol officers. They also remind officers of the unpredictable nature of the dispatch process and the need to do their own contextual analysis beyond what they are told by even their trustworthy colleagues.

Defining Citizen Roles

Who does the patrol officer meet after mobilization to an encounter? While he can assume that citizens will have a definite perception of his role, he must work out a definition of who *they* are in order to deal with them appropriately.

The initial definition of 'suspect' influences most proactive mobilizations, and the initial definition of 'complainant' influences most reactive mobilizations. However, these definitions are frequently altered during the encounter, and other people may enter the encounter to influence the role-typing and what is ultimately decided upon.

As enumerated in Table 4.5, the patrol officers we studied had direct dealings with 2,653 citizens. These citizens are categorized by role as defined by the patrol officers. 'Primary suspects' are persons treated as possible culprits for an offence and are candidates for investigative checks, and/or unofficial warnings, and/or official action. 'Primary victim-complainants' are individuals who lodge a complaint with a patrol officer and whose complaint is at least initially entertained by the patrol officer in making a decision about what further action might be necessary. 'Primary others' are people who play some role in encounters, but who are not treated as a suspect or victim-complainant, e.g. contributing witnesses or informants, and those having troubles not warranting investigation, e.g. 'service' matters such as assisting a person trapped in an elevator, and aiding someone who had fallen out of a wheelchair. 'Secondary' participants are people who play a peripheral role, such as supplying non-essential information about a matter, or being occupants of a car subject to a search where the driver is the primary individual under police investigation.

The figures in Table 4.5 reveal that encounters between patrol officers and citizens are visible to a large number of people. While the officers averaged slightly less than 4 encounters on each of the 348 shifts of observation, they had direct involvements with almost 8 citizens per shift. Moreover, not included in the table is the fact that there were 1,537 'bystanders' observing incident disputes even though they were not directly involved, so that on average 12 citizens per shift were seeing the officer's actions during encounters with citizens.

Obviously, patrol officers are highly visible to the public in handling troubles. First and foremost the officer must take into account who the citizens are and what actions might resolve the matter without producing citizen complaints. As we argue in the next two chapters, officers do this by taking into account the 'place' of the citizens within the community – assessing what they can do without having a citizen complain. While they can rely on the pervasive influence of their symbolic authority, patrol officers also develop situated strategies to achieve the outcomes they desire.

As Table 4.5 indicates, patrol officers placed the majority of primary citizens in the 'suspect' role, and most of the rest were victim-complainants. The majority (60.6 per cent) of suspects were encountered in citizen contacts, while the majority (73.6 per cent) of victim-complainants were encountered in incidents. Furthermore, 83.4 per cent of suspects in citizen contacts and 32.9 per cent of suspects in incidents were encountered through proactive

TABLE 4.5

Total number and role of citizens present in citizen contact and incident encounters, excluding bystanders

Citizen role	Citizen contacts (816 encounters)	Incidents (507 encounters)	Total (1,323 encounters)
Primary – suspects	603	392	995
Primary – victim-complainants	153	427	580
Primary – others	60	94	154
Secondary	590	334	924
Totals	1,406	1,247	2,653

mobilizations; overall, the majority (63.5 per cent) of suspects encountered were defined by patrol officers without the supporting mobilization of a victim-complainant. 86.9 per cent of victim-complainants in citizen contacts and 95.3 per cent of victim-complainants in incidents were encountered reactively. Thus, officers involved in encounters involving citizen complaints of trouble in need of investigation, usually did not initiate the matter themselves: only 6.9 per cent of victim-complainants were encountered after proactive mobilization.

In the following chapter we examine the dealings of patrol officers with victim-complainants in citizen-contact and incident encounters. In chapter 6 we consider their dealings with suspects in citizen-contact and incident encounters and the outcome for people charged in these encounters. As part of our analysis we show that once the encounter is engaged, the manner of mobilization recedes in importance. The patrol officer must deal with the immediate situation and order a resolution that can be justified and legitimated.

5

Dealing with Victim-Complainants

Citizens mobilize the police for a wide variety of purposes. In addition to reporting property-related troubles such as automobile accidents, lost property, and theft, they call the police to handle interpersonal conflicts because other forms of social control have failed, are unavailable, or are absent (Black, 1968: 117, 1972: 1099, 1976: 6; Meyer, 1974: 81–2). This failure of controls is especially frequent at particular times and places (Cumming et al, 1970: 187) and among the less powerful (Black, 1971: 1108; Bottomley, 1973: 45). The police are used as a power resource to help reproduce the order desired by the citizen.

For several reasons, the bulk of troubles complained about by the public do not result in a 'criminal' designation by the patrol officer. Citizens are about as likely to call the police for troubles they themselves define as 'non-criminal' as they are to call regarding 'criminal' troubles (Cumming et al, 1970; Punch, 1979). As we emphasize with case examples in this chapter, the types of things viewed by citizens as 'serious' enough to warrant police presence are typically not very serious at all when compared with conventional wisdom about the police and crime.

Furthermore, citizens only report to the police a small fraction of what they themselves regard as 'crimes' committed against them (Ennis, 1967; Biderman et al, 1967; Sparks et al, 1977). Moreover, as we saw in chapter 4, the communications bureau does not dispatch a substantial number of citizen calls (Jorgensen, 1979; Manning, 1979).

When they do encounter citizens, patrol officers do not routinely accept the citizens' definitions, whether 'criminal' or otherwise. Rather, they translate these requests within the framework of the police organization, employing 'recipe' rules, legal rules, and/or community rules to decide whether the matter could or should be transformed into police property (cf Christie, 1977; Ericson,

1981). In the survey by Sparks et al (1977: 156), '35 per cent of the survey-estimated crime appeared to have been reported to the police; but ... of these apparently reported incidents, only about a third appear to have been recorded in the police statistics.' Reiss (1971: 70 – 8) found that while 58 per cent of all calls for police assistance are initially defined as criminal matters by citizens, one patrol division recorded only 17 per cent of dispatches as criminal incidents.

Police officers have wide interpretive latitude in deciding what constitutes a crime and how the matter should be constituted. Ennis (1967) found that officers and lawyers agreed only slightly more than half the time on whether matters reported by respondents in a victimization survey actually constituted 'crimes.' Chappell et al (1977) found great variation between police departments in their definitions of 'forcible rape,' and this partly accounted for the difference in the incidence of forcible rape in the jurisdictions studied. The officer can transform what is initially reported as a 'service' matter into a 'criminal' incident if it appears possible or desirable to use the criminal law to handle the matter (cf Shearing and Leon, 1978).

In this chapter we examine the processes by which officers make decisions about citizen complaints. I initially describe general statistical patterns in the resolution of both minor (citizen contact) and major (incident) encounters with citizens. We then see how patrol officers construct encounters and the resulting official reports to legitimate their actions. Patrol officers may deflect complaints so that official reporting is not required, report in a way that justifies their decision not to initiate a 'criminal' occurrence, or report in a way that justifies the particular 'criminal' interpretation they give to an occurrence.

Our descriptive statistical portrayal is not an indication that we view the patrol officer as an automaton who follows unreflexively citizens' requests for action according to pre-established criteria. We look at the patrol officer *making* his judgments *within* the complexities of the encounter. He takes into account who the citizens are, their claims within the *context* in which they are made, expectations within the police organization, and the resources (legal and otherwise) available to reproduce order.

Equipped as he is with considerable authority, which routinely yields deference on the part of the public, he routinely achieves an outcome in accordance with his sense of order. His power allows him to make his definition of the situation stick; his authority usually means that the citizens involved readily accept his definition, at least to the point of not invoking an official complaint about it. As the United States National Advisory Commission on Criminal Justice Standards and Goals (1973) observed, police effectiveness depends upon 'the participant's belief that the police have more authority than they actually have.' This applies to both victim-complainants and suspects and is a key reason why the police control the reproduction of order on behalf of the state and its constituent interests.

Minor Complaints

As we saw in chapter 1, patrol officers make decisions on how to handle encounters by typing the individuals involved and using that to assess their claims. Encounters involve a 'negotiation of status claims' (Hudson, 1970: 190) which results in a situation where 'police activity is as much directed to who a person is as to what he does' (Bittner, 1970: 10). Do the citizens' characteristics indicate that they are tied into the order of things? Do their characteristics make their claims legitimate? What investigative actions might refute their claims? What final actions can citizens of this type be made to accept that will also allow police interests to be served?

One way of studying these questions is to categorize the citizens encountered according to criteria of status and role and to link these with characteristics of the encounter. We classified the 153 victim-complainants in citizen-contact encounters according to their personal characteristics, how their encounter was mobilized, the type of dispute, and the actions taken by the officer to terminate the dispute.

Age, *sex*, and *race* were categorized by the researchers. If a driver's licence was produced, or citizens gave their age, these sources were employed. Race was grouped in terms of 'white' and those from other racial backgrounds (black, East Indian, Pakistani, other Asian).

Socio-economic standing was determined by the researchers' judgments. In subsequent analysis these determinations were in turn categorized into 'lower,' 'working,' and 'middle.' This assessment proved difficult because the researchers were required to base their judgments on limited cues, such as the citizen's dress, speech, type of automobile, and/or place of residence. When they were unable to decide they omitted this item, resulting in a large proportion of 'do not know' responses.

Demeanour was judged by whether citizens were deferential to the officer and co-operative in questioning or at any point refused to afford the officer deference and did not co-operate.

Mobilization and *dispute type* were defined in the same way as described in chapter 4. Dispute type was split into 'traffic' and all 'others.' Citizen-contact disputes typically involved minor traffic accidents (damage under $200), interpersonal troubles (disputes between neighbours and domestic problems), and property-related troubles (found property, minor theft, apparent attempted theft, minor property damage).

Advice/assistance involves the officer responding to citizens' troubles by helping them in some way. Advice includes a wide range of counselling on how to obtain other remedies to rectify the trouble, e.g. informal compensation from the culprit concerning minor property damage or loss, alternative sources of help for interpersonal troubles, civil remedies available, etc. Assistance typically included speaking with the other party in a dispute, arranging transportation, providing transportation, etc. Patrol officers took this type of action in almost one-half of their dealings with victim-complainants in citizen contacts.

Official reports are general occurrence reports, property reports, or accident reports. This form of official action was undertaken for only 25 of 153 victim-complainants – on minor traffic accidents (e.g. 'failure to report an accident,' where the damage was slight), found property (e.g. 'found bikes'), minor property occurrences (e.g. 'attempt theft'), and neighbour disputes (e.g. 'barking dog').

As Table 5.1 documents, only three variables significantly differentiate those who received advice/assistance. There is a significant relationship between socio-economic status and advice/assistance. Lower-status persons were much more likely to receive advice/assistance than their higher-status counterparts. One probable reason is that persons of this type are more likely to *use* officers to help them with petty troubles because they have fewer other resources available to handle their problems.

Unco-operative people were significantly less likely to receive advice/assistance from the patrol officer. If a victim-complainant was requesting support and was subsequently not co-operative, the officer was likely to be unable and/or unwilling to offer advice/assistance. However, the 'demeanour' variable does not indicate when during the encounter the citizen became unco-operative or otherwise challenged the officer's actions. In some cases the citizen may have become unco-operative after the officer said he was unwilling to deal with a trivial trouble or something he deemed not proper police business.

Table 5.1 shows also that advice/assistance was more typically given as an alternative to official reports. Only 5 of 25 subject to offical reports also received advice/assistance, while 70 of 128 who did not have an official report taken received advice/assistance.

In Table 5.2 we consider mobilization, dispute type, and victim-complainant characteristics, as well as whether or not an official report was taken, in a stepwise discriminant analysis concerning whether advice/assistance was given.[1] The best predictor of whether or not advice/assistance was given is demeanour. Whether an official report was taken, the victim-complainant's socio-economic status, and his or her age also have influence. Victim-complainants in citizen contacts who received some form of advice/assistance were distinguishable as lower or working class, aged under 17 or over 24, co-operative, and not subject to an official report. These data, along with similar data for major complaints, support the view that in reactive work, patrol officers are often used by lower- or working-class people to handle their personal troubles (cf Downes, 1979: 12–13).

In Table 5.3 I relate mobilization, dispute type, victim-complainant characteristics, and whether advice/assistance was given to those subject to official

TABLE 5.1

Victim-complainants in citizen contact encounters: mobilization, nature of dispute, victim-complainant characteristics, and whether official report against proportion of victim-complainants given advice/assistance

		N	Percentage receiving advice/ assistance	χ^2	df
Total sample		153	49.0		
Mobilization:	Proactive	20	60.0	0.66	1
	Reactive	133	47.4		
Dispute type:	Traffic	47	42.6	0.79	1
	Other	106	51.9		
Victim-complainant characteristics					
Age:	17–24	17	58.8		
	<17 / >24	119	48.7	0.27	1
	Do not know	(17)	(58.8)		
Sex:	Male	100	50.0	0.03	1
	Female	53	47.2		
Race:	White	124	50.0		
	Non-white	28	46.4	0.02	1
	Do not know	(1)	(0.0)		
SES:	Lower	17	82.4		
	Working	55	40.0	9.38	2
	Middle	44	47.7		
	Do not know	(37)	(48.6)		
			*		
Demeanour:	Co-operative	121	56.2		
	Unco-operative	23	17.4	10.14	1
	Do not know	(9)	(33.3)		
Other patrol officer action					
Official report:	Yes	25	20.0	8.73	1
	No	128	54.7		
			*		

* $p < 0.01$
χ^2 corrected for continuity in 2 x 2 tables

reports taken on their complaints. Except for advice/assistance, none of these variables is associated with others at a statistically significant level. One reason is the small proportion subject to official reports.

In Table 5.4, a discriminant analysis employing the same variables indicates that the best predictor of whether an official report was taken is whether advice/assistance was given, followed by the additional influence of the citizen's demeanour and then type of mobilization. People receiving an official report on their complaint are grouped as being involved in reactive mobilization, being co-operative with patrol officers, and not receiving advice/assistance.

In summary, patrol officers handled most minor complaints without recording them. When advice or assistance was offered, it was usually after

TABLE 5.2

Victim-complainants in citizen contact encounters: stepwise discriminant analysis of mobilization, dispute type, victim-complainant characteristics, and whether official report taken against whether advice/assistance given

Step discriminant variables		F to enter	Discriminant function coefficients
Demeanour:	Unco-operative	9.97	+0.683
	Co-operative		
Official report:	No report	9.62	–0.504
	Report		
SES:	Middle	7.55	+0.527
	Lower/working		
Age:	17–24	1.39	+0.215
	<17/>24		

Centroids: Group I – No advice/assistance ($n = 51$) –0.497
Centroids: Group II – Advice/assistance ($n = 54$) +0.469
Percentage correctly classified – 70.5%
Wilk's lambda = 0.7646; $\chi^2 = 27.11$; df = 4; $p < 0.001$

complaints by lower-status citizens about troubles with neighbours, spouses, children, or other intimates. Official reports were taken usually for property matters such as minor accidents, attempt theft under $200, or minor property damage.

Obviously our analysis is limited by what we are able to quantify. We consider the influence of the police organization in detail in 'Citizen Requests and the Production of Organizational Accounts,' later in this chapter.

Major Complaints

The greatest proportion (74 per cent) of complaints by victim-complainants are dealt with more extensively. The officers we observed undertook three general forms of action. *Advice/assistance* involved them in giving immediate help or advice (e.g. advice to stay away from the suspect for a while; calling an ambulance service for medical assistance). *Advice to take other formal action* included suggestions that the citizen seek remedies through other 'formal' channels – e.g. consult a lawyer, contact a public welfare agency, make private security arrangements – as well as advising the citizen about proceeding by private prosecution (laying a private information). *Official reports* included general occurrence reports, accident reports, found-property reports, etc. Overall, 16.9 per cent (72) of victim-complainants received advice/assistance, 14.5 per cent (62) received advice to take other formal action, and 52.0 per cent (222) had their complaints officially accepted in the form of reports. Of course, these actions were not mutually exclusive; some citizens received two or all three actions during an encounter, which is taken into account in subsequent analysis.

TABLE 5.3

Victim-complainants in citizen contact encounters: mobilization, nature of dispute, victim-complainant characteristics, and whether advice/assistance given against proportion of victim-complainants subject to official report

		N	Percentage subject to official report	χ^2	df
Total sample		153	16.3		
Mobilization:	Proactive	20	0.0	3.22	1
	Reactive	133	18.8		
Dispute type:	Traffic	47	12.8	0.31	1
		106	17.9		
Victim-complainant characteristics					
Age:	17–24	17	23.5		
	<17 / >24	119	16.0	0.19	1
		(17)	(11.8)		
Sex:	Male	100	16.0	0.01	1
	Female	53	17.0		
Race:	White	124	16.1		
	Non-white	28	14.3	0.00	1
	Do not know	(1)	(100.0)		
SES:	Lower	17	5.9		
	Working	55	20.0	2.01	2
	Middle	44	20.5		
	Do not know	(37)	(10.8)		
Demeanour:	Co-operative	121	17.4		
	Unco-operative	23	8.7	0.53	1
	Do not know	(9)	(22.2)		
Other patrol officer action					
Advice/assistance	Yes	75	6.7	8.73	1
	No	78	25.6		
			*		

* $p < 0.01$
χ^2 corrected for continuity in 2 x 2 tables

In Table 5.5, whether advice/assistance was given is considered according to the same mobilization and victim-complainant characteristics analysed for victim-complainants in citizen contacts. We include two features of incidents that may also have affected decisions: whether or not the victim-complainant suffered any property damage or loss of any dollar value and whether or not the victim-complainant suffered any personal injury.[2] The types of disputes considered are automobile, property, interpersonal, and others.[3]

A number of factors are related at a statistically significant level to decisions to give advice/assistance. Those involved in interpersonal disputes were more than twice as likely as those involved in any other type of dispute to receive advice/assistance. This is consistent with the fact that those not

TABLE 5.4

Victim-complainants in citizen contact encounters: stepwise discriminant analysis of mobilization, dispute type, victim-complainant characteristics, and whether advice/assistance given against whether official report taken

Step discriminant variables		F to enter	Discriminant function coefficients
Advice/assistance:	Advice/assistance *No advice/assistance*	6.08	+0.823
Demeanour:	Unco-operative *Co-operative*	5.48	–0.642
Mobilization:	Proactive *Reactive*	2.11	–0.390

Centroids: Group I – no official report ($n = 86$) +0.164
Centroids: Group II – official report ($n = 19$) +0.740
Percentage correctly classified – 73.3%
Wilk's lambda = 0.8777; $\chi^2 = 13.24$; df = 3; $p < 0.004$

involved in property damage or loss were also significantly more likely to receive advice/assistance. Statistically significant relationships are apparent between advice/assistance and age, sex, and race. Older persons, men, and non-whites were much more likely to receive advice/assistance.

Advice/assistance was not usually associated with any particular circumstances or characteristics. Moreover, while it often consisted of advice regarding other formal action, it was relatively rarely employed along with the taking of official reports.

In Table 5.6 a discriminant analysis is documented to sort out on a predictive basis the characteristics of the group receiving advice/assistance from those who did not.[4] The best predictor on a stepwise basis is whether or not an official report was taken, followed by the addition in order of the dispute type, mobilization, race, sex, age, advice concerning other formal action, and whether personal injury occurred. Those receiving advice/assistance characteristically are also given advice concerning other formal action but do not have a report taken. They are typically in proactive disputes, interpersonal conflicts, and conflicts that do not involve injury. In terms of citizen characteristics, they are under 16 or over 24 years old, women, and non-white.

Turning to Table 5.7 we find that those receiving advice concerning other forms of action are differentiated several ways. As with informal advice/assistance, the vast majority of victim-complainants did not receive advice regarding other types of action.

Advice to take other forms of action was overwhelmingly likely to be in interpersonal disputes and likely to be in situations that did not involve property loss or damage, but did involve a degree of personal injury. People involved were significantly more likely to come from the lowest socio-economic

TABLE 5.5

Victim-complainants in incident encounters: mobilization, dispute characteristics, victim-complainant characteristics, and other patrol officer actions against proportion given advice/assistance

		N	Percentage given advice/ assistance	χ^2	df
Total sample		427	16.9		
Mobilization:	Proactive	20	30.0	1.69	1
	Reactive	407	16.2		
Dispute type:	Auto	81	8.6	22.17	3
	Property	137	11.7		
	Interpersonal	128	29.7		
	Other	81	13.6		
			**		
Damage/loss:	Yes	217	10.6	11.45	1
	No	210	23.3		
			**		
Injury:	Yes	89	18.0	0.02	1
	No	338	16.6		
Victim-complainant characteristics					
Age:	Under 16	26	3.8	6.94	2
	16–24	96	11.5		
	25+	293	19.8		
	Do not know	(12)	(16.7)		
			*		
Sex:	Male	259	12.0	10.37	1
	Female	168	24.4		
			**		
Race:	White	314	14.0	7.28	1
	Non-white	94	26.6		
	Do not know	(19)	(15.8)		
			**		
SES:	Lower	49	24.5	2.80	2
	Working	160	18.1		
	Middle	185	14.6		
	Do not know	(33)	(12.1)		
Demeanour:	Co-operative	368	17.1	0.02	1
	Unco-operative	48	16.7		
	Do not know	(11)	(9.1)		
Other patrol officer actions					
Advice re other formal action:	Yes	62	54.8	71.49	1
	No	365	10.4		
			**		
Official report:	Yes	222	9.5	16.99	1
	No	205	24.9		
			**		

* $p < 0.05$
** $p < 0.01$
χ^2 corrected for continuity in 2 x 2 tables

TABLE 5.6

Incident victim-complainants: stepwise discriminant analysis of mobilization, dispute characteristics, victim-complainant characteristics, and other patrol officer actions against whether or not advice/assistance was given

Step discriminant variables		*F* to enter	Discriminant function coefficients
Official report:	*No report*	19.54	+0.327
	Report		
Dispute type:	Other	10.15	−0.505
	Interpersonal		
Mobilization:	*Proactive*	8.22	+0.407
	Reactive		
Race:	White	6.33	−0.357
	Non-white		
Sex:	Male	5.44	−0.320
	Female		
Age:	*<16 / >24*	2.27	+0.210
	16–24		
Advice formal action:	*Advice formal action*	2.04	+0.204
	No advice formal action		
Personal injury:	Injury	1.39	−0.164
	No injury		

Centroids: Group I – advice/assistance (*n* = 64) –0.812
Centroids: Group II – no advice/assistance (*n* = 304) +0.171
Percentage correctly classified – 70.7%
Wilk's lambda = 0.8609; χ^2 = 54.21; df = 8; *p* < 0.001

status, and were somewhat more likely to be male than female. This group was particularly likely to use patrol officers in place of other agencies and/or officers were more willing to displace complaints from citizens in this category. However, as we learn from Table 5.8, the role of socio-economic status recedes when considered with other variables.

Table 5.7 also indicates that while advice concerning other formal action was often given in conjunction with other forms of advice/assistance, it was rarely combined with the taking of an official report.

From Table 5.8 we learn that on a stepwise basis, the overwhelmingly strongest predictor of advice to take other formal action was whether other informal advice was also given. The addition of dispute type to the equation is then of some importance, while the influence of the remaining variables – personal injury, official report, mobilization, and sex – is relatively less, though still statistically significant.

Those receiving advice concerning other formal action tend to receive other advice/assistance but not to have their complaints officially recorded. They are predictably more likely to be involved in interpersonal disputes, disputes that involve a degree of injury, and reactive disputes and to be men.

TABLE 5.7

Victim-complainants in incident encounters: mobilization, dispute characteristics, victim-complainant characteristics, and other patrol officer actions against proportion given advice concerning other formal action

		N	Percentage receiving advice to take other formal action	χ^2	df
Total sample		427	14.5		
Mobilization:	Proactive	20	15.0	0.07	1
	Reactive	407	14.5		
Dispute type:	Auto	81	8.6	45.38	3
	Property	137	6.6		
	Interpersonal	128	32.0		
	Other	81	6.2		
			**		
Damage/loss:	Yes	217	5.5	27.28	1
	No	210	23.8		
			**		
Injury:	Yes	89	27.0	12.79	1
	No	338	11.2		
			**		
Victim-complainant characteristics					
Age:	under 16	26	0.0	4.90	2
	16–25	96	14.6		
	25+	293	16.0		
	Do not know	(12)	(8.3)		
Sex:	Male	259	11.6	3.99	1
	Female	168	19.0		
			*		
Race:	White	314	12.1	3.31	1
	Non-white	94	20.2		
	Do not know	(19)	(26.3)		
SES:	Lower	49	30.6	13.65	2
	Working	160	15.6		
	Middle	185	9.7		
	Do not know	(33)	(12.1)		
			**		
Demeanour:	Co-operative	368	13.6	2.26	1
	Unco-operative	48	22.9		
	Do not know	(11)	(9.1)		
Other patrol officer actions					
Advice/assistance:	Yes	72	47.2	71.49	1
	No	355	7.9		
			**		
Official report:	Yes	222	5.9	26.53	1
	No	205	23.9		
			**		

* $p < 0.05$
** $p < 0.01$
χ^2 corrected for continuity in 2 x 2 tables

TABLE 5.8

Incident victim-complainants: stepwise discriminant analysis of mobilization, dispute characteristics, victim-complainant characteristics, and other patrol officer actions against whether or not advice concerning other formal action was given

Step discriminant variables		F to enter	Discriminant function coefficients
Advice/assistance:	*Advice/assistance*	104.58	+0.794
	No advice/assistance		
Dispute type:	Other	24.55	–0.323
	Interpersonal		
Personal injury:	*Injury*	3.44	+0.173
	No injury		
Official report:	*No report*	3.15	+0.168
	Report		
Mobilization type:	Proactive	1.35	–0.010
	Reactive		
Sex:	*Male*	1.36	+0.010
	Female		

Centroids: Group I – advice other formal action ($n = 53$) –1.299
Centroids: Group II – no advice other formal action ($n = 300$) +0.229
Percentage correctly classified – 84.4%
Wilk's lambda = 0.701; $\chi^2 = 123.6$; df = 6; $p < 0.001$

As indicated in Table 5.9, decisions by patrol officers to take occurrence reports in conjunction with victim-complainant reports of trouble vary greatly on a number of incident and citizen characteristics.

In contrast to informal advice, formal action via official reports was much less likely in interpersonal disputes than in any other type of dispute. Only 25.8 per cent of victim-complainants in interpersonal incidents had official reports taken by patrol officers, while the figure is 53.0 per cent in automobile disputes, 59.3 per cent in 'other' disputes, and 70.3 per cent in property disputes.

Official reports were much more likely to be taken in relation to victim-complainants involved in incidents where there was property damage or loss. Reports were also somewhat more likely when there was no personal injury to the victim. Reports were particularly likely for victim-complainants in property disputes and particularly unlikely for victim-complainants in interpersonal disputes. We find that men, and persons of higher socio-economic status, were significantly more likely to have official reports taken on their complaints.

Table 5.9 shows also that official reports were much less likely to be taken where informal advice/assistance, or advice to take other formal action, was given.

In Table 5.10 we present a discriminant analysis concerning whether or not an official report was taken. By far the most important predictor is the type of dispute. While eight other factors are also statistically significant, their additional influence is markedly less after the type of dispute has been taken into

TABLE 5.9

Victim-complainants in incident encounters: mobilization, dispute characteristics, victim-complainant characteristics, and other patrol officer actions against proportion subject to official reports

		N	Percentage subject to official reports	χ^2	df
Total sample		427	52.0		
Mobilization:	Proactive	20	50.0	0.00	1
	Reactive	407	52.1		
Dispute type:	Automobile	81	54.3	56.54	3
	Property	137	70.8		
	Interpersonal	128	25.8		
	Other	81	59.3 **		
Damage/loss:	Yes	217	67.3	40.09	1
	No	210	36.2 **		
Injury:	Yes	89	42.7	3.43	1
	No	338	54.4		
Victim-complainant characteristics					
Age:	Under 16	26	46.2	4.54	2
	16–24	96	61.5		
	25+	293	49.5		
	Do not know	(12)	(50.0)		
Sex:	Male	259	60.6	18.76	1
	Female	168	38.7 **		
Race:	White	314	54.1	3.44	1
	Non-white	94	42.6		
	Do not know	(19)	(63.2)		
SES:	Lower	49	28.6	20.56	2
	Working	160	47.5		
	Middle	185	62.7		
	Do not know	(33)	(48.5) **		
Demeanour:	Co-operative	368	53.0	2.54	1
	Unco-operative	48	39.6		
	Do not know	(11)	(72.7)		
Other patrol officer actions					
Advice/assistance:	Yes	72	29.2	16.99	1
	No	355	56.6 **		
Advice to take other formal action	Yes	62	21.0	26.53	1
	No	365	57.3 **		

** $p < 0.01$
χ^2 corrected for continuity in 2 x 2 tables

TABLE 5.10

Incident victim-complainants: stepwise discriminant analysis of mobilization, dispute characteristics, victim-complainant characteristics, and other patrol officer actions against whether or not an official report was taken

Step discriminant variables		F to enter	Discriminant function coefficients
Dispute type:	*Other* Interpersonal	40.31	−0.374
Sex:	*Male* Female	12.20	−0.339
Advice/assistance:	Advice/assistance *No advice/assistance*	8.06	+0.237
Damage/loss:	*Damage/loss* No damage/loss	6.94	−0.300
Age:	*<16 / >24* 16–24	6.10	+0.322
SES:	*Middle* Working/lower	5.47	−0.265
Race:	*White* Non-white	2.09	−0.153
Advice formal action:	Advice formal action *No advice formal action*	1.10	+0.121
Demeanour:	Unco-operative *Co-operative*	1.06	+0.111

Centroids: Group I – no official report ($n = 180$) –0.455
Centroids: Group II – official report ($n = 188$) +0.436
Percentage correctly classified – 68.8%
Wilk's lambda = 0.801; $\chi^2 = 80.18$; df = 9; $p < 0.001$

account. The addition of the victim-complainant's sex adds somewhat, followed in order by whether advice/assistance was given; whether there was property loss/damage; the victim-complainant's age, socio-economic status, and race; whether advice for other formal action was given; and demeanour. Those receiving official reports are involved in disputes other than interpersonal, involved in disputes with some degree of property damage and/or loss, male, aged 16 to 24, middle class, 'white,' co-operative in demeanour, and, not receiving advice/assistance or advice concerning alternative action.

The patterns we found were influenced also by police rules which we were unable to include in the quantitative analysis. Patrol officers handled most interpersonal disputes by means other than official reports. Their work in these situations is to patch up the citizen's disorder by various 'cooling-out' strategies – sometimes informal advice and/or assistance and advice concerning other formal remedies. 'Recipe' rules on interpersonal conflicts, especially among intimates ('domestics'), apparently instruct officers to deal with these situations by means other than the criminal law.[5] Citizens are to be advised about the private-information route and/or non-criminal legal remedies and/or welfare-agency remedies.

On the infrequent occasions when officers invoke a criminal law they are usually corrected by their superior officers. A patrol officer arrested and returned to the divisional station a man whose wife had alleged 'assault occasioning bodily harm' ('AOBH'). Equipped with apparent ample evidence, the patrol officer planned to charge the man with 'AOBH,' but the sergeant ordered him not to do so. The officer was told to write a record-of-arrest report using the non-chargeable 'breach of the peace' section – 31(1) – of the Criminal Code and to inform the complainant that if she wished criminal charges she would have to proceed via a private information.

The reasons for this practice are well discussed in the literature. Police officers know from experience what researchers have documented (e.g. Vera Institute, 1977): a prior relationship between a victim and suspect substantially decreases the probability that the suspect will be convicted if charged. Of course, compared with property-related offences, there are usually greater problems in sustaining a charge for assault arising out of interpersonal conflicts. Hence, officers routinely try to handle interpersonal troubles by informal means, while property-related troubles are more routinely handled by official reports.[6] As we learn shortly, official reports arising out of interpersonal conflicts are typically produced when the officer wants to 'cover' his decisions in writing.

The variability we have found can be explained in large part by factors we cannot quantify. Features of the encounter, including perceptions of it and police organizational influences, must be taken into account. We now turn to a consideration of these matters.

Citizen Requests and the Production of Organizational Accounts

In handling the complaints of citizens, patrol officers do interpretive work. They interpret who the citizens are and what their complaints are within the context in which they are made. They decide what outcomes they can legitimate to the citizens and to their superiors. While the wishes of the citizens may be taken into account and/or made part of an organizational account, they do not in themselves determine what the officer does.

The officer interprets the situation to make up his mind what he is going to do. He then seeks to justify what he does in terms of the rules of the organization, 'recipe' rules, and/or the law. Often his interpretations and attendant justifications coincide with the wishes of the victim-complainant. When they do not, he must work at getting the victim-complainant to agree with him. His pervasive and persuasive authority gives him the power to do this in a routine manner, although he is always aware that his routines can be upset by the victim-complainant or his superiors.

In this section, we initially establish that contrary to the image portrayed by some researchers (e.g. Black, 1968; Reiss, 1971; Pepinsky, 1975), patrol officers do not routinely accept the definition of the situation put forward by the complainant, and they do not routinely follow whatever action is dictated by the complainant. We present data concerning decisions not to follow citizens' requests and not to undertake any official accounting. Further examples reveal organizational reasons why an officer does take an official report. We examine how reports are written in light of organizational purposes and interpretations of citizen complaints. Finally, we consider the implications of our findings for understanding how matters, including crime, become officially recorded as police business.

Encounters of patrol officers with victim-complainants involve many complex requests, demands, interpretations, and reinterpretations on both sides. It is therefore difficult to quantify victim-complainants' requests and officers' actions. However, we decided to classify requests and actions in incidents if there was a dominant request from the victim-complainant which the patrol officer was asked to respond to in a particular way. We can show on a loose basis that officers frequently deflect these requests or do not respond to them at all. The processes involved can then be depicted through qualitative case materials.

Data for 'special requests' by victim-complainants and officers' actions are documented in Tables 5.11 and 5.12. The 'special requests' include 1) *arrest of suspect*, defined as taking custody of someone present or identified as a suspect; 2) *informal settlement*, defined as any means outside the criminal process for resolving the dispute (e.g. warning or caution of suspect; compensation from suspect to victim); 3) *surveillance*, defined as investigative checks or guarding of persons or property connected with the incident; and 4) *other* requests, including a wide range of favours sought from officers by the citizen. Patrol officers were judged to have followed these requests 1) *entirely*, carrying out what was requested of them; 2) *partially*, carrying out to some degree what was requested, but making some changes (i.e. not complying with all aspects of the request and/or taking some additional action not in accordance with the request); and 3) *not at all*, not carrying out any aspect of what was requested.

Among the 427 victim-complainants encountered in incidents, 38 per cent made a special request. Patrol officers acted *to some degree* on 95 per cent of requests for surveillance, 73 per cent of 'other' requests, and 71 per cent of requests for informal settlements. They followed only *to some degree* requests by victim-complainants for arrest of suspects in 45 per cent of such cases. For all types of requests the officers very often only followed them 'partially'. In sum, patrol officers do not routinely follow victim-complainants' requests. More often than not, they act only after altering the thrust of the request or do not act on the request at all.

Special requests were most likely in interpersonal disputes, followed in order by 'other,' property, and automobile disputes. There was widespread fluctuation in compliance according to dispute type: 90 per cent of requests in

TABLE 5.11

Incident victim-complainant special requests and patrol officer action on requests

Special requests	Total		Patrol officer action on requests (percentage)		
	N	%	Entirely	Partially	Not at all
Arrest suspect	38	100.0	26.3	18.4	55.3
Informal settlement	49	100.0	32.7	38.8	28.6
Surveillance	41	100.0	36.6	58.5	4.9
Other	33	100.0	48.5	24.2	27.3
Totals	161	100.0	35.4	36.0	28.6

No special requests: 262; missing information: 4

property disputes were complied with to some degree, 88 per cent in 'other' disputes, 58 per cent in automobile disputes, and 56 per cent in interpersonal disputes. In interpersonal disputes, only 2 of 15 requests for arrest of a suspect were complied with to some degree. Officers complied at least partially with 25 of 37 victim-complainants' requests for an informal settlement in interpersonal disputes. In contrast, in property disputes, they complied at least partially with 12 of 15 requests for arrest of a suspect, and all 5 requests for an informal settlement.

In summary, most (62 per cent) victim-complainants did not make a special request. When requests were made, only slightly more than one-third were followed outright, while a similar proportion were altered and almost one-third were not followed at all. Officers usually acted without taking into account special requests and ignored or altered requests to suit their organizational demands. Clearly victim-complainants were extremely compliant with the ordering brought to the encounter by patrol officers.

One of the accomplishments of patrol officers is to secure routine compliance from victim-complainants in accepting their decisions and the justifications that go with them. Especially when official reports are not taken, this is an important means of keeping their actions discreet and invisible to their superiors. Victim-complainants experience the 'high visibility' of direct dealings with patrol officers and yet routinely accept what officers do, thereby collaborating in keeping officers' activities hidden from the police organization.[7]

Manning (1979: 25) argues that the *context* of disputes is assessed by 'recipe' rules. 'Officers work to do two things: to accomplish work within the premises of the work as they understand them, and to create, if necessary, the proper official paper which will represent events within the official, sanctioned format for such events as they are administratively understood.' 'Paper' may be deemed unnecessary for a number of reasons. It is suspect because it invites scrutiny and can open up the problem of administrative support (Manning, 1979a: 56). The officer may be blamed for reporting a trivial matter, for labelling it one way rather than another, for writing it up as something it is later deemed not to be, and so on. In Rubinstein's view (1973: 40), 'Policemen regard

TABLE 5.12

Incident victim-complainant special requests and patrol officer action on requests, by nature of dispute

Dispute type	Special requests	N	Patrol officer action on requests (percentage)		
			Entirely	Partially	Not at all
Automobile	Arrest suspect	5	1	0	4
	Informal settlement	4	1	1	2
	Surveillance	6	3	2	1
	Other	4	3	0	1
	Totals	19	8	3	8
	No request: 62				
	Missing information: 0				
Property	Arrest suspect	15	8	4	3
	Informal settlement	5	4	1	0
	Surveillance	14	5	9	0
	Other	6	4	1	1
	Totals	40	21	15	4
	No request: 95				
	Missing information: 2				
Interpersonal	Arrest suspect	15	0	2	13
	Informal settlement	37	9	16	12
	Surveillance	3	0	3	0
	Other	13	2	6	5
	Totals	68	11	27	30
	No request: 58				
	Missing information: 2				
Other	Arrest suspect	3	1	1	1
	Informal settlement	3	2	1	0
	Surveillance	18	7	10	1
	Other	10	7	1	2
	Totals	34	17	13	4
	No request: 47				
	Missing information: 0				

anything requiring them to commit statements to paper as a threat.' Why write up something if it may create problems for the officer rather than gaining rewards for him and his fellow officers, or personal rewards (e.g. insurance claims) for the victim-complainant? This may be one reason why complaints involving interpersonal disputes are less often recorded than property complaints.

With a strict division of labour in investigative work, not reporting a matter may be a means of keeping something interesting for oneself rather than having it taken over by a superior or detectives.

Another reason for avoiding official reports is the common human desire to avoid work. Patrol officers frequently told research fieldworkers that they did not take an official report because they wished to avoid the work involved.

This practice is termed 'skating' – gliding with ease over the surface of the matter. Sometimes the easiest way to do the work, and avoid repercussions that might upset the routine, is to 'unfound'[8] complaints or otherwise make them unreportable.

Interpersonal disputes are particularly unlikely to result in official reporting and are often handled by offering advice and/or assistance, because they are complex and a wide variety of interpretations are equally believable and easy to legitimate if called into question. If the officer chooses an interpretation that does not call for official recording there is little the victim-complainant can do; he is likely to accept the officer's 'common sense' definition of the matter. The officer's judgment determines the case, and often there is no case at all.

For example, at 2:35 am a patrol officer drove at high speeds along a residential street in response to a dispatch regarding 'someone attempting to enter apartment.' Upon arrival, he was admitted by the 30-year-old female complainant, who explained that she lived there with her young daughter. She reported that someone had knocked on the door and had tried the door handle; when she peered through the door visor, she discovered it was a man dressed only in a bath robe. The complainant said that she feared a sexual attack and that police presence was necessary to investigate the matter. She became visibly upset and began sobbing. The officer immediately suggested that the man may have mistakenly thought it was his own apartment. He then strengthened the force of his interpretation, asserting that the man was 'obviously' a resident of the building, probably on the same floor, and was just a little lost. The officer checked the floor hallway and stairwell and told the complainant to call again if the man reappeared. He did not take an occurrence report; hence there could be no follow-up work by general-investigation detectives. In conversation with the researcher, he said the complainant was unduly alarmed by the circumstances.

In many interpersonal disputes, allegations and counter-allegations make it difficult to label 'victim' and 'suspect' and to generate evidence that would justify a 'criminal' label for the incident. These complexities again create an enabling framework for the officer to impose an interpretation that does not involve official action. The usual method is to recommend the private-information route to the 'victim' who is persistent or simply give up if the 'victim' is not persistent. For example, four people reported that they were assaulted by the bartender of a club 20 minutes prior to their report. The officer drove to the club. One customer told him that one of the complainants was banned from the club; when the bartender asked all four to leave, they refused, and he physically removed them from the premises. The officer accepted this account as a means of justifying to the complainants his decision not to lay a charge. He told them that they could lay a private information by appearing at the divisional police station the following day, but he did not produce an occurrence report on this incident.

Victim-complainants usually accept the officer's decisions, although sometimes their persistence necessitates extra work and the formulation of additional justifications. For example, a patrol officer was dispatched to the parking-lot area of an apartment building regarding 'youths fighting – disorderlies.' He and a back-up officer talked with four male youths and the wife of one of them. Three of the youths said that the fourth youth attempted to take their car for a ride without consent, while the fourth youth (the original complainant) and his wife alleged that one of the others had tried to 'kill' him for no apparent reason. The officers said they accepted the account of the three youths, and they told the fourth youth to 'go home and sober up.'

As far as the patrol officers were concerned, they had ably handled the situation without official paper. However, 25 minutes later they were dispatched to the address of the fourth youth, who had decided to pursue his complaint against the other three. The complainant again argued that the other three should be apprehended, pointing to his cut lip and 'bitten' finger as evidence of the assault. The officers again told him to sober up and added that he could think about laying a private information the next morning if he were still inclined to do so. However, they formulated the options in a way that indicated the only thing to do was to drop the matter. They explicitly advised the complainant not to lay a charge, saying that the other youths would in turn lay a charge against him. Back in the patrol car the officer, in conversation with the researcher, claimed that the encounter had been handled in this manner 'to avoid paper work.' In the unlikely event the complainant did persist, the officer was 'covered' by not being committed in writing to taking sides. If the complainant complained about him, he could discredit the complainant by mobilizing the majority support of the other three youths.

Sometimes patrol officers do not officially report an incident because, in spite of their efforts, they are frustrated by the complexities and the lack of citizen assistance in sorting them out. Even if the allegations are serious, they will not be reported if citizens cannot be mobilized to concur in a particular version of the truth that will legitimate official reporting by the officer.

For example, a patrol officer was dispatched at 1 am to a residential address concerning 'several anonymous complaints – a domestic,' which was relabelled en route as a 'fight.' Upon arrival the officer, backed up by three other patrol officers, discovered a party involving 30 persons of East Indian and Pakistani descent. There was considerable arguing among the citizens present, some of whom were standing on the front lawn.

As the officer was speaking with the owner of the home, another man approached saying, 'Someone hit me – do your duty.' When the officer inquired about the culprit, the complainant informed him that it was a white man who had left the party. The officer then took the owner aside and asked if there had been any white persons at the party. The owner replied that there were no white people present at any time and suggested that the complainant was lying: 'Nobody saw anything. One minute he was OK, the next minute he seemed to have fallen down a few stairs.'

The officer again approached the complainant and told him that if he wanted to lay charges he could do so at the divisional station in the morning. He did not act on 'noise' complaints from surrounding neighbours, justifying this on the grounds that they refused to give their names and addresses as complainants. He departed, making an entry in his notebook with no official report.

Forty minutes later, he was again dispatched to the same address regarding a 'fight,' with the added information that an ambulance had been dispatched. As he approached he saw the ambulance leaving, with another car pulling out behind it. He stopped this car, which contained the owner of the house and another man. A back-up patrol officer stopped the ambulance and said he learned from the attendant that the apparent 'victim' had been punched but was not seriously injured.

The patrol officer questioned the owner of the house, who claimed that he had no knowledge of what happened and added, 'Maybe he fell down the stairs.' The officer returned to the house and sought witnesses, but no one supplied any information. He left the scene and later contacted the 'victim' at the hospital, but the latter refused to provide any information on what had happened or on the identity of the culprit. The officer made no further inquiries. He noted the encounter but did not submit an occurrence report.

Officers also have occasion to write reports and pursue suspects in 'interpersonal' encounters, but tend not to because of 'recipe' rules for handling these disputes, especially 'domestics,' through non-official sources. Unless the officer or his superiors want to record the matter or to 'get' the suspect(s), he is likely to handle the matter without official documentation.

In the 'domestic' area in particular, requests for any type of action are often circumvented or ignored (see Kokis, 1977). For example, husband-and-wife counter-allegations of assault and demands for arrest were rejected by a patrol officer, who offered informal advice and did not take an occurrence report. The husband had called the police. Upon arrival of the officer, he claimed that his wife was very drunk and that when she was drunk she tended to be violent, destroying household property and attacking him and the children. The wife countered by saying that her husband had beat her up while their sons had held her to the floor; she pointed to multiple bruises on her arms and legs, as well as open sores, to support her claim. The patrol officer centred the discussion on the wife's drinking problem. The husband then demanded that the officer take the wife to a hospital 'to dry out,' but the officer said it was not his job to do so. The officer eventually convinced the couple that he could not take any formal action. Afterward another patrol officer, who had provided a back-up, told the officer and researcher that he had given this same couple the same advice on 'three or four' previous occasions. Rather than treating this as an

'AOBH' and possible charge, the officers treated it as a ritualized matter that they could do little about except to remind the citizens involved that they could do little about it.

In these circumstances the criminal law was not a viable option. This was not simply a matter of 'evidence problems,' typically referred to in public debate as a reason for not invoking the criminal law in domestic situations. Rather, the criminal law was an inappropriate means of dealing with the conflict, the origin and depth of which lay elsewhere, and might have exacerbated rather than resolved the problem. While the officers could expect to be called to this address again and have one party or the other attempt to use their authority to order their relationships, they would be likely to continue 'bracketing out' the use of the criminal law in reproducing this order.

While property and other types of disputes are much more often reported than interpersonal disputes, a substantial minority are not reported. The reasons again include the desire to avoid work and to avoid reporting something that will predictably turn out to be trivial or 'unfounded' if investigated further by detectives. Interpretive latitude and the power to make 'common sense' interpretations 'stick' permit officers to act thus.

Patrol officers sometimes submit occurrence reports on property-offence complaints even when nothing is taken or damaged, the loss or damage is minimal, or the complainant is suspected of false reporting. For example, a victim reported a 'break and enter' occurrence at his residence, showing the officer a window screen to his back bedroom that had been pushed in. The officer did not question this account or look for any alternative explanations and subsequently filed a 'break and enter' occurrence report.

In contrast, other officers in similar circumstances give interpretations and justifications that allow them to avoid taking an official report. For example, a patrol officer interviewed a 'break and enter' victim who reported that while she had been away working the previous two nights someone may have entered her house through the front door. The door had a missing panel of glass that would allow someone to slip a hand through and unlock the door. The victim told the officer that she was particularly nervous because she was the victim of a 'break, enter and theft' two weeks earlier. The officer suggested that an offence had not occurred and that she was overreacting. The victim seemed to accept this and appeared grateful when the officer placed a piece of cardboard over the broken pane and suggested that she tie a string across the doorway whenever she went out as a means of discovering if anyone entered during her absence. The officer later told the researcher that there obviously was 'no man around the house,' and he decided that he would not submit an occurrence report.

On another shift, a patrol officer was dispatched to a 'break and enter in progress' after a complaint from a neighbour. The officer sped to the scene with two back-up officers. They searched the residence inside and outside but found no occupants and no signs of an offence. The officer telephoned the complainant, who reported that the owners always left their back door open to allow access for their cat. The officer commented to the researcher, 'Fuck it, if they are going to be that irresponsible to leave their back door open for their cat, I'm not going to take an occurrence on the call.'

When citizens mobilize the police, they usually expect the responding officer to assist them in ways that serve their interests. The officer's organizational agenda sometimes produces actions that leave citizens dissatisfied (see Sparks et al, 1977: chapter 5).

Sometimes an outcome can be arrived at which serves mutual interests but at other times the interests conflict and the citizen is either knowingly, or more often unknowingly, put at a disadvantage. The citizen always invites this latter by calling the police, because he gives up most of his power to direct the course of the encounter and settlement. In Coleman's terms (1973: 3), the citizen who mobilizes the police gives up 'usage rights' (use of his own power resources to resolve the matter in his own interests) in exchange for 'benefit rights' (the right to benefit from the very powerful, organized resources of the police): 'The right to use resources is what is ordinarily meant by power, while the right to benefit is the right to gain from the exercise of power.'[9]

This does not necessarily mean the police are acting improperly when they take over the victim's complaint and use it as police property within their own organizational criteria of priorities, trade-offs, and so on (Christie, 1977; Ericson, 1981). The police and the wider process of criminal law are given a mandate to treat the matter as an offence against the state, to take control of the matter on behalf of the state, and to serve the interests of the state first and foremost over any individual interests.

As we have seen, officers frequently use their power to produce a settlement that is not brought to the attention of the police organization through a written report and does not lead to official investigation of possible suspects. They accomplish this through a 'common sense' redefinition of the situation which complainants come to accept. This redefinition may be accompanied by advice, assistance, and/or the declaration that the new definition of the matter now makes it into something which is not police business.

When patrol officers do decide to make the matter more widely known through official reports, they do so with a consideration for one or more interests: their own or those of the complainant, the police organization, or other bureaucratic organizations. Patrol officers may submit occurrence reports because it enhances their productive appearances. They may construct the proper paper in order to 'cover their ass,' especially where they need to control the definition of events organizationally because they were unable to control them adequately in the encounter.[10] They may produce paper for the direct benefit of a complainant when they perceive some property benefit (e.g. insurance claim) for the victim or to give the victim the *appearance* of something being done. Paper may also be generated to serve the police organization. Particular segments of it may want paper to justify a particular form of action. The division of labour regarding investigation means that paper will be produced to notify and guide supervisors and detectives about specific incidents that might be worthy of further investigation. Patrol officers also produce paper to serve the police organization's mandate to act on behalf of both public and private bureaucracies whose own procedures (for compensation, insurance, and so on) require an official accounting.

The police are sensitive to the need to perpetuate co-operation from citizens through public relations. One of the most obvious methods is by giving the appearance that something can be done even if little or nothing can be done. With very low probabilities for clearing most types of reported crime, especially property crimes, the best the patrol officer can do is record the matter and say that it will be passed on to detectives for investigation. A large part of the 'face work' between officers and victim-complainants involves a careful recording of detail, for appearances' sake (see Skogan, 1975; Greenwood et al, 1975; Sanders, 1977; Ericson, 1981). Patrol officers know that the vast majority of their reports will simply be written off by detectives after a brief follow-up contact with the victim-complainant, or even filed with no further action (see Ericson, 1981: chapters 4 and 5). They justify their efforts as placating the complainant.

On some occasions, patrol officers write reports to appease the citizens involved. For example, a patrol officer eventually took a report on a motor-vehicle collision with damage under $200 that occurred on private property. Organizational procedures and the Highway Traffic Act (see chapter 4, note 10) did not call for an official report. The officer took the report to defuse the hostility between the two drivers.

The officer was informed about the accident by a passing motorist. He drove to the scene and observed two vehicles stopped in the exit of a shopping plaza, one with obvious damage to the rear. As he drove up, one of the drivers approached and asked, 'Would you investigate this accident please?' This citizen (driver 2) was adamant that the other citizen (driver 1) was at fault. Driver 1 claimed that as he was about to leave the plaza, he stopped suddenly and driver 2 hit him in the rear. Driver 2 claimed that driver 1 had stopped suddenly, backed up, and hit him. The officer interjected that since the accident had taken place on private property and the damage was less than $200, he had no jurisdiction in the case. He added that he was not required to take a report, and if he did so it would not make any difference.

The argument worsened to the point where it, rather than the accident, became the problem. The officer separated the two and developed new tactics to enforce their compliance. He asked driver 1 how much he had to drink, implying that if he refused to acquiesce to an informal settlement he might be a candidate for an impaired-driving (or care-and-control) charge. Driver 1 denied having anything to drink. The officer then asked to smell his breath and after doing so again asked him how much he had to drink. Driver 1 replied, 'I just came home from work and I only had one beer.' The officer retorted that by looking at driver 1's face he could tell he had a lot more. Hoping this strategy would defuse driver 1, the officer called driver 2 to join them. Driver 2 suggested that each driver could look after the repair costs on his own car. An argument again ensued, and the officer exclaimed, 'OK, that's it, both of you get in the back of the car and I'll take a report.'

After the details were taken, the officer informed the drivers that he could not assign blame or be used as a witness. The drivers left, with driver 1 throwing his hands up in the air in apparent disgust. The patrol officer said 'You don't look too happy about this.' Driver 1 replied, 'I'm no further ahead than I was before.' The officer reminded him that he had told him taking a report would not change anything. Driver 1 then thanked the officer and departed. The officer, talking to the researcher, characterized driver 1 as a 'stupid asshole' and said, 'I'd bet anything he backed into him. [Driver 2] looked pretty honest.' The officer added that he hated to take accident reports.

Cases of this type illustrate that reports are sometimes taken for situationally specific reasons despite external influences which recommend against doing so. However, most such decisions reflect organizational influences, and the way the reports are written always reflects these influences.

The lack of investigative autonomy available to patrol officers is an impetus to report-writing in some matters. If the victim of an offence describes or even names the alleged culprit, the officer normally records the information for his report but does not pursue the culprit because the division of labour requires him to be back out on patrol. Moreover, the force prefers more experienced police officers (detectives) to investigate reported offences and to decide whether the case is 'founded.' Except in routine cases where the culprits are caught in the act by the complainant (e.g. shoplifting) or by the patrol officer himself (e.g. impaired driving, possession of marijuana), the job of 'making crime' is left up to detectives. Indeed, we saw several minor cases (e.g. shoplifting) turned over to detectives to produce additional information and charges (Ericson, 1981). As we saw in chapter 3, patrol officers generally resent the lack of investigative autonomy because it restricts them from doing interesting work. Yet the role of report-taker rather than investigator is sometimes welcomed because it allows the patrol officer to pass responsibility for key decisions to others.

Many incidents, especially in the property category, reflect the patrol officer's role as report-taker. For example, a woman reported the theft of jewelry worth $650. She suspected one of two workmen who had been doing contract work on her home. She was able to identify this suspect through the second workman, who was a friend of hers. The officer took details and submitted an occurrence report, but he made no effort to contact the suspect or to undertake any other investigative checks.

On another shift, the officer was dispatched to the address of a company that had gone bankrupt and was subject to demonstrations outside the plant by ex-employees who had not been paid. At the scene the complainant, a truck driver with the company, reported an estimated $2,000 damage to a company truck. The company owner was also present, and he demanded that the officer immediately arrest four ex-employees who were demonstrating on the property, and who the owner believed were the culprits for the property damage. The patrol officer – reluctant to aggravate the already tense conflict – took the names, addresses, and dates of birth of the ex-employees, but did not question them as suspects. He recorded their identities in the occurrence report, but only as 'employees' rather than as 'suspects.' The occurrence was eventually turned over to detectives; their reports indicate that they interviewed the ex-employees as suspects for this 'mischief' occurrence.

Specific orders from superior officers shape report-taking activity. The incidents in the last two paragraphs were among many in a division at a time when a senior officer was discouraging patrol officers from taking any form of investigation. To *report* a large volume of occurrences would overload the detective office in another division that also handled the detective work for this division; the added volume might give weight to the argument that a separate detective office was needed for this division.

Reports aimed at 'leaving it up to the detectives' are also taken on specific instructions from sergeants who become involved in the matter. When there is a specific order to take a report for 'covering' purposes, the patrol officer obliges. For example, a patrol officer was dispatched to a home where a woman wanted to lodge a complaint concerning a sexual assault and threats. The woman told the officer that she met the suspect at the hotel where she worked as a stripper. She said she invited the suspect home where she willingly allowed him to embrace and kiss her. He became increasingly aggressive, but was halted by her fiancé, who returned home and confronted the man. At this point the victim called the police and constructed the account to her fiancé that the suspect had grabbed her breasts and threatened to rape her. The fiancé apparently ensured the swift departure of the suspect and encouraged the victim to obtain assistance from the police.

During the interview, both the victim and her fiancé repeatedly asked what type of 'prosecution' would occur, and after a while told the officer to stop wasting his time interviewing them and to go out and catch the 'criminal.' The officer, in the presence of a patrol sergeant and two other patrol officers, took down the details for an 'indecent assault (female)' occurrence report. No attempt was made to apprehend the suspect.

The officer later told the researcher that his interpretation of the victim's characteristics and the nature of the complaint led him to discount the entire matter as something unworthy of an official report. He thought that the victim had constructed the allegations against the suspect when she was 'caught' by her fiancé. Her occupation, her drunken condition, and her statement that she had invited the suspect to her home discredited her account. The officer added that he would not have spent more than five minutes on the incident and would not have taken an official report even for 'covering' purposes if the patrol sergeant had not been present.

Official reports have a 'covering' function for both the patrol officer and the force as a whole. A written account allows the officer to select the facts he deems relevant to construct a version of the incident that is consistent with the decisions he has taken.[11] As long as he does this according to legitimate justifications for decisions, he is usually 'covered' even if later investigations by detectives lead to an alteration in his account. The problem for the patrol officer is to find, and to use appropriately, the correct justifications. As we noted in relation to dispatches (chapter 4), there is a strong tendency to err on the side of caution. Reports are typically constructed to present a negative image *in case* further investigation reveals that image is the correct one, e.g. to present the most serious offence that may have been committed.[12]

For example, patrolling at 3:30 am an officer observed two youths sitting on the parking lot of a closed gas station. As he approached them, he noticed a broken window in the front of the station. He called for a back-up officer and casually began to talk with the youths about their actions. When the second officer arrived the questioning became more accusatory, but the youths denied breaking the window or having any intention of entering the service station. They claimed that they had been drinking a lot and they had chosen this spot to rest. The officers called the gas station proprietor who checked the premises but found nothing missing. In spite of this investigation, the officer decided to submit an occurrence report. Moreover, he chose to label it 'attempt break and enter' rather than 'mischief,' 'damage,' 'suspicious circumstances,' or other less serious labels. He later told the researcher that an occurrence report with this particular label was the best 'cover' in the circumstances.

The favourite 'cover' in vague circumstances is to file a report labelled 'suspicious circumstances.' For example, a patrol officer was dispatched to a jewelry shop regarding a 'theft.' The manager, acting as complainant, stated that no theft had occurred, but he wished to report that three suspicious-looking men had been in the store and appeared to be 'casing' it. The officer accepted the complainant's account and wrote up a 'suspicious circumstances' occurrence report. In addition to the obvious public-relations function, this report covered the officer in the remote event that the complainant's suspicions would turn out to be founded. By reporting the matter according to the complainant's account, the officer provided an informational base to detectives. He had brought the matter to the official attention of the force, thereby displacing the possible allegation that it was his fault the matter had not been investigated more thoroughly.

Patrol officers often do not submit a report after dealing with 'suspicious circumstances.' They can simply make a note in their duty notebook in case they need to recall the matter if later called into account. A cleaner working after hours in a doctor's office called the police to report that when he arrived for work he discovered keys left in the office door and upon checking found that the cash box was unlocked. He did not think anything was missing, but he was very anxious to protect himself against any possibility that he or his cleaning crew might be wrongly accused. The officer did not hold the complainant under suspicion and did not make any other checks concerning the circumstances reported to him. He made a note in his duty book, but did not write an occurrence report.

Official reports can also be taken for reasons unrelated to a complaint. Sometimes they are written to account for time. For example, a man reported that his four-year-old daughter had been missing for slightly more than an hour. The officer initiated a search, which included citizens as well as four patrol officers, a patrol sergeant, a detective inspector, and the canine unit. When a citizen located the girl, the other officers left and the sergeant asked the officer to submit an occurrence report to account for the 'man hours' spent on the case. The officer, who spent one and three-quarter hours on the incident, submitted a report labelled 'assistance.'

Sub-units within the force sometimes encourage the reporting of particular types of incidents, in a particular way. The 'sex offence' detective team were compiling a file of several hundred 'obscene telephone calls' believed to be by the same person. Patrol officers routinely recorded these complaints, repeatedly describing the same mode of operation in their reports to the point where all that was needed to channel them to the detectives' files was writing the first and last name used by the culprit when he made his calls.

Sub-units also encourage reporting of incidents in particular places if they are trying to build a case against the establishment involved. For example, a patrol officer was dispatched to a 'fight in progress' outside a hotel bar. He was met by two badly beaten victims. Both had cuts on their faces and upper bodies, and one was barely conscious when the officer arrived. The victims claimed that they had been attacked by some youths who were refused further drinks after they became 'rowdy' in the hotel bar. The officer talked with the manageress, who said she had cut off the drinks of the culprits and they went outside and engaged in an unprovoked attack on the two victims. The officer, backed up by a duty inspector, patrol sergeant, and three other patrol officers, was very eager to pursue the suspects and lay charges. However, both victims were adamant that they did not want to pursue the matter. They were both reluctant to give the officer even their names, and when they agreed to do so, one victim said, 'I want to sign something that my name can't be used in court.'

Some officers pursued the suspects, who were reported by other youths to be walking along a nearby road. However, they did not arrest or charge them. The patrol officer was apparently not going to submit an occurrence report on the matter, but decided to do so upon instruction from a superior officer who stated, 'Morality [the morality detective squad] is trying to close this place down and they're collecting all the reports out of this place. Turn it over to them.' The officer wrote the occurrence report, using the heading 'Cause Disturbance (Information)':

> At the above noted time, a disturbance broke out downstairs in the [hotel]. Two of the patrons involved then left, and were attacked on the front parking lot by four males. The victims [names, addresses, birth dates] were knocked to the ground and kicked. Both received facial injuries, but refused medical aid.
>
> The four assailants had left upon the writer's arrival. but were walking north on — Road. Both of the victims stated that they did not wish the matter pursued and wished things left alone.
>
> This report is made by order of Inspector —.
>
> It is to be sent to the morality squad in order that they have the information on file.
>
> Attention – Morality Squad.

Another reason for taking official reports is because police forces serve large public and private bureaucracies. For example, industrial accidents are routinely recorded to provide the appropriate provincial ministry with an official independent account. Thus, a patrol officer took an occurrence report labelled 'Construction Accident,' after an incident in which a worker allegedly fell off a ladder and suffered head injuries requiring hospitalization. The officer spoke with a witness, who gave details of the accident and the identity of the victim. In his report, the officer offered the judgment that the accident came about because the ladder was not secured properly, and he added that an investigator for the occupational safety branch of the provincial government had been notified and was investigating the matter.

In the private sphere, insurance companies are served through the reporting of property loss, theft, and damage. When complainants mention the need for official reports to bolster their claims for compensation from insurance companies, officers usually oblige. For example, a patrol officer filed a 'property damage' report after an elderly couple complained that someone at some unknown time had apparently knocked paint off the aluminum siding of their house causing an estimated $20 damage. The complainants told the officer that their insurance agent wanted an official police report and that is why they had called the police department.

Patrol officers see report-taking in traffic accidents with damage over $200 as being primarily on behalf of the insurance companies involved. Although there are occasional attempts to avoid paper work by interpreting the damages as being under $200 when other parties claim the damage is over $200, most major accidents are routinely handled by taking accounts from each party and writing up a motor vehicle collision report. While patrol officers sometimes obtain a Highway Traffic Act charge against one of the parties, this is also seen as furthering the work of insurance companies, who thereby have the blame settled for them in working out who must pay the costs.

After a decision to produce an official report, the officer has to decide how he is going to label and describe the incident so as to justify his decisions. He has a great deal of autonomy in doing this. Of course, his definitions and constructions may be checked (and changed) by his supervisors and detectives; indeed, that is a primary function of further investigation by others. However, there is a tendency for other members of the police organization to accept the officer's constructions. The officer writes his reports according to 'recipes' which tell him how to write an acceptable account. Many occurrences are not further investigated by detectives, or are investigated in a cursory manner to 'write them off.' They are filed for statistical purposes without any questioning of the officer's report (Greenwood et al, 1975; Sanders, 1977; Ericson, 1981).

Patrol officers, along with others in the police organization, know the importance of producing and being committed to a particular version of an incident. Despite the many interpretations possible, officers must decide on one interpretation and stand behind it. When they decide to commit their interpretations to paper, the product takes on the status of 'fact' which the organization as a whole becomes committed to. Patrol officers and their colleagues know that 'social order depends upon the co-operative acts of men in sustaining a particular version of the truth' (Silverman, 1970: 134).

Patrol officers are regularly confronted with competing definitions of events from citizens with competing interests who are attempting to influence the patrol officer's judgment. The interests of the police force may demand particular definitions. These competing demands introduce a degree of relativity into decisions. Whose version of reality becomes dominant? How does this come about? This is the practical epistemology of everyday life: what knowledge, transmitted by whom, under what conditions, becomes accepted for the purposes of action?

The patrol officer defines and transmits information from the complainant to the police organization. He decides whether something will be recorded and recognized as official business, and what type of business it is. While he has considerable autonomy, which introduces a degree of arbitrariness, his actions are grounded in reporting rules which come from the law as well as the police organization.

When constructing an official report, the officer keeps in mind its likely route within the bureaucracy. He labels and describes the incident in a way that will influence supervisors and detectives in their decision about further investigation. He omits information that might lead to a type of investigation he deems inappropriate and uses labels and descriptions fitting his assessment of the seriousness of the case.

For example, a patrol officer was initially dispatched to a supermarket in a shopping plaza. The dispatcher labelled the complaint a 'fight,' described the two people involved in it, and instructed the officer to see the manager of the supermarket regarding a knife involved in the incident.

The officer was met in the plaza by a female 'victim' and a male 'complainant' (the victim's common-law husband). The victim reported that while she was shopping alone in the supermarket, she noticed a man 'looking at me funny and flicking his tongue at me.' When she attempted to walk past this man, he grabbed her breast. She jumped away and told the man to 'Fuck off,' to which he replied, 'That's exactly what I'm looking for.' The woman walked away, paid for her purchases, and telephoned her husband to tell him what had occurred.

The woman's husband immediately came to the plaza and had his wife point out the 'suspect.' The husband then confronted the suspect and a fight ensued. During the fight the husband pulled a flick-knife from his pocket, but it was immediately knocked out of his hand by the suspect. The suspect, who was much bigger than the husband, beat him, causing facial cuts and bruises on the face, arms, torso, and legs. As the husband was lying 'dazed' on the floor, the store manager approached and the suspect fled.

After receiving this account from the victim, the officer talked to the husband, who admitted after prompting that he had been aggressive in his approach to the suspect and had drawn a knife on him. In his questioning of the husband, the officer attempted to establish that he was the aggressor and had committed offences (at a minimum common assault/possession of a prohibited weapon). The husband continually asked 'Wouldn't you do the same if it was your wife?' He gave a detailed description of the suspect, adding, 'I hope you catch the guy – I want to charge him to hell.'

The officer retrieved the knife from the store manager, but did not attempt to obtain a detailed account from him or from anyone else in the store. He questioned the husband further about the use of the knife and then decided to consult with a back-up patrol officer who had subsequently arrived. The officers decided not to lay a weapons charge against the husband or to mention the weapon in the occurrence report. They also ignored the original dispatcher definition of a 'fight.' Instead, they decided to focus the report on the woman's original complaint and to label it 'possible sex offender.' While constructing the report, the patrol officer said to the researcher he was writing it in a certain way 'or else the Ds [detectives] will make a big issue of it':

> The victim reported she was shopping in the [store], and while in the area of the ice cream display she noticed the suspect staring at her, flickering his tongue at her. She walked away and while passing the suspect he tried to grab her right breast. She jumped out of his reach and went directly to the check outs. Her common law husband was summoned by the victim a few minutes later, and she pointed out the suspect to him. The complainant spoke with the suspect and warned him to stop his actions. A scuffle ensued, and a few kicks and punches thrown by both men, and the suspect fled on foot.

The complainant stated he could identify the suspect if he sees him again, however at this point he seemed hesitant in relation to charges.

The area around the mall was checked by uniform cruisers, for suspect, negative results.

Several features effectively controlled any chance for intensive future action. The officer indicated there was a fight, but did not say that the complainant had admitted to being the aggressor and had drawn a knife or that he had suffered bodily injury. Moreover, while the complainant had said, 'I want to charge him to hell,' the officer indicated he was 'hesitant in relation to charges.' The suspect's initial sexual overtures were also not described in detail. The officer reached a settlement he considered just. He confided to the researcher that he agreed with the complainant's way of handling the situation and that the 'score' seemed to be even. He also left this impression with the complainant, to whom he suggested that a charge could have been laid regarding the knife; by implication he should feel fortunate at resolution by means of 'summary justice.'

Officers 'patrol' the facts about the disputes they are called upon to deal with. What initially appears a complex matter with as many shades as a chameleon in a box of crayons ends up black and white in a few sentences in the official report. The many possibilities are reduced to one version which will influence decisions about whether there will be any further investigation, what investigation will be undertaken, the criminal charges likely if a suspect is traced, and the category used in the official version.

Further examples can be provided of different types of disputes. A patrol officer was dispatched to a rural side-road regarding 'vehicle in the ditch – possibly a PI [personal injury].' He discovered a damaged vehicle (estimated $500) but no driver. He suspected that the driver had been impaired and had left to avoid detection. A vehicle registration check uncovered the owner's identity and he proceeded to the owner's residence to interview him.

During the interview, the officer changed his suspicions. The driver, who had apparently not been drinking, said that as his car was rounding a corner he was confronted with an oncoming vehicle driving on the wrong side of the road. This vehicle forced him off the road, but continued on. The driver was now a victim-complainant in an accident with elements of 'careless driving' and 'fail to remain.' He reported that there were no independent witnesses. The officer used this to justify to the complainant his decision not to treat this as a case of 'fail to remain' and/or 'careless driving.' He submitted a motor vehicle collision report, but made no mention of the other driver in the brief description: 'Vehicle was east bound on ——; driver attempted to evade oncoming traffic and slid into the ditch. Seat belts prevented injury.'

Even when an officer reports the matter in a particular category (e.g. property offence), he can choose from a number of designations. Thus, he gives varying interpretations of break-and-entry offences. For example, a complainant reported that someone had entered the area of his catering company warehouse where he stored cigarettes. He could not tell if anything had been stolen, but demanded surveillance of the property and investigation of an ex-employee who was known to have a key to the area. The officer listened patiently and wrote an occurrence report for 'suspicious circumstances,' which said there was no clear evidence of an entry, and that the matter was not serious because nothing was reported as stolen.

A victim reported that at some time during the previous two days someone had entered the garage attached to his house and taken the four hub-caps (valued at $85) from his car. The officer, noting in his report that the garage was 'unlocked' (perhaps to indicate why he was not labelling it 'break, enter and theft'), submitted a report for 'theft under $200.'[13]

One victim reported that someone had entered his house and taken a guitar valued at $680, while leaving behind other musical and photographic equipment valued at $3,000. The officer acted surprised upon learning that there were no signs of entry and that the other valuable items had been left behind, but agreed to take a report after the victim claimed that he required a report for insurance purposes. Retrospectively, the officer concluded the victim was probably making a false report for insurance gains, but he nevertheless reported 'theft over $200' (but not 'break, enter and theft').

On another shift, a victim reported that $1,350 worth of coins were missing from his home. He had last seen them 26 days earlier; when he checked the hiding place for them on the day of his complaint, he found they were missing. He reported that there were no signs of entry into the house and that he had thoroughly checked the house but could not find the coins. The officer initially suspected that the victim might be falsely reporting a theft. However, when the victim mentioned that three neighbours bordering on their backyard had had break-and-enters on the same day that he and his wife were absent from their home, the officer shifted his interpretation and accepted the victim's account. Instead of possible 'lost property' or 'theft' reports, the officer submitted a report for 'break, enter and theft.'

In complaints about property loss with no entry victims sometimes insisted that the matter involved a 'theft' rather than 'lost property,' and police interpretations varied. One officer was dispatched to the office of a company district manager regarding a theft. The manager complained that he had been missing his wallet since the previous day and wanted it reported as a theft of $120 to $150 plus credit cards. The officer, questioning the delay in reporting and probing for evidence of theft, received rather vague answers. The victim said he last remembered having the wallet at a shopping plaza on the previous day. The officer convinced the victim that it was more appropriate to regard this as a 'lost property' occurrence and produced a report to that effect. By way of comparison, a gas-station employee reported that he had hidden the station keys while he took a car for a test drive; upon his return 15 minutes later, he found the keys were missing. He reported the matter as a theft, and the officer submitted an occurrence report for theft without any suggestion of 'lost property.'

The many subtleties in report-writing allow patrol officers to justify their actions to supervisors and other officers who might read their reports. There are words or phrases which 'everyone knows' are acceptable designations of how an incident was handled.[14] In our research, a common justification for 'writing off' complaints, particularly interpersonal ones, was to say that this was the wish of the complainant. However, these 'complainant wishes' were sometimes produced by the officer after the complainant had started the transaction with very different intentions.

For example, a patrol officer was checking a park at 6 am when he noticed a parked car with two occupants. His suspicions were aroused when he observed the passenger door open slightly and close again, as if someone wanted to get out but then for some reason decided not to. The officer approached the car and asked the male and female occupants for identification. He noticed that the woman was 'dishevelled' and decided to place the man in the rear of the patrol car while he questioned the woman. She reported that she was picked up by the man in Toronto and driven to this location. She alleged that he had indecently assaulted her and showed the officer that her trousers were torn from the knee to the crotch.

The officer called for a patrol sergeant, who interviewed the victim. The sergeant changed her view of the matter and secured a verbal statement that she did not wish to press charges but only wished a ride back to where she was originally picked up. The sergeant invited the victim to use his car to change into a dress she was carrying in her bag. In private conversation, the sergeant told the officer that 'she seems like a quasi-hooker who has gotten herself in a bit of a spot' and that no charges would be laid because of the victim's wishes. The sergeant and officer also agreed that the victim would fail to appear as a witness if they charged the suspect.

The officer told the man never to bring his 'pick-ups' into the area again and threatened to tell his wife about the incident. The officer drove the woman to the boundary of the police force's area. He later wrote an occurrence report that justified not charging in terms of the victim's 'request':

[Heading: 'Indecent Assault Female']
[The victim] got out of the car and stated that suspect had ripped her pants and showed writer that pants were torn in crotch area.

She stated she had been hitch-hiking on Yonge Street Toronto and had been picked up by suspect and driven to above location where he told her to 'put out' or 'she was a dead duck.' She had not been assaulted in any other way than the pants being torn. Suspect denied ripping pants and victim stated she did not wish to press charges. Victim was turned over to —— PD for transport into city and suspect cautioned and released.

'Requests' not to take official action were often sought by officers trying to justify 'writing off' domestic disputes without taking formal action against the alleged culprit. For example, a woman reported to the divisional station to lay a charge against her husband for a domestic incident patrol officers responded to the previous day. On instructions from a staff sergeant, a patrol officer proceeded to interview the victim with the expressed purpose of discouraging her from laying a charge. The main thrust of his statement was that a charge would worsen the conflict with her husband; he recommended she seek the assistance of a lawyer and said he could help her arrange accomodation at the Salvation Army. In a report, the officer said 'She agreed not to lay charges at this time; it was made clear to her that this Department would render all necessary assistance to lay such charges if required.'

In summary, patrol officers exercise considerable power in controlling whether or not a citizen's complaint will be recorded, how it will be recorded, and what its subsequent career is likely to be in the priorities of police business. Our findings have significant implications for the statistics on occurrences and crime the police bureaucracy uses as an indicator of its work and justification of its resources. They also have implications for the way in which criminologists, the media, politicians, and other citizens use police statistics in their assessments of the 'crime problem.' We now turn to an examination of these implications.

Implications for 'Controlology'

In a refinement of the 'labelling' perspective, Ditton (1979) has argued that crime exists only when people decide to seek an official designation of a person's behaviour as criminal. Something is not a crime until it is constituted as such by control agents (the police) and certified as such by the courts. Thus, the study of crime centres on the subject of control, which Ditton refers to as 'controlology.'[15]

There are a number of variable elements in the production of police business, including the discovery of behaviour which might be labelled and treated as police business, the reporting by citizens and patrol officers of that behaviour, and the recording and classification by officers of that behaviour. The great variations in control at each of these stages has been subject to increasing attention.[16] Researchers have concluded that there is a great need for study of the role of police in 'making' or 'unmaking' crime. Sparks et al (1977: 160) state their victimization study findings emphasize that 'there is plenty of scope for such research. They also emphasize the importance of interpreting official criminal statistics as the outcome of a series of social processes and organizational activities; and the extreme dangers of uncritically assuming that the statistics automatically reflect – even approximately – the amounts and types of criminal behaviour which do in fact take place.'

Many complaints are not officially logged. Many calls for service do not result in a dispatch; many dispatches do not result in an official report; many reports do not recommend further action or criminal designations; and, regardless of designation, many reports are filed without any further investigation (see Ericson, 1981: chapters 4 and 5).

The patrol officer clearly has the power to make citizen complaints into non-police business. In reactive minor complaints only 19 per cent resulted in an official report, while in reactive major complaints only 52 per cent did so. The figure for all reactive complaints is 44 per cent. This can be compared with figures of about one-half in a study of 26 American cities (Skogan, 1976), about one-third for London, England (Sparks et al, 1977: chapter 6), and approximately two-thirds in Black's 1970 study.

As both Sparks et al (1977) and McCabe and Sutcliffe (1978) have stressed, policies on reporting can have a substantial influence on the volume of what becomes publicly portrayed as 'crime' and other police business. The police have it within their power to commit 'control waves,' which are then portrayed publicly as 'crime waves' (cf Ditton, 1979: 24).[17] Our own data provide examples of this phenomenon.

The divison of labour increases the probability that patrol officers will submit reports and let their supervisors and detectives decide on further action. This can produce two effects. First, it may increase the number of occurrence reports submitted and thus swell the official statistics on police business. If the patrol officer has more investigative autonomy, he has the opportunity to 'unfound' more complaints; either he will submit fewer reports, or more reports will consist simply of his legitimations for 'unfounding' the complaint. Second, supervisors and detectives may dispose of a greater number of occurrences by marking them 'filed,' 'no crime,' and 'unfounded' (see McCabe and Sutcliffe, 1978: 73; Bottomley and Coleman, 1979: 14–18; Ericson, 1981: chapters 4–5).

Other features of the organization can have a temporary influence on reporting. I mentioned that a senior officer instructed patrol officers to file as many reports as possible, without investigation to 'unfound' them. This strategy was apparently aimed at overloading the detective office in another division which handled the criminal investigation for his division, thereby serving to produce the 'facts' he wanted to support his argument that the force should create a separate detective unit within his division.

One must also consider the 'recipe' rules of the occupational culture concerning the handling of disputes and the production of official paper. A number of features of an encounter, as well as influences external to it, are considered in the context of the 'recipe' rules in order to make a reporting decision. In addition to patrolling the streets, the officer patrols the facts by not reporting them or reporting them to produce an outcome he sees as both just and justifiable.

The quantified data describe patterns in actions by patrol officers in terms of external criteria, including mobilization, the matter in dispute, and status and role of citizens. The qualitative data instruct us how these elements are interpreted by officers and how they, along with aspects of the police organization, are taken into account in the making of decisions and accounting for them.

In the next chapter I document how similar considerations affect dealings of patrol officers with suspects and accused persons. In particular, I stress the importance of looking inside the police organization to see how police business, including the business of crime, is made, literally. Behaviour is just behaviour until it is defined; definitions are just definitions until they are made to 'stick.' 'Making them "stick" requires a different sort of "stick" – power. The more powerful the definer, the "realer" the consequences' (Ditton, 1979: 87). As an organized *force*, the police have the power to make particular definitions of citizens' troubles – and to make them 'stick.'

6

Dealing with Suspects and Accused Persons

Researchers have paid little attention to the 'career' of suspects and accused persons from the first contact with the police through to the point at which their cases are disposed of by the police or in court. Few researchers on the police follow what happens after charging the accused, while most researchers on the accused do not study what happens before charging. Nevertheless researchers (e.g. Baldwin and McConville, 1977: 105; Bottoms and McClean, 1976: 230; Ericson and Baranek, 1982) stress the importance of studying the accused from the *earliest* point of contact with the police because this strongly influences later stages in the criminal process.

In this chapter, we trace the careers of persons whom patrol officers place in the 'suspect' category. We initially consider transactions with the 603 suspects they encountered in minor (citizen-contact) troubles. We then examine transactions with the 392 suspects they encountered in more major (incident) troubles. We then study the disposition by the courts of suspects charged under the Criminal Code and/or Narcotics Control Act.

The focus of our inquiry is upon the power resources patrol officers have to effect a resolution justified to them and justifiable to others. In dealing with suspects – especially after proactive stops on suspicion – they base their decisions on the status claims of the suspects and the matter in dispute. They have enabling organizational powers, and substantive and procedural legal powers, to assist them in ordering suspects. When they make the decision to charge, they also have substantial influence over the court outcome of the case within the enabling framework of the court's organization. In sum, I show that from first contact to ultimate disposition of a case, the police have considerable power to define what is 'out of order' and to reproduce their organizationally filtered sense of 'order.'

Minor dealings

The most important area of organizational autonomy available to patrol officers is their mandate to 'order the streets.' This involves regulating traffic and troublesome individuals who are at the most offensive rather than offenders. This regulation is effected by stops of vehicles and, occasionally, of pedestrians. Among the 603 suspects in minor troubles, 503 were encountered proactively in this way.[1]

Most of this activity consists of stopping vehicles. It is thus extremely difficult to determine whether the person is a 'suspect' for a traffic violation or for some other reason. A patrol officer might stop a vehicle to investigate the occupants on suspicion, but the outcome might be a traffic warning or summons which he uses to justify his intervention. Traffic violations often provide an excuse for investigations directed at developing other violations, with no traffic warning or summons being issued.[2]

Even the person 'objectively' stopped after a speeding violation recorded by radar can have his person and vehicle 'seen through' by the patrol officer. If the officer's suspicions are aroused, he has powers he can use to take control over the suspect's person. He can detain him for the time it takes to obtain CPIC information and can search him and his property. If a violation can be uncovered, he may choose to assert his authority by charging. A warning can be equally useful to remind the citizen of the order of things. As Rubinstein (1973: 233) stresses, 'a stop is an exercise in pure power.'

From the patrol officer's perspective, the purpose of proactive stops is as much to keep these people in their place, and to keep 'his' territory in order, as it is to uncover violations. Any action he takes towards these people is useful as an 'ordering' device. CPIC checks and searches may appear routine investigative actions, and warnings and charges appear to be resolutions; but they all serve to assert police power as an end in itself. They are devices for reproducing the economy of power relations between the individual and the state.

Of course, just because they are uniformed patrol officers does not mean that they have a mandate to treat all citizens uniformly in these matters. They are likely to take increasingly strong steps against people who threaten the 'order of things,' symbolically or otherwise, by being the wrong types in the wrong places at the wrong times (cf Cohen, 1979: especially 130–2). 'The law' as constituted by patrol officers in many proactive stops is specifically aimed at reproducing the order of things, including some aspects of structural inequality. Particular groups of persons are stopped on suspicion and differentially subjected to patrol officers' actions. In particular, men whom officers term 'pukers' (in their late teens or early twenties and of lower socioeconomic background) are frequently stopped and checked. The fact that they are more likely to produce an investigative 'payoff' may encourage officers to stop them. These checks rarely produce a charge, but officers deem their time well spent simply reminding these people of their place.

Our point can be furthered by considering CPIC checks. They are a means of providing additional information about a suspect which, along with his observable characteristics, can be used to make decisions about other actions to be taken.[3] They are a means of detaining the suspect for the several minutes it takes to obtain the information. Suspects usually accept this reason for detention. This detention is an assertion of authority by the patrol officer and opens up the opportunity for questioning and searches during the waiting period. CPIC checks occasionally reveal that the suspect is 'wanted' by the police. Patrol officers refer to this as a 'hit,' indicating both the lottery and 'targeting' aspects of CPIC checks.[4]

Among the sample of 603 suspects, 40.1 per cent were subject to CPIC checks. Given the advantages just outlined, it is surprising that checks were not carried out on more suspects. However, several factors militate against such checks. First, the time it takes may not appear to be worth it given the officer's predictions based on the suspect's characteristics and taking into account other things he might prefer to do. Second, dispatchers sometimes discourage officers from doing CPIC checks by saying that the communication centre is too busy. Third, the CPIC system is sometimes temporarily out of order. Fourth, 'recipe' rules discourage excessive use of CPIC checks. A zealous officer is sometimes criticized by his colleagues for not using the personal skills which supposedly enable him to get all the information needed without the 'crutch' of technological aids.

As documented in Tables 6.1 and 6.2, a very definite population is selected for CPIC checks. On an individual variable basis (Table 6.1), suspects most likely to receive CPIC checks were those in the 17 to 24 age category.[5] Men were almost two and one-half times as likely as women to have checks. People of the lowest socio-economic status were more likely subjects; indeed, the 'lower' group was three times more likely to be checked than the 'middle' group. Furthermore, suspects who became 'unco-operative' were significantly more likely to be checked than those who 'co-operated' throughout.

Table 6.1 also suggests the influence of other variables. Suspects stopped in a proactive mobilization were almost twice as likely to be checked as those in a reactive mobilization: in proactive encounters there are often fewer sources of information, i.e. there is no one else to provide relevant information, as there often is in reactive encounters. Furthermore, detention through CPIC checks is a tool of harrassment in the patrol officer's work of ordering the streets.

CPIC checks were equally likely in traffic and non-traffic encounters. This supports our earlier contention that patrol officers see traffic stops and stops on suspicion equally as opportunities for investigative checks.

TABLE 6.1

Suspects in citizen contact encounters: mobilization, dispute type, suspect characteristics, and other patrol officer actions related to proportion of suspects subject to CPIC checks

		N	Percentage of suspects subject to CPIC checks	χ^2	df
Total sample		603	40.1		
Mobilization and dispute type					
Mobilization:	Proactive	503	43.5	13.80	1
	Reactive	100	23.5		
			**		
Dispute type:	Traffic	366	39.6	0.06	1
	Other	237	40.9		
Suspect characteristics					
Age:	17–24	294	50.0	18.00	1
	<17 / >24	266	32.0		
	Do not know	(43)	(23.3)		
			**		
Sex:	Male	550	42.4	11.93	1
	Female	53	17.0		
			**		
Race:	White	485	40.6	0.00	1
	Non-white	110	40.9		
	Do not know	(8)	(0.0)		
SES:	Lower	119	60.5	33.56	2
	Working	262	38.2		
	Middle	69	18.8		
	Do not know	(153)	(37.3)		
			**		
Demeanour:	Co-operative	388	37.1	8.96	1
	Unco-operative	153	51.6		
	Do not know	(62)	(30.6)		
			**		
Other patrol officer actions					
Warning:	Yes	348	39.9	0.00	1
	No	255	40.4		
Traffic summons:	Yes	143	48.3	4.71	1
	No	460	37.6		
			*		

* $p < 0.05$
** $p < 0.01$
χ^2 corrected for continuity in 2 x 2 tables

Table 6.1 also records that CPIC checks were no more likely when the suspect was subject to a warning, but they were more likely to be used with a traffic summons than when no summons was issued. As we shall see later, when officers decide to take formal action they are usually more likely to include other investigative actions. When official action is taken it raises the visibility of the matter; the patrol officer might be embarrassed if he charged and

TABLE 6.2

Citizen contact suspects: stepwise discriminant analysis of mobilization, dispute type, suspect characteristics, and other patrol officer actions against whether or not a CPIC check was undertaken

Step discriminant variables		*F* to enter	Discriminant function coefficients
SES:	Middle/working	17.03	+0.458
	Lower		
Traffic summons:	*Summons*	15.37	–0.408
	No summons		
Sex:	*Male*	6.30	–0.301
	Female		
Age:	*17–24*	5.43	–0.275
	<17 / >24		
Demeanour:	*Unco-operative*	3.71	–0.318
	Co-operative		
Mobilization:	*Proactive*	3.90	–0.282
	Reactive		

Centroids: Group I – CPIC ($n = 178$) +0.394
Centroids: Group II – no CPIC ($n = 239$) –0.294
Percentage correctly classified = 64.8%
Wilk's lambda = 0.8840; $\chi^2 = 50.82$; df = 6; $p < 0.001$

released the suspect without a CPIC check and later discovered that the suspect was 'wanted.'

The stepwise discriminant analysis in Table 6.2 informs us that the best predictor of CPIC checks is the suspect's socio-economic status. Whether a traffic summons was issued has an important additional influence. Following this, the suspect's sex, age, and demeanour, and the type of mobilization, separately add to the equation. As a group, suspects subject to CPIC checks are men of lower socio-economic status, aged 17 to 24, and unco-operative. They are predictably more likely to be encountered proactively and to have received a traffic summons. Our analyses support the argument that CPIC checks are typically made on 'pukers' after they have been stopped on the initiative of patrol officers.

In the relatively rare instance when a CPIC check provides criminal information on a suspect, the officer does not always take further action. Sometimes the information appears to spur other action, while at other times it is bypassed. For example, on several occasions suspects were proactively stopped and subject to CPIC checks which revealed records for Narcotics Control Act violations. However, the officers made no effort to search these individuals and took no further action against them. On several other occasions the officers decided to search vehicles after CPIC checks revealed criminal records.

Searches provide similar functions to CPIC checks: generating further information to assess the suspect, asserting police authority, and uncovering something to justify a charge (mainly liquor and narcotics, but also stolen property and weapons). Unfortunately, the researchers did not systematically record searches in citizen-contact encounters, making impossible quantitative analysis using this variable. However, our observations support the claim that searches, like CPIC checks, were especially likely for 'pukers' and others of 'marginal' status. This is documented by case data later in this section and in our quantitative analysis of searches in major troubles.

CPIC checks and searches were principally ordering devices against people of lower status. Warnings were most often given to people of higher status in traffic-violation disputes. Warnings were given to 57.5 per cent of suspects.

As documented in Table 6.3, warnings were significantly more likely for people involved in traffic disputes, of higher socio-economic standing, non-white, and in the under 17 and over 24 age category. Warnings were equally likely to be given whether or not a CPIC check was undertaken, and they were almost equally likely with a traffic summons or as an alternative resolution when no summons was issued. The discriminant analyses summarized in Table 6.4 show that the most significant predictor of warnings is the type of dispute. The race and socio-economic status of the suspect add marginally to the predictive power. On a group basis, those who received a warning were involved in traffic disputes, were non-white, and of middle or working class.

The only variable that did not vary significantly according to the suspect's demeanour was 'warnings.' Co-operative suspects are more likely to receive warnings as an *alternative* to other actions, whereas unco-operative suspects receive warnings along with those other actions. As we learn later, the unco-operative suspect becomes subject to the full range of patrol-officer actions.

The only frequent form of official action in minor troubles is traffic summonses, notices, and CV3 (vehicle-inspection) notices. These were taken against 23.7 per cent of the suspects in citizen-contact encounters. In Table 6.5 we see that a number of variables taken individually are significantly related to the traffic-charge decision. Traffic charges are much more likely to arise out of proactive encounters, although there were eight charges laid after reactive mobilizations (e.g. minor traffic accidents). Traffic summonses were more likely in what were primarily traffic stops, although in 4.2 per cent of 'other' types of encounter traffic charges were used as a substitute to handle the situation. A patrol officer found a man sleeping in his car and questioned him extensively about his activities. When the man said he did not have his licence with him, the patrol officer charged him for failing to produce a licence under the Highway Traffic Act.

Table 6.5 documents that taken individually, race and demeanour of suspects are significantly related to traffic-charge decisions. Traffic charges were not substantially more likely when there was a warning issued, but were marginally more likely with CPIC checks than without them.

TABLE 6.3

Suspects in citizen contact encounters: mobilization, dispute type, suspect characteristics, and other patrol officer actions related to proportion of suspects receiving warnings

		N	Percentage of suspects receiving warnings	χ^2	df
Total sample		603	57.7		
Mobilization and dispute type					
Mobilization:	Proactive	503	59.8	5.12	1
	Reactive	100	47.0 *		
Dispute type:	Traffic	366	71.0	66.38	1
	Other	237	37.1 **		
Suspect characteristics					
Age:	17–24	294	54.6	3.86	1
	<17 / >24	266	63.2		
	Do not know	(43)	(46.5) *		
Sex:	Male	550	57.3	0.31	1
	Female	53	62.3		
Race:	White	485	55.7	4.48	1
	Non-white	110	67.3		
	Do not know	(8)	(50.0) *		
SES:	Lower	119	49.6	12.81	2
	Working	262	66.0		
	Middle	69	72.5		
	Do not know	(153)	(43.1) **		
Demeanour:	Co-operative	388	62.4	0.28	1
	Unco-operative	153	59.5		
	Do not know	(62)	(24.2)		
Other patrol officer actions					
CPIC checks:	Yes	242	57.4	0.00	1
	No	361	57.9		
Traffic summons:	Yes	143	59.4	0.15	1
	No	460	57.2		

* $p < 0.05$
** $p < 0.01$
χ^2 corrected for continuity in 2 x 2 tables

A discriminant analysis indicates that traffic summonses are predictably used in traffic disputes. The suspect's demeanour then enters the equation, followed in turn by whether a CPIC check was taken, the suspect's race, the type of mobilization, and whether a warning was given. Those who are summonsed are involved in traffic disputes, involved in proactive disputes, do not receive a warning, are subject to a CPIC check, are non-white, and are unco-operative. The suspect's demeanour had a substantial bearing on

TABLE 6.4

Citizen contact suspects: stepwise discriminant analysis of mobilization, dispute type, suspect characteristics, and other patrol officer actions against whether or not a warning was given

Stepwise discriminant variables		F to enter	Discriminant function coefficients
Dispute type:	*Traffic*	77.38	0.899
	Other		
Race:	White	3.28	−0.193
	Non-white		
SES:	*Middle/working*	3.02	+0.194
	Lower		

Centroids: Group I – warning ($n = 270$) –0.304
Centroids: Group II – no warning ($n = 147$) +0.558
Percentage correctly classified – 72.2%
Wilk's lambda = 0.8301; $\chi^2 = 76.98$; df = 3; $p < 0.001$

decisions to charge for traffic violations, as it did concerning the CPIC decisions. On several shifts, researchers recorded general statements by patrol officers that the prime factor in deciding to give a traffic summons is the 'attitude' of the violator. Officers generally see traffic enforcement as the principal area of discretionary latitude.

The citizen who looks respectable and acts with respect is likely to be subjected to fewer investigative measures and to avoid the full use of the law. In the main suspects are very compliant, even when subjected to delay for questioning or CPIC checks, or to searches. When they do protest too much, they are likely to heat up the dispute to the point where the patrol officer takes charge, literally.

Typing of citizens as 'respectable' and 'respectful' is done in terms of a variety of criteria. Sometimes a person's special status appears influential in the decision not to investigate further. For example, an older car being driven erratically was stopped for investigation. The driver, a man aged about 50, got out of the car and introduced himself as a justice of the peace from another jurisdiction. The officer explained why he made the stop and then said 'good evening' without making any further inquiries. Similarly, two police officers from other police forces who were candidates for driving charges were not charged.

Typing is particularly evident in decisions to summons for traffic violations. For example, a patrol officer using radar made three stops of speeding vehicles and made different judgments in each case. A late-model car driven by a higher-status man in his mid-fifties was clocked on radar at 43 mph in a 30 mph zone. The officer warned the driver to slow down but issued no summons. Later he noted to the researcher the driver's deference and apologetic approach, and he commented that people of this type are the main basis

TABLE 6.5

Suspects in citizen contact encounters: mobilization, dispute type, suspect characteristics, and other patrol officer actions related to proportion of suspects receiving a traffic summons

		N	Percentage of suspects receiving traffic summons	χ^2	df
Total sample		603	23.7		
Mobilization and dispute type					
Mobilization:	Proactive	503	26.8	15.34	1
	Reactive	100	8.0 **		
Dispute type:	Traffic	366	36.3	80.27	1
	Other	267	4.2 **		
Suspect characteristics					
Age:	17–24	294	23.1	0.33	1
	<17 / >24	266	25.6		
	Do not know	(43)	(16.3)		
Sex:	Male	550	24.0	0.13	1
	Female	53	20.8		
Race:	White	485	21.0	7.27	1
	Non-white	110	33.6		
	Do not know	(8)	(50.0) **		
SES:	Lower	119	21.0	2.98	2
	Working	262	27.9		
	Middle	69	20.3		
	Do not know	(153)	(20.3)		
Demeanour:	Co-operative	388	18.6	11.74	1
	Unco-operative	153	32.7		
	Do not know	(62)	(33.9) **		
Other patrol officer actions					
CPIC checks:	Yes	242	28.5	4.71	1
	No	361	20.5 *		
Warning:	Yes	348	24.4	0.15	1
	No	255	22.7		

* $p < 0.05$
** $p < 0.01$
χ^2 corrected for continuity in 2 x 2 tables

of police support. In another stop, the citizen was again an older, higher-status man driving a late-model car travelling 45 mph in a 30 mph zone. This driver was polite, and he was politely issued a summons for being 10 mph over the speed limit. The officer said he normally reduces a ticket unless the citizen is 'a real asshole.' He then commented, 'Hell, guys like this are where the police get all their support. You don't want to make them mad.' A man in

TABLE 6.6

Suspects in citizen contacts: stepwise discriminant analysis of mobilization, dispute type, suspect characteristics, and other patrol officer actions against whether or not a traffic summons was issued

Step discriminant variables		*F* to enter	Discriminant function coefficients
Dispute type:	*Traffic*	73.24	+0.796
	Other		
Demeanour:	*Unco-operative*	16.50	+0.354
	Co-operative		
CPIC:	*Yes*	10.68	+0.286
	No		
Race:	White	2.60	–0.176
	Non-white		
Mobilization:	*Proactive*	2.92	+0.178
	Reactive		
Warning:	Warning	1.06	–0.106
	No warning		

Centroids: Group I – summons (*n* = 106) –0.795
Centroids: Group II – no summons (*n* = 311) +0.271
Percentage correctly classified = 73.6%
Wilk's lambda = 0.7842; χ^2 = 100.16; df = 6; $p < 0.001$

his late twenties driving an older car was clocked at 56 mph in the 30 mph zone. The officer was polite to him, but the driver became argumentative. As the officer issued a summons for 49 mph in a 30 mph zone, the driver said he would dispute the summons in court. The officer later characterized the driver as 'an asshole trying to argue against the radar,' and he contemplated sending a summons in the mail for the clocked speed of 56 mph.

Of course, in making these decisions the officer is also taking into account his position in the police organization. He may feel a need to increase his productivity and thus be reluctant not to summons, or vice versa. He may be sensitive to public good will and the desire to avoid having his decision challenged. The reduction of the speeding level in writing a ticket has many similarities with the pre-trial negotiation of reducing charges and sentence in exchange for a guilty plea. By giving a concession the officer may improve the co-operative spirit of the citizen, who may think that he has received a break and is therefore likely to pay the fine without question. This in turn over-comes the work of having to produce evidence and appear in court. It also overcomes problems in evidence associated with the accuracy of the speed readings, especially in speedometer-clocked stops. Furthermore, even on a reduced charge the officer can still get production credit. In sum, this process allows the officer to minimize his work and ring up a charge credit while at the same time producing a compliant citizen.

Particular considerations sometimes override the factors we have already looked at. A patrol officer may believe that the suspect has already been inconvenienced enough from other police actions. For example, a patrol officer observed a speeding vehicle and gave pursuit. The motorist did not stop immediately and once stopped he verbally resisted the officer's request for identification. The officer obtained the motorist's driver's licence and ran a CPIC check which revealed that a man of the same name was wanted for questioning by another police force regarding a 'false pretences' investigation. The officer called for a more experienced patrol officer to question the suspect, who was detained for 20 minutes while the other officer drove to the scene and questioned the man. The second officer decided that this was not the same person as the one listed as wanted on CPIC. The first officer then decided not to charge for the speeding violation, apologizing to the suspect for the delay caused by the investigation. On another shift, the officer decided not to charge a youth for having illegal tires on his car after the youth produced two summonses issued the same day for the same offence.

Citizens stopped proactively for investigative checks are very compliant and usually respectful. These citizens perhaps believe that the police have pervasive authority to do what they want in these situations (cf Ericson and Baranek, 1982). This belief is not without foundation. For example, the law is apparently silent on the legal status of the person who is detained while the patrol officer awaits the result of a CPIC check. Since none of these checks in citizen contacts involved an announced arrest, the suspects were presumably free to leave, but none did. Because of the general aura of the police office, and the possibility of 'obstruct police' charges, among other actions, which might be forthcoming if they tried,[6] they probably did not feel free to leave.

In the case of searches the law is more clear. The patrol officer has a number of enabling provisions from different statutes to legitimate searches of the person and property concerning drugs, e.g. Narcotics Control Act sec 10(1); liquor, e.g. Liquor Licence Act sec 48(a); and prohibited or restricted weapons, Criminal Code sec 103(1). In the vast majority of encounters the patrol officer makes no reference to these provisions because the suspect consents to the search. It is only on the rare occasion when his power of search is challenged by the suspect that he might refer to these legal justifications. However, on these rare occasions, the challenges are not handled by legal references but with the threat or use of other actions aimed at enforcing compliance; or the officer uses other justifications for the search. An example of the latter occurred when a patrol officer stopped a car driven by a person resembling a suspect wanted for robbery; a subsequent search was justified by pointing to a beer-bottle cap in the ash-tray, which apparently provided 'reasonable grounds' for a search under the Liquor Licence Act sec 48(2).

Since most of these searches do not lead to a charge the suspects are unlikely to take legal action. When searches do produce a charge officers can retrospectively reconstruct 'reasonable grounds' for legal purposes. Moreover, even if these grounds cannot be established officers can still have the items they seize admitted as evidence in court because of the absence in Canada of an exclusionary rule.[7]

Suspects' consent to searches is the norm. In 47 citizen-contact and 33 incident encounters involving 90 searches of the person and 52 searches of vehicles not incident to arrest, there were only 19 encounters in which citizens objected to a search, and only 2 in which the objections were followed by decisions not to search.[8] Normally, suspects appeared to accept searches routinely as part of the order of things. For example a patrol officer, noticing a vehicle containing four long-haired youths, exclaimed, 'I don't know who those pukers are. I'll shake them a bit.' He searched all four and their vehicle, but found nothing. The suspects just stood by nonchalantly while this took place. On another shift, the officer spotted a youth walking along a residential street in mid-afternoon. He drove around the block and then approached the youth, who was by this time standing at a bus stop. The officer opened with a series of general questions and learned from the youth that he had just moved from Newfoundland to a nearby address, that he had no police record, and that he was now awaiting a bus. The officer then searched all of the youth's pockets, his boots, frisk-searched his pant legs, and looked through his wallet. Finding nothing, the officer apologized for the 'inconvenience'. The youth in turn thanked the patrol officer, putting his hand on his shoulder in a friendly gesture.

One of five youths sitting in a vehicle on the parking lot of a plaza told the officer that his father was an inspector in the police force. Upon learning the youth's identity, the officer, who initially indicated to the researcher that he intended to search for drugs, immediately decided not to search and did not undertake any other investigation.

A patrol officer encountered five youths standing beside two vehicles in a community-centre parking lot. He requested the ownership and insurance permits for one vehicle. One of the youths gave his permits to the officer, who then started some 'small talk' before asking one of the youths, 'Do you have any grass or anything on you tonight?' This youth said, 'No,' and the officer then asked jokingly, 'You don't even know what it is?' The youth replied that he knew what it was but he did not have any. The officer reached into the youth's shirt pocket but the youth pushed away. The officer appeared surprised but made no further attempt to search him; instead, he asked the youth what the trouble was. The youth replied, 'I'm tired of this shit. You can't go anywhere without getting hassled.' The officer returned to his previous friendly manner, telling the youths to enjoy themselves. Back in the patrol car, the officer commented to the researcher, 'That kid sure knows his rights. That's the first guy that's ever refused to let me search him. Normally I would have insisted but I don't want to get into any hassles tonight.'

Normally patrol officers do insist with unco-operative, unrespectful suspects. This is reflected in the greater likelihood of CPIC checks and traffic summonses for these people, as well as in the following illustrations.

A patrol officer observed a motorcyclist sitting at a curbside talking with three children. She informed the man that it is a violation to drive a motorcycle without a helmet. The motorcyclist became very upset and told her, 'Mind you own business.' The officer reacted in kind and asked the motorcyclist for his licence. With the licence in hand the officer returned to the patrol car to do a CPIC check, commenting to the researcher that she hoped the suspect had an outstanding warrant because this person was 'a real asshole.' While the CPIC check was being run, the motorcyclist walked back to the patrol car and 'yanked' open the door, saying in a sarcastic tone, 'If you're finished playing your little games, I have to go to work.' The officer became more visibly upset, gave an icy, 'Excuse me, sir,' slammed the door, and rolled down the window. The motorcyclist stood beside the cruiser, leaning one arm on the roof and keeping up a steady drumming with his fingers on the roof. The officer decided to run a CPIC vehicle-registration check as well. When both checks came back without anything against the citizen, the officer said, 'Thank you, sir, have a nice day.' This came across quite sarcastic and appeared to be interpreted as such by the man, who returned to his motorcycle without saying a word.

On another shift the officer stopped a vehicle travelling 60 mph in a 30 mph zone and issued a summons to the co-operative 25-year-old male driver for 41 mph in a 30 mph zone. Later on the same shift, a male youth on a motorcycle was stopped after being speedometer-clocked at 63 mph in a 30 mph zone. The youth became argumentative as the officer explained the speeding violation. The youth denied that he was travelling that fast. The officer wrote a summons for 63 mph in a 30 mph zone while the youth continued to argue and called the officer a 'fucking pig.' The officer did not allow for an out-of-court settlement and informed the youth of the court date. The youth then threatened that he would some day retaliate against the officer, who in turn threatened the youth with other charges.

An encounter in which the patrol officer decided to use a range of actions against the suspects developed after he stopped two youths driving along in an expensive car. The officer categorized the driver as 'out of place' – not the type of person who normally drives a car of this quality. In response to the officer's inquiry, the driver said he owned the vehicle and could afford it because he was a real estate agent. The officer replied, 'Sure kid, my ass you're a real estate salesman' and ordered the youths out of the car while he searched for liquor and drugs. One youth objected that his 'rights' were being violated, but was countered by the officer's assertion, 'Since when have you assholes become aware of your rights?" The search and a subsequent CPIC-check on the vehicle produced nothing. However, the officer issued a traffic notice to the driver, who was unable to produce his licence or proof of car ownership. Furthermore, the officer ordered him to park the car and not to drive it. The officer commented to the researcher that he 'shook up these pukers and told them where they belonged.'

A significant part of the patrol officer's work involves ordering the streets by proactively stopping and checking those who appear 'out of order.' A particular segment of the population is the prime candidate for this ordering. Patrol officers are equipped with symbolic and legal authority to accomplish this task. Suspects typically comply in order to keep the matter as a brief contact rather than having it grow into an incident. However, some of these proactive encounters – and many more reactive ones – do evolve into more major incidents with more serious consequences at stake for the suspect. We now turn to an examination of these major incidents.

Major Dealings

Many of the features of incidents are similar to those we have outlined in contacts. However, there are two fundamental differences. First, in incidents patrol officers were much more likely to confront suspects on someone else's definition of trouble rather than their own. While only 19.2 per cent of suspects in citizen contacts were encountered after reactive mobilization, 54.3 per cent of suspects in incidents were encountered that way. Furthermore, victim-complainants were frequently present at incident encounters with suspects: in 152 or almost one-half of the incidents recorded, both suspect(s) and victim-complainant(s) were present. Also, incidents more frequently involved the possibility of resolution via charges.

In the following analysis of major dealings with suspects, I initially present a quantitative analysis of dispute characteristics (how mobilized, type, property damage/loss, injury) and citizen characteristics (age, sex, race, SES, demeanour) as they relate to actions by officers (CPIC checks, searches, warnings, arrest and/or charge). I then consider the resources officers use to secure routine compliance from suspects, paying particular attention to compliance with search and arrest. Following this, I analyse decisions to charge in terms of factors not apparent in the quantitative analysis.

PATTERNS IN MAJOR DEALINGS WITH SUSPECTS

I have already outlined the nature and function of CPIC checks in the discussion of minor dealings between patrol officers and suspects. Many of the same factors influence CPIC checks in major dealing, although there are some notable exceptions.

As enumerated in Table 6.7, CPIC checks were much more likely in proactive encounters. Proactive encounters are unlikely to involve victim-complainants or other citizens who can provide additional information about the suspect; the CPIC check is usually the only alternative in such encounters. CPIC checks were most likely in automobile or 'other' disputes and least likely in property and interpersonal disputes. This is consistent with the variation on the mobilization variable – since the former were much more

TABLE 6.7

Suspects in incident encounters: mobilization, dispute characteristics, suspect characteristics, and other patrol officer actions related to proportion of suspects subject to investigative CPIC checks

		N	Percentage of sample subject to investigative CPIC checks	χ^2	df
Total sample		392	39.3		
Mobilization and dispute characteristics					
Mobilization:	Proactive	129	63.6	46.0	1
	Reactive	263	27.4		
			**		
Dispute type:	Automobile	91	53.8	34.18	3
	Property	69	24.6		
	Interpersonal	87	19.5		
	Other	145	49.0		
			**		
Damage/loss:	Yes	141	28.4	10.30	1
	No	251	45.4		
			**		
Injury:	Yes	44	20.5	6.51	1
	No	348	41.7		
			*		
Suspect characteristics					
Age:	Under 16	35	5.7	20.06	2
	16–24	187	46.0		
	25+	164	39.6		
	Do not know	(6)	(16.7)		
			**		
Sex:	Male	326	44.2	18.18	1
	Female	66	15.2		
			**		
Race:	White	302	40.7	0.42	1
	Other	78	35.9		
	Do not know	(12)	(25.0)		
SES:	Lower	91	49.5	18.22	2
	Working	126	41.3		
	Middle	111	21.6		
	Do not know	(64)	(51.6)		
			**		
Demeanour:	Co-operative	244	41.8	0.08	1
	Unco-operative	131	39.7		
	Do not know	(17)	(0.0)		
Other patrol officer actions					
Search:	Yes	98	62.2	27.61	1
	No	294	31.6		
			**		
Warning:	Yes	174	39.1	0.00	1
	No	218	39.4		
Official action:	Yes	215	48.8	17.34	1
	No	177	27.7		
			**		

* $p < 0.05$
** $p < 0.01$
χ^2 corrected for continuity in 2 x 2 tables

likely than the latter to be proactive – and with the fact that CPIC checks were less frequent when there was property damage/loss or personal injury.

Individual cross-tabulations on characteristics of suspects reveal that CPIC checks were most likely for men, people aged 16 to 24, and those of lower-socio-economic status. Demeanour does not differentiate suspects receiving CPIC checks during incidents, although it does in citizen contacts. Apparently, when more substantial matters are involved, the influence of demeanour recedes. As we shall learn, demeanour has little influence on searches and formal actions.

Table 6.7 also indicates that CPIC checks were twice as likely when there was a search as when there was no search. They were also much more likely to be employed along with official action than when no official action took place.

Table 6.8 presents the results of a discriminant analysis on whether a CPIC check was undertaken against dispute characteristics, suspect characteristics, and other action by patrol officers. Clearly, the most influential predictor on a stepwise basis is whether a search was undertaken. Type of mobilization and then the suspect's socio-economic status add substantially to the equation. These in turn are followed by some additional influence from whether there was official action, age, sex, personal injury, race, dispute-type, and damage or loss. As a group, suspects subject to CPIC checks are involved in proactive encounters, in other than interpersonal disputes, in disputes that do not involve injury, and in disputes without property loss or damage; are also subject to searches and to official action; and are of the lower socio-economic statuses, aged under 16 or over over 25, male, and white.

Comparing the data on CPIC checks with the data on searches, we discover some similarities in the 'target' population and circumstances. As revealed in Table 6.9, suspects searched were three times more likely to be encountered proactively than reactively. They were particularly likely to be searched in relation to 'other' disputes (e.g. liquor and drug 'suspicion' searches) and relatively unlikely to be searched if involved in interpersonal disputes. Searches were more likely where there was no property damage or loss and in incidents not involving personal injury to any party. This is consistent with the fact that they were particularly likely in 'other' types of disputes which typically involved 'suspicious' persons and circumstances.

In terms of individual suspect characteristics, searches were most common for suspects 16 to 24, those of lower socio-economic status, and men.

Table 6.9 also informs us that searches were more frequently conducted when CPIC checks were also conducted. Comparing this with data in Table 6.7, we find that the majority of searches were done in conjunction with CPIC checks, while the majority of CPIC checks were done without attendant searches. Searches were significantly less likely when there was a warning

TABLE 6.8

Incident suspects: stepwise discriminant analysis of mobilization, dispute characteristics, suspect characteristics, and other patrol officer actions against whether or not a CPIC check was undertaken

Step discriminant variables		*F* to enter	Discriminant function coefficients
Search:	*Search*	32.40	+0.312
	No search		
Mobilization:	*Proactive*	17.68	+0.369
	Reactive		
SES:	Middle	18.04	−0.435
	Lower/working		
Official action:	No action	7.36	−0.290
	Action		
Age:	*<16/>25*	7.14	+0.373
	16–24		
Sex:	*Male*	5.33	+0.292
	Female		
Personal injury	Injury	3.15	−0.123
	No injury		
Race:	*White*	1.92	+0.158
	Non-white		
Dispute type:	*Other*	1.81	+0.196
	Interpersonal		
Damage/loss:	Damage/loss	2.16	−0.159
	No damage/loss		

Centroids: Group I – CPIC ($n = 117$) −0.661
Centroids: Group II – no CPIC ($n = 194$) +0.399
Percentage correctly classified = 74.3%
Wilk's lambda = 0.7358; $\chi^2 = 93.26$; df = 10; $p < 0.001$

issued by the patrol officer and significantly more likely when the suspect was also subject to official action.

In the discriminant analysis presented in Table 6.10, the best predictor of a search is formal action. Whether there was a CPIC check and the suspect's age then add substantially to the equation. Following this, some additional predictive influence comes from adding whether there was a warning, the suspect's sex, and the type of dispute. Those searched are grouped as also receiving formal action, also being subject to CPIC checks, also being given a warning, involved in proactive encounters, involved in other than interpersonal disputes, being men, and age 16 to 24.

Another frequent action against suspects was the issuing of 'informal warnings.' These consisted of admonishments, cautions, verbal threats, and/or physical threats. As documented in Table 6.11, warnings were most likely for suspects in interpersonal disputes, followed by 'other' disputes and property disputes, and substantially less likely in automobile-related disputes. Consistent with this is the fact that warnings were more likely where

TABLE 6.9

Suspects in incident encounters: mobilization, dispute characteristics, suspect characteristics, and other patrol officer actions related to proportion of suspects subject to searches

		N	Percentage of suspects subject to searches	χ^2	df
Total sample		392	25.0		
Mobilization and dispute characteristics					
Mobilization:	Proactive	129	41.1	25.27	1
	Reactive	263	17.1		
			**		
Dispute type:	Automobile	91	19.8	24.5	3
	Property	69	26.1		
	Interpersonal	87	9.2		
	Other	145	37.2		
			**		
Damage/loss:	Yes	141	18.4	4.52	1
	No	251	28.7		
			*		
Injury:	Yes	44	15.9	1.67	1
	No	348	26.1		
Suspect characteristics					
Age:	Under 16	35	14.3	13.44	2
	16–24	187	33.7		
	25+	164	18.3		
	Do not know	(6)	(0.0)		
			**		
Sex:	Male	326	28.5	11.76	1
	Female	66	7.6		
			**		
Race:	White	302	25.8	0.01	1
	Other	78	25.6		
	Do not know	(12)	(0.0)		
SES:	Lower	91	35.2	11.81	2
	Working	126	24.6		
	Middle	111	14.4		
	Do not know	(64)	(29.7)		
			**		
Demeanour:	Co-operative	244	25.0	0.06	1
	Unco-operative	131	26.7		
	Do not know	(17)	(11.8)		
Other patrol officer actions					
CPIC checks:	Yes	154	39.6	27.61	1
	No	238	15.5		
			**		
Warning:	Yes	174	35.1	15.93	1
	No	218	51.8		
			**		
Official action:	Yes	215	37.2	36.43	1
	No	177	10.2		
			**		

* $p < 0.05$
** $p < 0.01$
χ^2 corrected for continuity in 2 x 2 tables

TABLE 6.10

Incident suspects: stepwise discriminant analysis of mobilization, dispute characteristics, suspect characteristics, and other patrol officer actions against whether or not a suspect was searched

Step discriminant variables		*F* to enter	Discriminant function coefficients
Formal action:	No action	43.73	+0.549
	Action		
CPIC:	*Yes*	19.21	−0.355
	No		
Age:	<16 / >25	15.57	+0.323
	16–24		
Warning:	*Warning*	4.93	−0.197
	No warning		
Mobilization:	*Proactive*	3.53	−0.160
	Reactive		
Sex:	*Male*	1.94	−0.167
	Female		
Dispute type:	*Other*	2.29	−0.164
	Interpersonal		

Centroids: Group I – search ($n = 77$) +0.865
Centroids: Group II – no search ($n = 234$) −0.285
Percentage correctly classified – 75.9%
Wilk's lambda = 0.7530; $\chi^2 = 86.67$; df = 7; $p < 0.001$

there was no property damage or loss. Warnings were more likely to be given to younger persons, especially juveniles, and to people who were unco-operative. They were proportionately more often a part of transactions that included a search than when no search took place.

The stepwise discriminant analysis summarized in Table 6.12 indicates that the best predictor of warnings is whether or not a search was undertaken, followed by the addition of the suspect's demeanour, then the dispute type, and then the suspect's sex. The discriminant analysis groups those who received a warning as being involved in interpersonal disputes, also being subject to a search, female, and unco-operative.

The fourth major type of action has been labelled 'formal action.' It is a category developed out of a wide range of official actions, summarized in Table 6.13.

'Formal action – further processing' includes all people who were subject to investigative dealings beyond preliminary questioning. In the sense that they were detained for further investigation on either an implicit or explicit basis, all of these people were arrested. However, this empirical definition does not totally accord with the legal definition, which is highly problematic. In Canada, case law has evolved in which arrest is defined as occurring at the point a police officer places his hand on the suspect and states he is under arrest or at the point at which the suspect submits to police directions whether

TABLE 6.11

Suspects in incident encounters: mobilization, dispute characteristics, suspect characteristics, and other patrol officer actions related to proportion of suspects subject to informal warnings

		N	Percentage of suspects subject to informal warnings	χ^2	df
Total sample		392	44.4		
Mobilization and dispute characteristics					
Mobilization:	Proactive	129	41.1	0.66	1
	Reactive	263	46.0		
Dispute type:	Automobile	91	28.6	16.90	3
	Property	69	42.0		
	Interpersonal	87	58.6		
	Other	145	46.9 **		
Damage/loss:	Yes	141	36.9	4.57	1
	No	251	48.6 *		
Injury:	Yes	44	47.7	0.10	1
	No	348	44.0		
Suspect characteristics					
Age:	Under 16	35	62.9	6.03	2
	16–24	187	46.0		
	25+	164	40.2		
	Do not know	(6)	(0.0) *		
Sex:	Male	326	42.6	2.00	1
	Female	66	47.0		
Race:	White	302	46.0	0.45	1
	Other	78	41.0		
	Do not know	(12)	(25.0)		
SES:	Lower	91	45.0	0.52	2
	Working	126	50.0		
	Middle	111	48.6		
	Do not know	(64)	(25.0)		
Demeanour:	Co-operative	244	37.3	20.9	1
	Unco-operative	131	62.6		
	Do not know	(17)	(5.9) **		
Other patrol officer actions					
CPIC checks:	Yes	154	44.2	0.00	1
	No	238	44.5		
Search:	Yes	98	62.2	15.93	1
	No	294	38.4 **		
Formal action:	Yes	215	47.0	1.07	1
	No	177	41.2		

* $p < 0.05$
** $p < 0.01$
χ^2 corrected for continuity in 2 x 2 tables

TABLE 6.12

Incident suspects: stepwise discriminant analysis of mobilization, dispute characteristics, suspect characteristics, and other patrol officer actions against whether or not a warning was given

Step discriminant variables		F to enter	Discriminant function coefficients
Search:	*Search*	16.99	–0.748
	No search		
Demeanour:	*Unco-operative*	14.97	–0.553
	Co-operative		
Dispute type:	Other	12.94	+0.536
	Interpersonal		
Sex:	Male	2.53	+0.233
	Female		

Centroids: Group I – warning ($n = 154$) +0.373
Centroids: Group II – no warning ($n = 151$) –0.380
Percentage correctly classified – 65.6%
Wilk's lambda = 0.8578; $\chi^2 = 46.18$; df = 4; $p < 0.001$

TABLE 6.13

Patrol officer formal action against suspects in incident encounters

	N	%
Formal action–further processing	(170)	(43.3)
Explicit arrest and charge	53	13.5
Implicit arrest and charge	26	6.6
Summons–liquor	7	1.8
Execution committal warrant	2	.5
Juvenile processing	19	4.8
'Voluntary' processing and no charge	3	.8
Implicit arrest and no charge	51	13.0
Explicit arrest and no charge	9	2.3
Formal action–no further processing	(45)	(11.5)
Summons–traffic	37	9.5
Summons–liquor	2	.5
Committal warrant collection	4	1.0
Private information summons	2	.5
Report only	(40)	(10.2)
No formal action and no report	(137)	(35.0)
Totals	392	100.0

or not he is touched or told he is under arrest. The general test is whether the suspect perceives he is free to depart the presence of the police officer if he so wishes. Obviously, this is highly problematic for empirical researchers to settle in any given case because it involves judging what is going on in a suspects's mind.

Since very few suspects attempted to depart and were prevented from doing so, the researchers were left with the hypothetical question: did this suspect want to depart but felt he could not do so, or did he feel free to depart but decided to co-operate voluntarily?[9]

The 170 persons subject to 'further processing' were categorized in terms of their charges, if any, and the nature of their arrest, if any. Among this group, 53 were explicitly arrested (e.g. told they were under arrest and/or clearly taken hold of to indicate an arrest) and charged under the Criminal Code and/or Narcotics Control Act, 7 were arrested and charged under the Liquor Licence Act, 2 were subject to arrest in connection with the execution of a committal warrant, 19 juveniles were apprehended prior to having their cases turned over to the youth bureau for further investigation, 3 persons were judged to have willingly gone along with processing after it was made explicit that they were not under arrest and therefore under no obligation to submit to investigation, 51 were implicitly arrested but later released without charge, and 9 were explicitly arrested but later released without charge.

'Formal action – no further processing' refers to those suspects charged or subject to warrant execution without being detained for further processing. In this group of 45 suspects, 37 were issued Highway Traffic Act summonses, 2 were issued Liquor Licence Act summonses, 4 paid the fine in connection with an outstanding committal warrant, and 2 received summonses under warrants issued as a result of charges laid via private informations. These 45 suspects were added to the 170 subject to 'further processing' to yield the total of 215 who were counted as having been subject to 'formal action.'[10] Among the remaining suspects, 40 were involved in encounters where official reports were taken on the dispute but no further action was taken and 137 were not subject to either formal action or official reports.

From Table 6.14 we learn that formal action was undertaken against approximately two-thirds of suspects in automobile disputes, two-thirds in property disputes, one-half in 'other' disputes, and two-fifths in interpersonal disputes. The greater proportion of formal action in automobile and property disputes is consistent with the fact that formal action was more likely where property loss and/or damage occurred. These findings are in turn continuous with a trend reported in chapter 5 regarding victim-complainants: patrol officers were most likely to take official action in property conflicts, especially compared with interpersonal conflicts.

On an individual basis, formal actions are not substantially differentiated by characteristics of the suspects. The only statistically significant variable is socio-economic status, with lower-status people being more often subject to formal action.

Official action was substantially more likely with than without investigative checks. Over two-thirds of those subject to CPIC checks were dealt with formally, while less than one-half not checked were subject to formal action.

TABLE 6.14

Suspects in incident encounters: mobilization, dispute characteristics, suspect characteristics, and other patrol officer actions related to proportion of suspects subject to formal action

		N	Percentage of suspects subject to formal action	χ^2	df
Total sample		392	54.8		
Mobilization and dispute characteristics					
Mobilization:	Proactive	129	57.4	0.35	1
	Reactive	263	53.6		
Dispute type:	Automobile	91	65.9	16.77	3
	Property	69	66.7		
	Interpersonal	87	40.2		
	Other	145	51.0		
			**		
Damage/loss:	Yes	141	62.4	4.62	1
	No	251	50.6		
			*		
Injury:	Yes	44	59.1	0.19	1
	No	348	54.3		
Suspect characteristics					
Age:	Under 16	35	65.7	4.07	2
	16–24	187	58.3		
	25+	164	50.0		
	Do not know	(6)	(16.7)		
Sex:	Male	326	57.1	3.30	1
	Female	66	43.9		
Race:	White	302	55.0	1.25	1
	Other	78	62.8		
	Do not know	(12)	(0.0)		
SES:	Lower	91	64.8	8.24	2
	Working	126	57.1		
	Middle	111	45.0		
	Do not know	(64)	(53.1)		
			*		
Demeanour:	Co-operative	244	55.7	0.00	1
	Unco-operative	131	56.5		
	Do not know	(17)	(29.4)		
Other patrol officer action					
CPIC checks:	Yes	154	68.2	17.34	1
	No	238	46.2		
			**		
Search:	Yes	98	81.6	36.43	1
	No	294	45.9		
			**		
Warning:	Yes	174	42.0	1.07	1
	No	218	47.7		

* $p < 0.05$
** $p < 0.01$
χ^2 corrected for continuity in 2 x 2 tables

Over four-fifths of suspects searched were subject to formal action, while less than one-half not searched were subject to formal action. As we noted in our discussion of minor (contact) dealings, CPIC checks and searches are more likely when official action is taken because the visibility of the encounter is 'raised' within the police organization and the officer does not want to be reprimanded for not uncovering something relevant to the investigation. In particular, personal searches in arrests are a routine protective device for the officer, as well as a means of generating further evidence and/or further charges.

From the discriminant analysis presented in Table 6.15, we learn that the most important predictor by far is whether or not the suspect was also searched. This is followed in turn by the successive additional influence of whether there was any damage or loss, whether there was a CPIC check, whether there was any injury, the dispute type, whether a warning was also issued, the suspect's race, and the suspect's socio-economic status. The discriminant analysis groups those subject to formal action as also receiving searches, also receiving CPIC checks, not also receiving warnings, subject to property loss or damage, subject to injury, involved in other than interpersonal disputes, being non-white, and being of lower or working class.

To this point I have mainly given a descriptive overview of actions by patrol officers in relation to characteristics of disputes and suspects. Other data at our disposal inform us about power resources available to patrol officers to gain compliance from suspects and to charge in conformity with expectations in the police organization. We now examine these data as a means of addressing the central question of who controls the process and how this control is accomplished.

COMPLIANCE OF SUSPECTS

As I documented in relation to minor (contact) dealings between patrol officers and suspects, there is routine compliance by the suspect when the officer conducts CPIC checks and searches. Suspects are apparently aware that a refusal will be met with increasing action, including the possibility of an arrest for obstructing police, breach of peace, causing a disturbance, or other general legal provisions which enable the police to assert *final* control over suspects. In the case of searches there are several enabling legal provisions which ensure that the officer has the power to enforce compliance. While these powers are rarely spoken of in the encounter, they are always 'there' to be called upon if someone calls the officer's actions into question.

As indicated in the quantitative data, searches are significantly more likely in conjunction with some form of official action than when no official action is undertaken. Most of these searches can be made legally legitimate because they are incident to arrest. They are often conducted as an integral part of the process of arrest, interrogation and charge.

TABLE 6.15

Incident suspects: stepwise discriminant analysis of mobilization, dispute characteristics, suspect characteristics, and other patrol officer action against whether or not formal action taken

Step discriminant variables		F to enter	Discriminant function coefficients
Search:	*Search*	43.73	−0.653
	No search		
Damage/loss:	*Damage/loss*	8.78	−0.271
	No damage/loss		
CPIC:	*Yes*	9.47	−0.328
	No		
Injury:	*Injury*	3.18	−0.210
	No injury		
Dispute type:	*Other*	3.24	−0.253
	Interpersonal		
Warning:	Warning	1.94	+0.173
	No warning		
Race:	White	1.63	+0.131
	Non-white		
SES:	Middle	1.11	+0.129
	Working/lower		

Centroids: Group I – no official action ($n = 135$) –0.514
Centroids: Group II – Official action ($n = 176$) +0.394
Percentage correctly classified – 67.5%
Wilk's lambda $= 0.7968$; $\chi^2 = 69.28$; df $= 8$; $p < 0.001$

For example, a patrol officer was dispatched to a 'theft in progress' at an underground parking garage in an apartment complex. The apartment superintendent met the officer and stated that four youths were in the garage breaking into vehicles. The superintendent pointed out one youth who was sitting behind the wheel of a car. The officer approached this youth, ordered him out of the car, and frisk-searched him. He asked this suspect where the other youths were but received no answer. A back-up patrol officer then began looking for the other youths, while the officer searched the suspect's vehicle and discovered a number of articles that he suspected were stolen.

While the back-up officer 'rounded up' the other suspects over a 10-minute period, the officer began interrogating the first suspect. His initial tactic was to refer to a baseball bat he had found under the front seat of the car as an 'offensive weapon,' thereby leading the suspect to believe that this offence might be charged if confessions were not forthcoming concerning the vehicles allegedly broken into and articles stolen.[11] The suspect immediately identified the vehicles entered and with the other three suspects identified articles in their possession that were stolen. When the original suspect stated that some other articles in his possession were not stolen, the officer told him that he did not believe him and then said, 'OK, let's go over it one more time. I asked you before if you'd taken anything else and you said no. Now you tell me you took some of this other stuff. If you clean all this shit up now, the judge, he'll go easier on you.' The suspect then identified more items as stolen.

The officer arranged for the owner of each car entered to be contacted by the superintendent and to come to the garage to identify their property. There was no questioning to ascertain whether the victims wanted charges to be laid; rather, the officer had each victim identify his own property and then informed him that the property would be kept for evidence. The officer produced 48 charges out of these circumstances: 10 counts of theft under $200, 1 count of mischief (for alleged damage to one car), and 1 count of possession of stolen property over $200 (for an item admitted by one suspect to have been stolen elsewhere) against each suspect.

As this example illustrates, resistance from suspects is readily overcome with threats that carry real or imagined consequences. The nature of the threats employed depends on what is available within the situation to construct a threat about. The compliance the threats produce eases the officer's task; lack of compliance only means more work (and usually more threats) aimed at producing what he wants.

If a suspect who is apparently not under arrest refuses to allow a search, an arrest may be effected in order to legitimate the action needed to accomplish the search. For example, a patrol sergeant, backed up by a patrol officer, stopped to assist a motorist who had apparently stalled his car in the roadway. The occupants, a man and woman aged 16 and 17, ignored the officers. The male driver was then forced out of the car. The youth began staggering, indicating that he had been drinking. The youth continued his belligerence, e.g. telling the officer to 'go fuck himself,' to take his uniform off so he could 'kick his ass,' and asked for a 15-second 'headstart.' The youth refused to allow a search of the car trunk, and the officers responded by telling him that if he did not co-operate he would be taken to the station for a breathalyser test. When the officers tried to obtain the suspect's car keys, a physical struggle ensued with the suspect yelling, 'Fuck you, I don't have to give them to you,' and the officers responding with further threats of charges and physical abuse. When the suspect then demanded his 'rights,' he was told, 'You don't have any rights, you're under arrest,' and the officers proceeded to conduct their search. The suspect was returned to the divisional station and given a breath test, which produced a reading of 100 mg. The suspect was charged with both 'impaired' and 'over 80 mg.'

Searches are also covered by enabling narcotics and liquor legislation. Sometimes patrol officers go to excessive lengths to uncover what they are looking for, usually with co-operation from suspects. For example, a patrol officer spotted an older car parked off a rural sideroad. The car contained five 'pukers.' As he approached the car, he commented to the researcher, 'Whatever they're doing here, they've got to be up to something illegal.'

The officer asked the driver for his licence and other papers and then told him to get out of the car. He asked the driver to open the trunk; the driver complied without question. The search revealed nothing. The officer followed with a frisk-search of the driver and then asked him to stand on the other side of the road. Each of the other suspects was in turn asked to produce identification and to get out of the car and was frisk-searched. The officer discovered some cigarette papers in the pockets of the third youth. Upon making this discovery, he took this individual into the back of the paddy-wagon he was using on patrol and skin-searched him, but this revealed nothing.

He placed all five suspects in the rear of the paddy-wagon and locked them in. He searched the suspects' car and eventually discovered some marijuana seeds and a roach clip. Equipped with something he could retrospectively use to make his original beliefs 'that they've got to be up to something illegal' appear reasonable, the officer exclaimed, 'Where there's a roach there's more,' and he searched the entire vehicle once again but found nothing. The officer had CPIC checks run on all five suspects while he returned to the paddy-wagon and skin-searched each suspect. No evidence was forthcoming, although one suspect eventually admitted they had smoked a joint just prior to the officer's arrival.

None of the suspects questioned the officer's right to conduct the search. Indeed, they were quite friendly and took the encounter as a joke, especially the searches, despite the fact that they were detained for 34 minutes, including 10 minutes locked in the paddy-wagon. The officer terminated the encounter by issuing a traffic notice to the driver concerning proof of insurance.

While suspects usually consent to searches without question, officers frequently uncover items during the search which can be used to legitimate it even though the thing found is not directly related to the original purpose of the search. The baseball bat 'weapon' and roach clip described above are examples.

Another cover is the enabling legal provision allowing for searches in conjunction with offences believed to be in progress.[12] These situations are sometimes additionally covered by the fact that patrol officers are acting on the complaint of a third party (see note 11). For example, a patrol officer was dispatched as a back-up to another patrol officer regarding a 'domestic' at an apartment. Upon arrival the patrol officers were met in the hallway by the complainant, who said she had heard a woman in an apartment screaming over a 45-minute period. She also expressed concern for the safety of a two-year-old child who lived in the apartment. The officers then approached the apartment and knocked. They received a reply from a male voice behind a closed door: 'Fuck off.' No one opened the door, and one officer then forced the door open and both officers entered the apartment. In these circumstances, the officers could retrospectively rely upon the complainant's statement about the screaming and the child's safety to justify the entry if it were subsequently questioned.

Most often, suspects readily admit patrol officers, even when there is obvious evidence available to condemn them. For example, a patrol officer was dispatched to an apartment regarding an anonymous complaint of an 'NCA [drug] party.' A resident in the building had detected a strong odour of marijuana in the hallway and decided that a drug party was taking place in a particular apartment. The patrol officer and a back-up knocked on the door of this unit and asked a man and woman if they could enter and talk with them. The couple, who were alone in their own apartment, willingly admitted the officers. The officers immediately spotted a burning cigarette and a bag sitting on a coffee table. The officers seized the bag (later determined to contain 19 grams of marijuana) and had the man admit ownership. He was arrested and returned to the divisional station where he was charged, processed, and released on a promise-to-appear notice.

Patrol officers also use entry gained to residences after a reactive call to conduct searches unrelated to the complaint. For example, a patrol officer was dispatched to a 'fight' at an apartment. He disovered that the complainant was a woman who wanted to prevent her common-law husband from continuing to live in the apartment, which was in her name. The officer advised her that since the apartment was hers, she could legitimately force the man out. He then went into the kitchen to use the telephone and discovered a hooka pipe. He returned to the living-room area with the pipe and said to the complainant, 'I have grounds to search. Can I search?' The complainant willingly complied, and the officer thoroughly searched the apartment. This search produced two more pipes, as well as a substance believed to be hash oil. The officer then confronted the man with his findings; the man admitted that the substance was his, but argued that it was petulia oil (perfume) and not hash oil.

At this point the officer ignored the 'domestic' complaint and dealt with the matter as a narcotics violation. Unsure of himself, he seized the items and returned to the divisional station where a patrol sergeant advised him to lay a charge but to ensure that the substance was later thoroughly analysed. The officer returned to the apartment and charged the suspect through the issuance of an appearance notice. The suspect remained incredulous that he was being charged for being in possession of petulia oil; his position was confirmed in a later analysis, and the charge was eventually withdrawn.

Any invitation to enter private space opens up the opportunity for the patrol officer to cast a suspicious eye around the premises. A call about one type of trouble can be radically transformed. The officer's resolution may also contribute to a resolution of the original trouble. In this case the charge was a means of asserting control over the man in what was a very hostile domestic situation. One could, however, argue that the charge might aggravate the original trouble or may indicate that the police have ignored the original trouble.

One enabling legal provision which patrol officers generally did not use in their searches was the search warrant. Only one incident involved obtaining and executing search warrants. In this case, the patrol officer took out a warrant regarding suspected marijuana in a home after another patrol officer reported an odour of marijuana coming from the residence. The matter eventually turned into a property crime investigation, and a second warrant was taken out to recover property allegedly stolen from another residence.

Patrol officers are not deterred by the process of applying to justices of the peace for a search warrant, since justices of the peace 'rubber-stamp' virtually all requests for a warrant (Ericson, 1981: chapter 6). Rather, they know they have sufficient legal and/or symbolic authority to secure the consent of suspects. Moreover, they know that if they go to their superiors with a request for a search warrant, the case might be taken out of their hands and turned over to detectives for further investigation. If patrol officers want to maintain investigative autonomy, they have to develop strategies for 'consent' searches which do not raise the visibility of their actions to superiors. As we have seen, patrol officers often accomplish what they want on their own because of the range of strategies and attendant legal legitimations available to them.

Many of the same elements are present when one considers decisions to further process suspects. Patrol officers have legal powers to employ whatever force is necessary to effect an arrest and to charge for resisting arrest. This alone usually ensures compliance where the arrest is clearly based on 'reasonable' evidence in the eyes of both suspect and officer (e.g. the suspect is caught in the act or is in possession of stolen property or illegal substances). Moreover, even when the arrest appears to be on vague suspicion or largely for investigative purposes, compliance can usually be ensured because of symbolic authority (Manning, 1977) and by the act that the officer can usually find some charge to legitimate an arrest (e.g. LaFave, 1965; Bittner, 1967, 1967a; Chevigny, 1969; Rubinstein, 1973; Chatterton, 1976).

Patrol officers could use what would otherwise have been viewed as 'cheap' charges as a pretext for investigative arrests. For example, a male youth walking along a main shopping street at 2:15 am was stopped for questioning and searched. He was found to be carrying $200 in small bills as well as one marijuana cigarette contained in a cigarette package. When questioned about the money he said he was beginning a vacation and was hitch-hiking to a nearby city. When questioned about the marijuana cigarette, the youth claimed the cigarette package had been given to him by someone he had hitched a ride with and added that he did not use marijuana.

The officers were faced with deciding what further action they should take (could legitimately take) in the circumstances. They wanted to run a CPIC check but the system was temporarily inoperable. They discussed whether they should charge the youth 'for one lousy joint' of marijuana. What appeared crucial was the officers' belief that the youth was suspicious in other ways and a possible candidate for interrogation about other offences. His claim that he had $200 for a vacation was not believed because he was not carrying luggage. Moreover, he had no personal identification, apparently did not know where he was, and generally seemed 'spaced out.' The officers decided to detain the suspect for further investigation, justifying the detention via arrest and charge for possession of marijuana. The accused was detained overnight for a bail hearing the following morning, and during that period he was interrogated regarding property offences in the area.[13]

Most often suspects comply with an arrest even if they are not given a reason for it (cf Asworth, 1976). As recorded in Table 6.13, of the 60 people arrested but not charged, 51 were not explicitly arrested; yet they went along with the police investigation. People who were eventually charged under the Criminal Code and/or the Narcotics Control Act were much more likely to have been explicitly arrested at the beginning (53 of 79). Patrol officers vary their strategy for taking control over the suspect according to the means at their disposal; regardless of the means, they nearly always attain their end of in-custody investigation.

These enabling features ensure that patrol officers gain compliance during and after detention. As documented in Table 6.16, two-thirds of suspects subject to physical and/or verbal constraints did not raise any objections, and if they did so it was usually verbal resistance rather than active physical resistance. Moreover, physical resistance was only forthcoming in response to physical constraints placed upon them by patrol officers.

The 'symbolic stick' of his office means that the patrol officer rarely has to use the physical stick of striking the suspect. Most physical constraints involve taking the suspect by the arm or handcuffing him or placing him in the rear of the patrol car where there are no inside door-handles to enable escape. The physical stick was only observed to be in use when the suspect took some resistance which officers judged to be abusive.

An example of this occurred when a patrol officer was dispatched to aid a patrol sergeant at a fight in a tavern. Upon arrival, the sergeant asked the officer to assist him in finding the suspect, who had left the tavern. The officer learned that the suspect had been drinking with several friends in the tavern when he was 'cut off' by the waitress serving the table. Angered by this, the suspect allegedly jumped over a railing and confronted the manager. A bartender then came over to assist the manager, and the suspect allegedly took a swing at him but missed. The bartender punched the suspect in the face, cutting his lip and bloodying his nose, and the tavern staff called the police.

TABLE 6.16

Patrol officer constraints placed on suspects subject to further processing and suspects' objections to these constraints

		Suspects' objections to constraints						
		None		Verbal resistance		Physical resistance		Physical and verbal resistance
Police officer constraints	*N*	*N*	%	*N*	%	*N*	%	*N*	%
Physical	71	60	84.5	9	12.7	0	0.0	2	2.8
Verbal	21	15	71.4	6	28.6	0	0.0	0	0.0
Physical and verbal	41	14	34.1	16	39.0	3	7.3	8	19.6
Totals	133	89	66.9	31	23.3	3	2.3	10	7.5

No patrol officer constraints: 37

When the suspect and his friend were confronted at the rear of the tavern they argued that the suspect did not swing at the bartender first but rather had been hit without provocation. The sergeant did not investigate this, but asked the suspect to come to the nearby divisional station for a chat. When the suspect began arguing against doing this, the sergeant took him by the arm. The suspect in turn took a swing at the sergeant, but missed as he lost his balance and banged against a door. The sergeant then punched the suspect in the stomach and along with the officer took a firm grip on him and ushered him on foot to the station. Entering the station, the suspect was pushed down a stairwell and literally thrown into a report room where three other officers sat. When the suspect continued to hurl verbal abuse at the officers he was slapped hard in the face, with blood spraying around the room. When the suspect began shouting again, he was grabbed by two officers who bent his back over a counter top and held his hair and throat, while a third officer pressed the suspect's testicles against a chair. He was thrown into the cells to sober up before questioning.

Once brought under control, suspects are also quite responsive to questioning in spite of the right to remain silent and to have legal assistance (for recent empirical evidence in Britain, see Royal Commission on Criminal Procedure, 1980, 1980a). There is an extensive literature on the ineffectiveness of legal rules (United States) and judicial guidelines (Britain, Canada) which attempt to protect the suspect's right to silence in face of police questioning (see Morris, 1978). A clear message in this literature is that regardless of the type of formal rules which exist, the *practice* is that the police arrange secret questioning without much, if any, resistance from suspects. As Morris (1978: 13n) notes, there is a contradiction in the fact that secret questioning is routinely accomplished within a system of criminal law which recognizes privilege against self-incrimination and the right to counsel.

Only 24 per cent (40 of 170) of the suspects further processed were known to have objected in any way to the patrol officer's questioning. Furthermore, the vast majority did not attempt to obtain access to a third party to assist them in their dealings with the police. The researchers recorded only 14 of 170 suspects further processed who were observed asking patrol officers for access to a third party.[14]

Moreover, the requests were just as often for contact with non-lawyers as they were for lawyers, indicating that suspects very rarely sought legal assistance. Seven asked for lawyers, two for a family member, one for a friend, and four for other parties. Officers did not always comply with the requests. Among the seven requests for lawyers, two were granted immediately, one was granted after a delay, and four were refused. The two requests to contact family and one request to contact a friend were all granted without delay, while two requests to contact other third parties were granted, one was delayed, and one was refused.

Suspects were rarely observed trying other forms of counter-resistance. Three suspects attempted to offer patrol officers material favours (bribes) in exchange for turning a blind eye. All three attempts involved persons caught driving while prohibited: one offered money, one offered fillets of beef, and one suggested sexual favours. None of these offers was accepted. Patrol officers occasionally trafficked in the currency of criminal information, using charges as a threat for the purpose of 'levering' the information from the suspects.[15]

Compliance is nearly always achieved, although occasionally it must be worked at. Once the suspect is put 'in order,' the patrol officer is left with the task of deciding whether to charge and of ascertaining what charge is both just and justifiable in the circumstances.

GETTING A CHARGE

Similarly to decisions on whether or not to record a complaint (see chapter 5), decisions on whether to charge and what to charge are framed within the *context* of the dispute and organizational expectations about how the dispute is to be handled. Who are the disputants? What are their claims? Is invocation of the criminal law an appropriate way to reproduce order? Is there an appropriate criminal law that is usable? Can invocation of the law be justified to police supervisory officers? Can invocation of the law be justified to the crown attorney? Can the citizen(s) involved be made to accept the decision? In sum, the patrol officer makes up his mind about what is just in the circumstances while keeping in mind how he is going to justify it to the various parties who will react to his decision. His actions are framed, and ultimately bound, by the need to tailor his conception of justice to the available justifications.

When an officer handles a matter without a charge, he can ease his concern about organizational justifications because of the 'low visibility' of the decision. When the suspect is encountered after a proactive mobilization and the decision is made not to charge, the suspect is likely to remain quietly thankful and no one else in the organization is likely to know what happened. In a reactive encounter, the officer may have to 'cool out' the complainant. However, as we learned in chapter 5, a number of enabling resources and strategies usually allow the officer to accomplish this with ease. Victims can be talked into a 'request' not to invoke the criminal law, especially in interpersonal disputes, particularly among intimates. There is encouragement from the police organization not to charge in this type of encounter; if the complainant later protests to the force about the officer's actions, he is well covered. Indeed, in only one case did we observe a patrol officer arrest a suspect in direct response to a 'domestic' assault complaint. The officer arrested the suspect and intended to charge him with 'assault occasioning bodily harm,' but when he arrived at the divisional station with the suspect his actions were countered by the sergeant. The sergeant instructed him to substitute a 'breach of the peace' arrest to justify the fact that the suspect was in custody; to release the suspect; and to inform the complainant that if she wanted charges laid she would have to proceed by a private information.

The patrol officer has considerable autonomy in meeting the needs of at least some of the citizens involved in a dispute and in producing the appearance of meeting the needs of the police force. For example, he can take into account the special-status claims of some suspects and use 'low visibility' conditions to cover his decision not to charge. Off-duty police officers stopped on suspicion of impaired driving or for traffic violations are regularly given grace. If they become involved in something which the officer feels compelled to report, then 'covers' must be found by formulating the matter in a way which accords with the interests of the suspect. Thus, a supervisor from another police force was involved in an accident with another car, causing $1,000 damage to each vehicle. He immediately approached the patrol officer and said that while he could obviously be charged with 'failure to yield' under the Highway Traffic Act and thereby be judged the culprit, he thought this would blemish his record on the force, especially because he was using a police vehicle on non-police business. The investigating officer said he was willing to go along with not charging as long as the other citizen could be made to accept it. The patrol officer then spoke with both drivers together and indicated that while both parties were at fault, he was willing to give them both 'a break' by not laying any charges. The other driver appeared pleased with this resolution, and the patrol officer took an accident report that made no mention of fault.

The sympathies of patrol officers because of other criteria of status can be expressed in decisions not to charge. Older people involved in Liquor

Licence Act violations, or Criminal Code impaired driving, are given special consideration. For example, at 12:30 am a patrol officer decided to go 'fishing' for some 'pukers' whom he could put in 'order.' He checked along a dirt road that ran into a park, this being a place frequented by 'pukers,' who are deemed likely candidates for liquor and narcotics violations. During the check, the officer spotted an old car. It contained an older man asleep in the front seat, and a dog asleep on a mound of pillows, clothing, suitcases, and other paraphernalia in the back. There was an open six-pack of beer on the front floor. Being awakened, the man appeared very drunk, and the first thing he did was attempt to finish drinking a beer that was already opened. He appeared quite apathetic, and initially it seemed he did not know where he was or what was happening. He said he had been to a pub and then decided to drink six more beers in his car but did not get that far.

The officer took the man's driver's licence and the remainder of the six-pack and told him he had a choice of a charge of 'being in care and control of a motor vehicle while impaired' or letting the officer keep the keys until the morning. The man selected the latter option. The officer checked the suspect on CPIC and found him clear. Without the apparent knowledge of the suspect, the officer hid the keys and the six-pack under the rear seat of the car. He promised to return in the morning at the end of the shift and told the man to go back to sleep, saying 'My only concern is that you don't go for a drive tonight.'

A 'puker' found in similar circumstances probably would have been dealt with in quite a different way. During our fieldwork, patrol officers were observed sneaking and flitting from tree to tree in secluded areas of parks in order to catch youths drinking. Yet older people appearing respectable and orderly were not prevented from engaging in prohibited activity. For example, a patrol officer was dispatched to a parking complaint in a public park and adjacent private property. He was met by the complainant who outlined his complaint and received the officer's agreement to have the vehicles moved. Upon getting out of the unmarked cruiser the officer noticed a flurry of activity and the rattle of bottles being hidden in picnic coolers. He commented to the researchers, 'I hope they're not stupid enough to be drinking here too.' He laughed as he watched a group of 'respectable' middle-aged men and women hide the bottles, and he called out, 'That's it fellows, hide the beer, hide the beer.' He asked the group to move their cars but he did not tag any. He noted to the researcher that one of the men had quite a lot to drink and commented, 'Let's get out of here before he starts to drive. The last thing I want today is an impaired.'

The patrol officer's general task in the reproduction of order is not to enforce the law mechanically; it is often possible to reproduce order by using other resources. His work *approaches* mechanization in some areas because the decision to arrest has already been taken by others (e.g. a store employee 'turns over' a shoplifter to him; a CPIC check reveals an outstanding committal warrant). However, the officer usually has the leeway to *use* the law as an 'all-purpose control device.' Here, his organizationally filtered perception of what is 'out of order' and of what laws are useful to reproduce order comes into play. If the suspects are of a *type* generally seen as 'out of order,' or are 'out of order' in responding to the officer's commands, they are likely candidates for a charge. When the charge is formulated for the police organization and prosecution in court, it bears few if any signs of what led to the charge.

A patrol officer spotted six youths sitting on a bench and taking turns sipping beer from a can. As soon as he approached, a confrontation began to brew. One youth placed a beer can between his legs. When the officer demanded that he put the can in the beer case, he put it to his mouth and tried to drink some. The officer grabbed at the can to prevent the youth from drinking the beer, and after a brief struggle the youth let go. The youth then warned the officer, 'I'd better see that stuff when we get to court,' suggesting that the officer was confiscating it for his own use. The officer collected identification from all six youths. Saying that he could charge all six, he asked who owned the beer. He asserted that the youth who had refused to give him the beer would definitely receive a sumons. This youth then stated, 'OK it's my beer' and started to argue, at which point he was placed in the rear of the patrol car while the officer ran CPIC checks on all six youths.

This youth was issued a summons for 'consume liquor in other than licensed premises or residence' – Liquor Licence Act sec 46(2) – and a vehicle-inspection summons regarding his car. None of the other five was formally dealt with; the officer clearly selected this one person who had challenged his authority and used him to bring order to the situation. The record-of-summons report did not refer to the other five, who were also consuming beer under the same circumstances. It only hinted at the suspect's resistance as the basis for the charge: 'The accused was observed by the writer to be sitting on a park bench in — Park, drinking from a can of Labatts 50 ale. The accused continued to drink from this can after the writer instructed him to stop. Subsequently charged Sec 46(2) LLA.'

In handling troublesome situations, any law will do. The fact that the person can be charged with *something* is usually sufficient for the officer's purposes. His legal resources are ample, but his resourcefulness is more important.

A patrol officer joined two other patrol officers to observe a strike picket-line. He talked continually about the need to assert police authority over the picketers, especially those he singled out as potential troublemakers. He spent his time trying to develop charges against these people. His efforts ranged from checking their cars for possible parking violations to requesting a patrol sergeant to charge some picketers in the 'union goon squad' for not wearing seat-belts while driving.

Another officer was dispatched to join approximately 15 other officers at a picket-line where 60 picketers were attempting to block entry to the plant. The picketers were arguing with the police, claiming the police were wrong in acting for management against union interests by allowing 'scabs' to enter the plant. As the shouting continued before the watchful eyes of media representatives, the officer and a sergeant began arguing with one of several vociferous picketers. They decided to select this person and remove him from the situation, hoping that putting him 'in order' would caution the others. This arrest was eased when a CPIC check revealed an outstanding committal warrant of $350 or 30 days against this person. He asked if he could go home and obtain the money but was refused; he was returned to the divisional station where he was also charged for 'causing a disturbance.'

As we have repeatedly stressed, there is a strong tendency to handle interpersonal disputes without charges or official reports. When officers decide charges are necessary, they often choose one that can be laid and prosecuted with police evidence, rather than those directly related to the original complaint and dependent on the testimony of the complainant or witness.

For example, a patrol officer was dispatched to a hotel regarding a 'dispute.' Upon arrival, he learned from the dancer in the hotel lounge that she had been assaulted. At the beginning of her act she turned off a juke-box and started her own music; this angered the customer who had been playing the juke-box, and he threw a chair at her, breaking it against her foot and causing substantial swelling.

The officer interviewed the manager, who appeared reluctant to have the police pursue the matter and did not want them to enter the lounge to talk with the suspect. However, the officer and a back-up proceeded to the lounge and selected a person they knew from previous contacts. They took this person to the hotel office for questioning. The suspect both verbally and physically resisted the officer's efforts and on entering the office smashed a chair. The victim identified this man as the one who had assaulted her, and the officer informed him that he was under arrest for 'cause disturbance.' When the suspect asked 'Who was disturbed?,' the officer replied, 'We were.' The follow-up report made no mention of the dancer's original complaint or the property damage to the chair. It briefly mentioned the accused's 'abusiveness' while he was being questioned about an unspecified complaint.

On another shift, the patrol officer was dispatched to back up another patrol officer at the scene of a reported fight involving six youths. Upon arrival, he discovered a barely conscious woman lying on the floor. He interviewed a witness who said the woman, who was married with children, was out drinking with him, three other men, and another woman; one of the other men began arguing with the victim and his associates after making sexual overtures to the victim. A fight ensued and the one youth kicked and punched the victim and fled. The officers decided to treat the matter as an 'assault occasioning bodily harm.' One escorted the witness back to the divisional station and took a written statement, while the other accompanied the victim to the hospital to learn more about the suspect's identity and to obtain her account of the assault. However, the victim refused to provide any information and said she wanted nothing to do with the police or the hospital. Another officer later located the suspect after a search through a field and charged him for being drunk in a public place under the Liquor Licence Act.

'Substitute' charges were also used in the few domestic conflicts in which officers took formal action.[16] For example, a patrol officer was dispatched with a back-up to the scene of a 'domestic' after a complaint from the culprits' neighbour (see p 164). The wife told one officer that she feared her husband would harm her because he had been smashing up bottles and furniture. She also said that he had previously been charged with common assault on the basis of her complaint. The officer interviewing the husband was later joined by the second officer, who became increasingly aggressive with the husband. This brought on a fight, and the husband was placed under arrest for 'breach of the peace' as a means of removing him from the apartment. He continued to struggle as he was led to the patrol car, and his wife began pushing at the officers and alleging 'police brutality.' She was arrested and subsequently charged on two counts of 'obstruct police officer' – Criminal Code sec 118(1)(a) – while the husband was later charged with assaulting a police officer – Criminal Code sec 246(2)(a). Again, the arrests and charges used to handle the situation were produced by the police.

Patrol officers also use charges to 'lever' suspects into giving information about activities unrelated to the arrest and charge. Again, the pretext for the arrest can be any charge which justifies it, while the reason for the arrest lies elsewhere. For example, an officer parked his patrol car on a residential street and kept surveillance on a house inhabited by a well-known offender (see p 88). He knew the citizen was a drug offender prohibited from driving. The suspect eventually did come out of the house and drive the car about 20 yards before parking it. The officer immediately drove up to the suspect and at the same time called for back-up assistance.

Upon approaching the suspect, the officer stated, 'Well, well, well, Detective — will be pleased to see you.' The suspect initially denied any offence and then made several appeals to the officers, offering them money to turn a blind eye to the matter and asking if they would consider beating him up in lieu of charging him. The officers spurned these suggestions, but became interested when the suspect offered names of drug users and suppliers. As the suspect provided names, the officers kept stating that this was not enough, and that they were after 'traffickers.' They then told the suspect that he was being arrested for driving while prohibited. They handcuffed him, placed him in the rear-seat 'cage,' and arranged for his car to be impounded.

On the way to the station the suspect was continually threatened with other charges and told that his vehicle would be impounded 'permanently' if he refused to produce further information about drug dealers. Upon arrival at the station, he was turned over to the detective referred to at the beginning of the encounter. According to the patrol officer, the detective was successful in having the suspect 'agree' to be an informant in exchange for no charges being laid. In this encounter, the officers created the role of informant for the suspect by proactively producing the 'drive while prohibited' charge as a lever. Although no charges were ultimately laid, the officer wrote up a 'motor vehicle report' regarding the seizure of the car and a 'record of arrest' which, among other things, accounted for the detention of the suspect. The arrest report made no mention of the suspect's role as informant as being the primary basis of the transaction. It was constructed to hint that the suspect had given a legitimate excuse for driving, although this was not directly tied in as the justification for not charging: 'On [date and time] the accused was observed driving east on [street]. When approached by police the accused readily admitted driving and the fact that he had no licence as it had been suspended. Accused states that the car had broken down while his girl was driving and after had only parked it properly as it was sitting out on the road. And he thought it would be alright. No charges laid at this time.'

Arresting suspects and threatening charges as a 'lever' is also a technique employed to have them turn informant on their accomplices. Lacking other facts, patrol officers use these informants to produce the facts needed to justify charging their accomplices. For example, two patrol officers were dispatched to a high-rise apartment residence to assist a man locked out of his apartment on the balcony. After assisting him they returned to their patrol cars and discovered eggs splattered over the hood of one car. They looked up and noticed two people peering from an apartment balcony, but decided to take no action.

An hour later, one of the officers was dispatched along with a sergeant regarding beer bottles being thrown from a balcony at the same address. Upon arrival, the officers were bombarded with full beer bottles being thrown from a balcony several stories up. The sergeant called for two more back-up officers. Upon their arrival, the officers entered the building and obtained the key to the unit in question from the superintendent. They entered the apartment and arrested four of the five occupants: two youths aged 18 and 19 and two juveniles aged 14 and 15. The fifth occupant, a woman who apparently lived in the apartment, was not asked to leave.

All four suspects denied responsibility. They were all told they were under arrest for 'criminal negligence,' and were returned to the divisional station in separate patrol cars. At the station, the officers had the two juveniles turn informant on the two youths, one of whom was a well-known offender the officers seemed particularly eager to charge. The juveniles gave written and signed witness statements against the two youths and were turned over to their parents. The two youths were ultimately charged with 'common nuisance' (Criminal Code sec 176).

In writing up the records of arrest on this incident, the officer referred to the juvenile suspects' 'co-operation' in providing statements. While all four suspects denied the offence, the two juveniles' denials were accepted as justifications for no charges. The two youths' denials were countered by the statements of the juveniles, which were used as evidence in charging the youths:

[Suspect's name] was arrested and returned to — Division. At the
station, [the suspect] admitted being in the apartment at the time of the
incident. Further, he co-operated with us in giving a witness statement which
incriminated [names two youths].

It is felt by the writer that no charges should be laid due to the fact that
this [juvenile] did not throw any bottles. This [juvenile] realizes that he
should not associate with the two accused parties. [The suspect] was turned
over to his parents who were made aware of the situation and appeared
genuinely concerned. They advised that they would take matters in hand. It
is unlikely that this [juvenile] will be in any future trouble with the police ...

[Record of arrest, juvenile suspect 1]

[The suspect] was arrested and returned to — Division. At the station, [the
suspect] admitted being in the apartment at the time of the incident. Further,
after some discussion, [the suspect] was co-operative in giving a statement
incriminating [the two youths]. This youth was not directly involved in the
incident and thus it is felt no charges should be laid.

[The suspect's] mother attended — Division and was made aware of
the situation. She advised that she would ensure that [the suspect] would be
made aware of the error of his ways and that he would not be involved with
Police again.

[Record of arrest, juvenile suspect 2]

In the record concerning juvenile suspect 1, the officer spoke of the 'fact' that this [juvenile] did not throw any bottles. The evidence for this 'fact' was apparently nothing more than the officer's strategic acceptance of the suspect's denial as fact. Written statements by the two juveniles were used to construct facts against them.

In summary, patrol officers sometimes find it appropriate to use the criminal law to reproduce order. Such occasions are relatively rare, and their occurrence certainly does not indicate that the officers' primary task is criminal-law enforcement. Rather, the law is occasionally invoked because it comes in handy as an enabling device to assert order. While some people are selected out and others are ignored, all are reminded of the 'order of things.'

As we documented in chapter 5, patrol officers have great interpretive latitude. In ordering their lives, and the lives of others, they can choose to ignore possible criminal-law violations, charge some persons and not others, charge for particular things and not others, and produce some facts while ignoring others. These decisions fundamentally affect what becomes officially known as police business and what the courts are able to do with their business.

While patrol officers produce charges to handle immediate troubles, they are also half-watching in terms of another show. That show is the production of outcomes in court. They realize that they will be monitored in this show, and their charging practices reflect their desire to give a commanding performance.

Charging and the Production of Court Outcomes

As noted previously (chapter 3), patrol officers frequently have their cases worked on, or even taken over, by more senior officers and/or detectives when criminal charges are laid. However, along with their more senior colleagues, they can influence the production at the court stage by the way they construct the 'facts' that come to stand for the reality of the case, by the charges laid, and by pre-trial dealings with the defence lawyer and crown attorney.

As recorded in Table 6.13, 79 persons 'further processed' were charged on one or more counts under the Narcotics Control Act – all sec 3(1) possession offences – and/or the Criminal Code. We were able to follow 73 of these people to the point of court disposition using data from the research program of which the present study is a part.[17]

The cases of these 73 indicate that in the majority of instances, charges are laid in the expectation they will be altered at the court stage. Once they have decided to charge, officers and their colleagues charge everyone possible with everything possible as an initial 'levering' position from which they and the crown attorney can work out a pre-trial plea settlement with the accused and/or the accused's lawyer. Alteration to the charges becomes the norm during pre-trial deliberations.

Data supporting this view are presented in Tables 6.17 and 6.18. As documented in Table 6.17, among the 73 accused only 28 (38 per cent) had their charges unaltered, 1 had a more severe charge, 3 a less severe, and 41 (56 per cent) had one or more charges withdrawn. The data in both tables suggest that 'charging up' categories, leading the crown attorney and/or judge to reduce them, was infrequent; multiple and/or questionable charging leading to withdrawals was common.[18]

TABLE 6.17

Change in charges after originally being laid by police up to court determination of guilt or innocence for accused persons charged under the Criminal Code and Narcotics Control Act

Change in charges		N	%
No changes		28	38.5
Charge category increased		1	1.4
Charge category reduced		3	4.1
Number of charges withdrawn:	One	22	30.1
	Two	10	13.7
	Three	2	2.7
	Four	2	2.7
	Five	1	1.4
	Six	2	2.7
	Seven	2	2.7
Totals		73	100.0

TABLE 6.18

Plea, change in charge(s), and finding for accused persons charged under the Criminal Code and Narcotics Control Act

	N (=73)	%	Cumulative percentage
Guilty as originally charged	15	20.4	20.4
Guilty to some charge(s) after other charge(s) withdrawn	28	38.3	58.7
Guilty to reduced charge	1	1.4	60.1
Guilty to one charge after withdrawal of others; not guilty to one charge and found guilty	1	1.4	61.5
Not guilty to one charge and found guilty	5	6.8	68.3
Not guilty to one charge and found guilty to lesser included offence	2	2.7	71.0
Not guilty to one charge and found guilty after other charges withdrawn	1	1.4	72.4
Not guilty to two charges and found guilty to one charge after other charge dismissed	3	4.1	76.5
Not guilty to all charge(s) and all charge(s) dismissed	4	5.5	82.1
Not guilty to two charges and found not guilty to one charge after other charge dismissed	1	1.4	83.5
Not guilty to one charge and charge ultimately withdrawn	4	5.5	89.0
Not guilty–accused failed to appear for subsequent hearing and bench warrant outstanding	1	1.4	90.4
No plea–charge(s) withdrawn	7	9.6	100.0

'Charging up' in anticipation of reduction to lower categories in exchange for guilty pleas was not frequent among the cases in the follow-up sample. In one case the crown attorney decreased the charge: the suspect was originally charged with 'fail to remain at the scene of an accident' under

Criminal Code sec 233(2), and the crown attorney reduced the charge to come under the 'fail to remain' provisions of the Highway Traffic Act. In another case, the two accused both went to trial under the 'cause disturbance' provisions of the Criminal Code, sec 17(a)(iii), and were eventually found guilty by the trial judge for the lesser (included) offence of 'attempt cause disturbance.' It is highly unlikely the police anticipated this reduction. As we have previously observed, 'cause disturbance' charges were already vaguely constructed out of problematic 'order maintenance' situations; for patrol officers to have constructed 'attempt cause disturbance' charges the definition would have to be even more vague (although the order-maintenance function of charging would obviously have been served). In other words, this case was handled by the trial judge in an idiosyncratic manner and is not indicative of police 'charging up' practices.

In Table 6.18 we show the range of alterations in charges that took place in relation to the plea and finding for each accused person. Seven accused had all their charges withdrawn without entering a plea; 4 had the one charge against them withdrawn after they entered a plea of not guilty; 1 had charges withdrawn after pleading not guilty and was found guilty on one other charge; 1 pleaded guilty to one charge after other charges were withdrawn and pleaded not guilty to another charge and was found guilty; and 28 pleaded guilty to some charge(s) after other charge(s) were withdrawn. Overall, 62 per cent entered a plea of guilty and were found guilty on at least one charge, 14 per cent were found guilty on something after entering not-guilty pleas, and 24 per cent were able to avoid a registered conviction altogether.

Several factors lead officers to try multiple charges even though they know that a large number of the charges will be withdrawn. First, the police organization uses, as one measure of its collective performance, the number of offences cleared by charge. If there are charges laid against every possible person for every possible offence, this rate is obviously improved. Not incidentally, the personal credit rating of the individual patrol officer is also improved by laying many charges against many persons.

Second, the goal of convicting the offender is more likely to be achieved if there are a number of charges available from which to 'lever' a guilty plea. As we have learned in our previous analyses, the patrol officer's concern is less often with the specific offences charged than with the fact that the charges laid serve to assert control over a troublesome individual. In this light, officers are content to get a conviction on *something* (although not just *anything*) among a number of charges they have laid.

Third, multiple charges provide a good framework from which to begin discussions of a pre-trial plea agreement. As Alschuler (1968) states, 'The charge is the asking price in plea bargaining, and the drafting of accusations is therefore an integral part of the negotiating process.' If we define 'plea bargaining' as 'any agreement by the accused to plead guilty in return for the promise of some benefit' (Law Reform Commission of Canada, 1975: 45), the withdrawal of charges will perhaps be seen as a benefit which will at least reduce the accused's conviction record and might also reduce the sentence.[19] It is to the advantage of the police to avoid a full trial: the officer avoids the extra work needed to prepare an acceptable brief for the crown attorney, subpoena witnesses, and appear in court (cf Martin and Wilson, 1969; Laurie, 1970; Ericson, 1981). A guilty plea confirms the wisdom of earlier decisions to arrest and charge and prevents the propriety of police decisions from being called into question during a trial.

The criminal law, and the organization of the pre-trial discussion process, have enabling elements which allow the police to be assured that multiple charging and related practices are not challenged. The police thus have considerable control over outcomes from the contacting of suspects through to the court disposition of cases.[20]

The criminal law enables the police to lay multiple charges even if convictions cannot be sustained legally on more than one count. There have been a number of legal cases dealing with questions of multiple convictions arising out of the same circumstances. None of these cases seems to question seriously the propriety of laying additional charges at the outset. Rather, it is a question of them being *alternative* charges in which conviction can be sustained for one *or* the other, but not both. This was clearly put by Laskin in *Kienapple* v *The Queen* (1974) 15 CCC (2d) 524, in which the appellant was originally convicted of both rape and unlawful sexual intercourse with a female under 14 years for the same incident of sexual assault.[21]

In relation to 'drinking and driving' situations, it was held in *R.* v *Houchen* – 1976 31 CCC (2d) 274, 71 DLR (3d) 739, 5 WWR 182 – that a person could be convicted either of impaired driving or over 80 mg, but not both, because both charges arose out of the same cause or matter and thus should be viewed as alternative charges. Again, this is not saying that it is not legitimate to lay both charges; indeed, it invites multiple charging in order to ensure that if there is an acquittal on one charge the second can be used as a back-up to secure a conviction.

Another practice in multiple charging is to charge for both an illegal act and possession of items connected with that act, e.g. 'theft' and 'possession of stolen property.' Police officers can use the 'possession' charge as a back-up with solid evidence in case the main charge is successfully challenged. For example, if 'theft' cannot be proven then the stolen property seized can be used to obtain a possession conviction. Prior to 1955, the offence relating to stolen property was 'receiving or retaining' stolen property, and the prevailing view was that courts could not convict for both theft and receiving because one could not receive what one had stolen. In 1955, the offence was changed to 'possession' of stolen property, but the courts continued to use the same analogy in holding that a person could not be convicted for both theft and possession of the property taken in the theft, e.g. *R.* v *Siggins* (1960) 127 CCC 409. However, in a 1974 ruling by the Supreme Court of Canada – *Côté* v *The Queen* (1974) 18 CCC (2d) 321 – it was held that the reasoning in *Siggins* and earlier cases was not applicable under the new 'possession of stolen property' provisions of the Criminal Code because the offence of possession was markedly different from the former offence of receiving or retaining stolen property. In *Côté*, the Supreme Court legitimated the possibility of conviction for both theft and possession of the property taken in the theft. If the person continues to keep the item he has stolen, he can be convicted for both theft and possession.

The criminal law enables multiple-charging practices. The organization of pre-trial discussions enables the police to have some control over which charges will result in convictions and which ones will be dispensed with as an apparent concession in exchange for guilty pleas.

As Klein (1976) has pointed out, the police are very often involved in plea discussions. Our data also indicate that this is the case. However, patrol officers tend to be less involved than detectives.[22] Many criminal cases which patrol officers initially develop are taken over by detectives for further investigation and processing of the accused. When patrol officers alone are involved in bringing a case to court, the charges are either minor (e.g. causing a disturbance, a 'possession' charge under Narcotics Control Act sec 3[1], theft under $200, 'shoplifting') or involve driving-related charges (e.g. impaired and/or over 80 mg, or impaired and/or refusal to provide a breath sample).

Police officers are involved in plea discussions with the accused, the defence lawyer, and/or the crown attorney at the court stage because of their familiarity with the case and its construction. At the provincial-court level, crown attorneys often are not well informed about a case because they often do not receive the case until the morning of the court appearance. Moreover, if the case goes through several court appearances, the same crown attorney frequently does not stay with the case but passes it on to whomever is handling the cases for the courtroom that case comes up in the next time around. As a result, crown attorneys often defer to police assessments of the case and to police judgments about what combination of charge reductions, charge withdrawals, and sentencing recommendations would make an appropriate settlement. Moreover, lawyers tend to consult with the police to 'make a deal' because they know the police officer is better informed about the case and that he is in a position to influence the crown attorney.[23]

While in theory the crown attorney can still inquire deeply into how the police produced the charges and constructed the facts, in practice he is very unlikely to do so. Moreover, since this arrangement helps to produce plea settlements without a full trial, there is unlikely to be any inquiry from the judge (cf Grosman, 1969; Klein, 1976; Law Reform Commission of Canada,

1976). In sum, *the* truth about a case and the charges involved in it are usually synonymous with the *police* version of the truth.

This situation is of major consequence for what happens at the court stage. The police maintain and perpetuate a positional advantage (Cook, 1977) among the organizations of criminal control. This allows them to reorder the assumed hierarchy of control which ideally places the judge at the pinnacle followed by the crown attorney and then the police (Heydebrand, 1977). The police gain this advantage through their control over knowledge and through the need for this knowledge in order to proceed without the constant disruption that would come from systematic questioning. 'Both the pre-trial procedure and what goes on in court represent a kind of dishonest game – everyone knows that the situation being described is not *quite* what happened, but somehow because the game is played within certain rules, it is accepted' (Morris, 1978: 30; see generally Carlen, 1976). Since one of the basic ways to control what rules and attendant sanctions are applicable is through control over the production of meaning,[24] the police have considerable de facto power to produce outcomes that are in conformity with their own organizational interests.

This is not to say that the police are omnipotent. Rather, they are structurally able to 'frame' the charges and attendant 'facts' in a way which creates a strong propensity for the other actors in the process to accept them. What is then left to discuss is a tinkering with the details. This tinkering is worked out in pre-trial discussions according to a web of relationships among police officers, lawyers, crown attorneys, and judges.[25] The 'bargain' – if one can call it that – is to plead to 'over 80 mg' and have the 'impaired' withdrawn; to have five superfluous theft charges withdrawn instead of three, or four; to plead guilty to possession of stolen property and have the charge for theft of that property withdrawn.

From the police viewpoint, the practice of multiple charging followed by a plea discussion and settlement is useful for all parties. It allows the officer to get his charges, the crown attorney to avoid 'compromising his convictions,' and the lawyer to assure his client that 'justice' has been done (although not seen to be done because the client is usually excluded from plea discussions – see Ericson and Baranek, 1982), through the justification that he has apparently 'got off' at least something. It is because they see the court process as functional in this way that police officers become upset on the relatively infrequent occasions when their charges and attendant decisions are called into question by one of the other participants (Reiss, 1971: 135; Wilson, 1968: 52). They do not expect the rules of the organizational game to be upset just because there has been a minor – and to the police, irrelevant – bending of rules or overcharging of an accused who is seen as 'obviously' guilty.

In sum, there are enabling features in both the law and the organization of the court which allow the police to produce multiple charges aimed at securing plea settlements that serve their own organizational interests. The following detailed case examples illustrate the process at work.

A patrol officer was dispatched to the residence of a victim who reported a $100 theft of meat from his freezer as well as damage to his freezer. After interviewing the victim, the officer stated that the suspects probably resided in an adjacent townhouse (he believed 'undesirable' persons associated with a motorcycle group lived there). The officer seemed particularly anxious to pursue the investigation to 'get at' these people and therefore decided to develop further information on them through interviewing the superintendent of the townhouse complex.

The superintendent reported that he had been trying for a long time to evict the residents of the townhouse in question, as the original tenant had sublet it and the individual whom he sublet it to had in turn gone, leaving several 'boisterous' friends as residents. When the superintendent discovered that it would take three months to secure an eviction he went to a justice to obtain a private-information charge for 'trespass.' The superintendent asked the officer if he would serve the private-information summons and also arrange to have the occupants' car towed away. The officer obliged, seeing this as a means of gaining entry for his own investigations.

The officer's first strategy to contact the suspects in the townhouse was to ask the researcher to pose as a board of education officer inquiring if there were any school-aged children resident there. However, there was no response after ringing the doorbell, and the officer concluded that no one was in. Another patrol officer appeared and reported that the suspects' residence was directly across the hall from her own residence. The investigating officer then asked the second officer if she had ever smelled marijuana coming from the suspect residence, and when he received an affirmative reply he exclaimed, '*Now* we have grounds for a search warrant!'

The officer returned to the divisional station and obtained the sergeant's permission to take out a search warrant regarding narcotics in the residence. Joined by a patrol sergeant and four other officers, the officer obtained the key from the superintendent and conducted a 40-minute search, which revealed a few shreads of marijuana, cigarette papers, and roach clips. In the mean time, the patrol officer learned that one of the occupants had been arrested the previous night for 'causing a disturbance' and was being detained in the divisional police cells.

After the search, the patrol officer received a radio call stating that occupants of the townhouse had just arrived at the divisional station and were attempting to arrange for the release of their friend who was being detained there. The patrol officer immediately returned to the station and confronted one of the persons, asking him if he had 'ever been in trouble.' The man replied he had a record for theft and for possession of marijuana. The patrol officer then told him that he was under arrest for theft. A woman and another male member of the party, as well as the suspect in the cells, were all treated as suspects for the theft and the marijuana found in the townhouse.

Separate interrogations produced information that in addition to having stolen the meat, the suspects were also in possession of a further small amount of marijuana, as well as a tape deck and two tennis racquets that were apparently stolen property. The patrol officer took one of the suspects and seized these items from their hiding spot under a car and then obtained and executed a search warrant to recover the stolen meat from a freezer at a residence belonging to a friend of the suspects.

The patrol officers decided to charge all four suspects. One suspect admitted to theft of the tape deck and was also charged with possession of this and the other stolen property (meat) (accused 1). One admitted to possession of the marijuana and was also charged with two counts in relation to the stolen property (accused 2). One was charged on two counts in relation to the stolen property (accused 3). The suspect who had been arrested the previous night for 'cause disturbance' was also charged across a range of other available offences ('theft under,' 'attempt theft,' 'possession of marijuana'), but not with possession of stolen property (accused 4).

As the case reached court, the patrol officer indicated to the lawyer representing accused 4, the lawyer representing accused 1 and accused 2,[26] and to the crown attorney, that he was content to have each accused plead guilty to one charge on a 'take your pick' basis. In the crown attorney's office before the beginning of court on the trial date, the patrol officer (PO) chatted with the provincial court crown attorney (CA):

PO: I think there's going to be some pleas on that anyhow.
CA: On this?
PO: I think so, I think we'll see if we can take ...
CA: We've got pretty good statements.
PO: Oh statements, they're dead on it the whole works ah ...
CA: Yeah ...
PO: *I think we can get one charge apiece out of them or something, wiggle it around* [emphasis added].
CA: Well that's ah [accused 4] on theft.
PO: Yeah, [accused 4] is dead on the theft and attempt theft.
CA: Yeah.
PO: Ah ... and the cause disturbance.
CA: Right.
PO: Ah ... [accused 2] is dead on the ah ... possession of the grass.
CA: Yeah.
PO: And ah ... [accused 3] is good for any of the possessions 'cause he carried the stuff up to his place, eh?
CA: Yeah.

PO: And [accused 1] is good for the theft of the tape deck.
CA: Yeah.
PO: I was talking to one of the counsel ah ... for [accused 1] and, ah, as far as he was concerned he was going to try to plead guilty to one or both of them.
CA: Yeah.

After court started and during a recess period, the lawyers talked in the hallway with the crown attorney and patrol officer about a negotiated settlement. The lawyer for accused 4 stated that his client would plead guilty to 'cause disturbance' and 'theft under,' adding that the 'attempt theft' charge was a duplicate (lesser included offence) charge and that there was not sufficient evidence to sustain the Narcotics Control Act charge. The patrol officer interjected that the 'attempt theft' pertained to a theft of meat separate from the 'theft' charge, but added that he was nevertheless agreeable to the plea agreement.

In a later interview with a researcher, the lawyer for accused 4 stated that the 'attempt theft' *or* the 'theft' should have been charged, but not both, and added that this was an example of over-charging by the police. The lawyer also stated that his client should not have been charged under the Narcotics Control Act because the marijuana was found in a bedroom that was not occupied by his client. The lawyer added that in his view, this case illustrated the 'broadside' technique of police charging. He defined this technique as 'slap[ping] the accused with everything and hope that he will plead to something.'

During the recess, the crown attorney and patrol officer also spoke with the counsel for accused 1 and accused 2. In relation to accused 2, the lawyer indicated that his client would plead guilty to one Narcotics Control Act charge, and the crown attorney said he should speak to the federal crown attorney to arrange this. The patrol officer said he would be willing to have the two charges for possession of stolen property withdrawn on this accused since one of the co-accused 'would take them.' In relation to accused 1, the parties readily agreed to a guilty plea on one count of possession of stolen property (regarding the seized tape-deck) in exchange for a withdrawal of the other possession-of-stolen-property charge and the 'theft under $200' charge.

The research interview with the lawyer for accused 1 and accused 2 reveals the lawyer's view that the charges were 'obviously' open for discussion and that the patrol officer was clearly content to obtain a conviction on any one charge against each accused:

> The only part that in a sense disturbed me about the information the police had was with respect to [accused 2], that they had lumped in some narcotics that they found elsewhere and were trying to slough it off as though they had been found in her residence – until you pressed them, you discovered that it was from somewhere else.
>
> ...
>
> [The lawyer mentions that it was the patrol officer who first contacted him about a possible plea settlement].

[We] discussed, to a certain extent, what he was looking for which was quite nominal. He was looking for basically a plea to something from each of the parties and it then became my task to determine whether or not there should be a plea by both [clients]. [Accused 1], they had his fingerprints and he knew it, so there was obviously – he was going to get caught with either theft or possession. With [Accused 2] the linkage was not nearly so good.

...

[What] had happened and what usually happens in most of the criminal cases I have, is that you will find out what the police officer is prepared to recommend and if he recommends it then there's usually no problem with the crown. Now there are cases where the crown will say 'No,' he'll think you're taking advantage of him. But you usually don't have a chance to speak with the crown as readily as with the police officer. I think you have to start with the police officer. The police officer recommended it so really it was no problem.

The researcher (R) next asked the lawyer (L):

R: How was it that you managed to get the crown to withdraw the one theft under and one possession under [against accused 1]?

L: All right. The theft under was related to the 8-track stereo or whatever it was –

R: That he pled to ...

L: That he pled to on the possession.[27] On the other charge which was the possession of the meat, there was a defence to it – as to whether the defence would be successful or not is a different matter – but the police officer accepted the evidence that neither [accused 1] nor [accused 2] had anything to do with the actual theft of the meat and their sole role was to take it from a freezer somewhere else where the freezer was working. Now they had to communicate with [accused 4] with respect to that meat and the police were able to verify that through their investigations, so that I think they took the position that it was a pretty inactive part of the crime.

R: In retrospect, then, what factors would you suggest in this case made it negotiable?

L: Well, I think the main factor was that the police had statements which implicated all four people one way or another. A second core factor was that you had an officer who was not vindictive, that he wanted to make certain that there were convictions against each of the people but without trying to overload it, especially in view of the fact that [accused 2] had not had a record in the past and [accused 1]'s record was four to five years old I think ...

Another example of this process is provided from a case which developed after a patrol officer was called to the scene of 'thefts in progress' at an apartment underground garage. Upon apprehending four suspects there, ten theft charges, one possession-of-stolen-property charge, and one mischief charge were laid against each suspect. As the case proceeded to court, the detective who conducted follow-up investigations on the accused after they were arrested by the patrol officer took an active part in producing a plea settlement. As a result of plea discussions involving the detective, defence lawyers, and the crown attorney, one accused entered guilty pleas on five counts of 'theft under $200,' and three accused each entered guilty pleas on five counts of 'theft under $200' and on one count of 'possession of stolen property over $200.'

In this case, accused 2 and accused 3 each had his own separate lawyer, while accused 1 and accused 4 retained the same lawyer. In separate interviews with a researcher, all three lawyers were of the opinion that the patrol officer laid as many charges as possible in a somewhat questionable manner, and that from the outset the task before them was to 'dicker' with the crown attorney and detective for withdrawal of some charges in exchange for guilty pleas on others.

> [Lawyer for accused 1 and accused 4]:
> I personally feel that they should have been charged with one count of theft over and one count of possession over, and perhaps a count of mischief ... I just don't understand exactly why they would go on ten counts [of theft]. It's one, it was one transaction. It's like somebody grabbing a bag of money that's got $50 in pennies in it and charging them with 50 separate counts of theft under ...
>
> ...
>
> [Lawyer for accused 2]:
> Oh I think the police were justified in charging him with them all but as a practical matter I think they could well have charged fewer counts. Once you get to that many, it's sort of meaningless. I think that they could have laid one general charge against him, and for that matter, the others, of stealing articles, various articles, property of various persons. That would have been one count as it was really one transaction on that evening when they were caught in the garage.
>
> R: Why do you think they chose to do it this way?
> L: Oh it looks more impressive. But it's really one theft on that evening at that place.
>
> [Later, in response to questions about plea discussions] ... I asked them how many convictions they wanted and I know they like numbers – whether it was one or five counts, it didn't mean a thing. It should have been one count because it was all one transaction ...
>
> I knew it wouldn't make any difference in the sentence anyways. But the accused might think it's great ...
>
> In retrospect, the negotiation was only to the extent of the number of counts that he was to plead guilty to. I think that I made it clear that it was really only one count. So it was meaningless. It was just a play of numbers or words.
>
> ...

[Lawyer for accused 3]:

[after stating that the 'mischief' and 'possession' charges were legitimate]: The other ten charges of theft under, these I, the police use this tactic, you know – hit 'em with so many and negotiate. You know, negotiate out so you drop out some ... We probably could have successfully defended at least four or five of them ... They were charging them with theft of those items even though they didn't, couldn't link it to anybody. There was about three or four other items that they could not link with any particular individual but of course the crown would have ... started off with their strongest one and they would have worked down from there and to their weaker ones and would have ended up with ... conceivably ten mini-trials or twelve mini-trials with at least ten of theft under ... Somebody, particularly my client having no previous record or anything like that ... if he does run into problems again, even if they may be of a minor nature again, they'll look at his record sheet and it'll be a full sheet even though it was virtually taken from the one offence. It's similar to if you want to charge a bank robber going into a bank and charge him for each till he cleans out, charge him with a theft over of each till he cleans out.

R: It was the same incident.

L: Yeah ... there might have been two theft overs or something like that instead of these multiplicity of charges of theft unders ... The police have a great habit ... of charging you with as many things as possible and in hoping you're going to negotiate some of them off and plead guilty to the others to save – I don't know – to save their time and their investigation because this course would have meant a lot of investigation for them and summonsing in a number of witnesses to get them all in.

In approaching the question of plea discussions, the lawyers separately contacted the detective at various points prior to the trial date to obtain disclosure and an indication of the detective's willingness to discuss a plea settlement. The lawyer for accused 1 and accused 4 mistakenly believed that the 'possession' charge was laid in relation to the property taken in all of the alleged thefts, rather than for a separate item admitted by his clients to have been stolen in an earlier theft in another jurisdiction. Based on this mistaken assumption, this lawyer approached the crown attorney and requested that all charges be withdrawn except for the 'possession' charge, to which his clients would plead guilty. In the crown attorney's office, the lawyer stated, 'As I say, we're ready to go with that, with a plea to the possession over, all these goods are ...' At this point the crown attorney interjected, 'Yeah, well I'm going to have to get the detective here, 'cause I'm not buying that at all.'

The lawyer engaged in an argument with the crown attorney, but then realized his mistake and decided it would be better to have the lawyer for accused 3 seek a plea settlement.

[Lawyer for accused 1 and accused 4 in research interview]:

I just spoke before I thought, but in any event I then went and spoke to the police officer because I had alienated myself from the crown and I didn't want that to hinder my client. So I told [lawyer for accused 3] to speak with the crown – 'I'll stay out of the picture and I'll speak with the investigating officer'. [The investigating officer] more or less said that he was amenable to anything the crown thought was reasonable under the circumstances. I told him ... I didn't expect any pleas that they might take or any charges they might withdraw in any way to affect the outcome of this proceeding ... I indicated that they could read the entire circumstances so the judge knows the whole deal. It's just in the interest of the future it just seemed to me that [the withdrawals wouldn't] give him quite so many strikes and it really did arise out of one occassion, you know, and yet someone looking at that sheet would just get the feeling like, 'gosh you know,' and it really all took place in half an hour.

The lawyer (L) for accused 3 proceeded to talk with the crown attorney (CA) and the detective (D) about a plea settlement. As indicated by the following discussion in the crown attorney's office, the crown attorney was still hesitant about the withdrawal of several charges, but the detective indicated his willingness to settle:

D: How many of these do you want?

CA: Well that's what I want to talk to you about. They [lawyers] are suggesting now a plea to six counts of theft.

D: The mischief, I'm not worried about, but I'll take the six thefts and that possession because that's an [town out of jurisdiction] situation and I think we should have that in there. He had taken that prior to coming to [this jurisdiction].

CA: Which six thefts are you talking about?

D: Well, this, exclude that one 'cause he says that's his, so I'm going to get some kind of proof on him before I turn it back. So one through four, six and seven, eh? They are all similar in value, they are all under [$200]. But I think that possession should be in there because that's a situation [town out of jurisdiction].

L: No I think it's [another town].

D: As far as I know there were no charges laid by [the police in that jurisdiction]. They came down and talked to the guy [accused] to see if they had done anything else in that area, but I don't think they had.

L: On that possesssion over, you ought to get the value for the thing, the wrench.

Second Detective: There isn't a possession over is there?

D: Oh yeah, for the 'over, that was worth quite a bit of dough.

CA: That's the [describes item in detail].

L: I didn't even notice that, yeah.

D: It was a valuable piece of equipment.

CA: As far as I'm concerned, you've got evidence on all ten of them?

D: Well I've got the property and I've got most of the victims. I can't exactly say which ones, like I turned back [some property], probably thinking that it was all over, I turned back one of his radios.

CA: He's still got the radios.

D: That was just two days ago. And this chap here [accused 2] is asking for a remand 'cause he's on his third lawyer or fourth lawyer.

CA: Yeah, except that it's the same lawyer he's got. It's [names lawyer].

D: He's from [another city] or something like that.

[the CA is called to a courtroom]

D: I don't want to hang these guys but you know I think that that possession is ...

CA: Yeah, well he's [lawyer] suggesting six [thefts] and one possession.

L: Is that what you're saying, six and one possession?

D: I think that definitely should be included because ...

L: How about five and one?

At this point the settlement was worked out in detail. Accused 1, accused 3, and accused 4 each entered guilty pleas to five 'theft under' charges and one 'possession over' charge on this date, while accused 2 had his case remanded because his lawyer was not present. The lawyer (L) for accused 3, who was involved in the above discussion, provided a researcher (R) with a retrospective account of his discussions with the detective and crown attorney:

L: I eventually ended up doing the negotiation and it became just a numbers game – how many you're going to knock off ...

R: In terms of disclosure, did you get most of the disclosure you wanted and need from the police officers or most of it from the crown, or was it a combination of both?

L: Got most of it from the police officer and a little bit from the crown, but it's the type of situation where a lot of time the crowns haven't looked at the sheet until they've walked in that day and they really don't know much about it. [In contrast] the police officer has been following the case from day one and they've got a little more insight into what happened and what it's all about ...

R: The five 'theft unders' were most provable, is that the way it turned out?

L: It became, yeah the most probable ones ... We more or less just went from one down but we knocked out the ones that actually [belonged to the other accused] There was a couple, I think, one in there that the police might have difficulty proving but it doesn't make any difference ... Number seven they could have proved because they had the person that owned that tape deck and number three they didn't have the person. So it did, it became a numbers game. Most of it, the crown discussed it with ... the investigating officer and said OK and it became a numbers game – how many you going to knock off –

R: So was the detective there when you had the discussion?

L: Yeah, when he came down to the final – you know, how many we were going to plead to and how many –

R: And what role would you say he played in these discussions?

L: Oh, I'd say he was running, it looked like he was almost running the show at that time and the crown just did – whatever he [the detective] was happy with they were going to take.

While lawyers stated critically in interview that the police charged regularly for everything possible against as many persons as possible, they accepted this practice as part of the organization of criminal control. In an isolated case where extra charges filtered into the trial process, a judge did have occasion to object.[28] However, in most cases the extra charges had been withdrawn and the judge did not inquire into the reasons for the withdrawals.

As indicated by the cases we have discussed, the various parties expect that there will be a withdrawal of some charge(s). The plea discussion simply involved a working out of the details, confirming mutual expectations about what is just and justifiable in a case of the particular type before them. Much of the process operates on a taken-for-granted basis and involves routine confirmation rather than prolonged negotiation; for further examples, see Ericson (1981), Ericson and Baranek (1982).

Of course, many cases do not involve either multiple offenders or the possibility of a large number of multiple offences. However, when multiple charges are possible the practice of charging 'automatically' for as much as possible and then tinkering with the details during plea discussions remains the same. For example, it is standard procedure to charge for both 'impaired' (driving, or care and control) and 'over 80 mg' on the breathalyser. Since legally one charge must be withdrawn upon conviction for the other, the plea discussions centre on which charge will be withdrawn. Most defence lawyers prefer a plea of guilty on 'over 80 mg' because it is viewed as less serious even though it carries the same penalty. In eight cases, three pleaded to 'over 80 mg,' four pleaded guilty to 'impaired,' and one pleaded not guilty and had the case dismissed. Similarly, it is standard procedure to charge for both 'impaired' and refusal to give a breathalyser sample. In this situation it is legally possible to obtain a conviction on both counts. In four cases, two accused were convicted on both counts while two accused were convicted on refusing to give a breathalyser sample only.

It is highly likely that a conviction will be registered, although what the conviction will be on is open to the forum of pre-trial plea discussions. For example, an accused who pleaded guilty to refusal to provide a breath sample while the impaired-driving charge was withdrawn had a lawyer who persisted in making this settlement. The lawyer initially obtained the patrol officer's agreement, but the crown attorney balked. The case was then put over until the afternoon, by which time, according to the lawyer, the patrol officer was anxious to get home because it was his day off and the crown attorney was anxious to clear his cases because he had an airplane to catch within a short time. The crown attorney changed his mind and accepted the agreement that had originally been proposed by the lawyer and patrol officer.

In another case, the accused and his privately retained lawyer decided it would be advantageous to enter guilty pleas to both impaired care and control and refusal to provide a breath sample because of circumstances they became aware of upon their arrival in court. The accused had previous convictions for impaired driving, and he was facing a mandatory jail term if convicted this time. The initial strategy of the lawyer was to obtain a remand in order to allow time for a defence to be developed. However, upon arrival in court he learned that the crown attorney had no knowledge of the accused's previous record. He therefore decided to have his client plead guilty to both counts as a 'first offender.' Moreover, in order to convey the impression to the judge that the accused was poor (i.e. too poor to hire his own lawyer), the lawyer arranged for a duty counsel to make the representations regarding sentence. The accused was fined $250 for impaired care and control and $50 for refusal to provide a breath sample.

In summary, the charges available to patrol officers provide a framework which predictably ensures that convictions will be forthcoming, although what the conviction will be on and its link to sentencing are open to situated elements and discussion among the police, lawyer, and crown attorney. Moreover, the police have considerable input into these plea discussions.

The fact that 17 of 73 accused were not ultimately convicted (see Table 6.18) should not be taken as an indication that the police 'failed' in a substantial minority of cases. An examination of the cases of these 17 accused reveals that 5 were not brought to the point of making a plea decision because the charges and the ultimate withdrawal of the charges served other purposes for the police. All 3 accused in one case had the 'mischief' charge against them withdrawn in exchange for an agreement from 1 of the accused to serve as a police informant. In another case a staff sergeant arranged for the withdrawal of the charge after an informant claimed that he had been unfairly dealt with. In another case there was no objection to the lawyer's request for a withdrawal of the charge because the purpose of the charge had been to justify an arrest for investigative purposes regarding other offences.

Two accused were not brought to the point of a plea decision for administrative reasons. One accused failed to appear in court and a bench warrant for his arrest remained outstanding. Another accused was subject to the withdrawal of both charges against him after the crown determined that the matter was being dealt with through the family court.

Among the other 10 accused who were not convicted, 7 were involved in cases in which there was no co-accused. In five of these cases there were apparent problems with the crown's evidence before the case went to court: a lab analysis of a substance used to justify a charge of possession of marijuana revealed that the substance was not a narcotic; a crown witness was unavailable and the judge rejected a request for a remand; a crown witness changed her mind about pursuing the complaint; the crown lacked proof of having served the suspension notice on two persons charged for driving while disqualified. In the other two cases the accused were charged with one count of theft under $200. The accused pleaded not guilty and the judges accepted their accounts at trial to justify dismissal of the charges.

The remaining three accused were involved in cases which did not result in a conviction for them, although co-accused were convicted in relation to charges arising out of the same incident. One accused did not go along with the plea agreement package accepted by his three co-accused, and the three charges against him were eventually withdrawn. One accused went to trial on an altered charge and eventually had the charge dismissed while his co-accused pleaded guilty to the original charge in a 'package' with other charges. One accused did not go along with the plea agreement package accepted by his three co-accused; one of the charges against him was dismissed and he was acquitted on the other charge.

The majority of persons not convicted either 'dealt' their way out with the police, were the victims of improperly laid charges, or were the beneficiaries of problems the crown had in organizing the evidence. Moreover, in three of the five cases where there were successful challenges at trial, the prosecution was still successful in gaining convictions on other accused involved in the incidents in question.

These findings are testimony to the fact that in the vast majority of cases patrol officers, along with other police officers who take over their criminal cases, are able to confirm their charging decisions with a conviction against somebody for something. In producing this outcome, the police have considerable control from the beginning to the end of the process. In most cases, the organization of the court is a supportive resource for the police if they choose to charge. In constantly reproducing the legitimaccy of police actions, the court gives weight to actions by police 'on the street' when they wish to threaten or use the criminal sanction as a lever for reproducing order in troublesome situations.

This is not to say that the rules of the court organization do not permeate the police organization and influence police actions. It is not our contention that the courts will take serious abuse by the police, but neither will they seriously abuse the police by routine inquiry into practices. Similar to their use of the structural resources and rules available to them in other spheres, the police use the court organization to accomplish their work as they see it.

The criminal law apparatus functions both symbolically and pragmatically to ease the patrol officer's work. Very often the patrol officer decides that he does not need to use criminal charges in dealing with suspects. Sometimes his symbolic authority, backed up by the perceived *possibility* that he *could* invoke the criminal sanction, is sufficient for putting things 'in order.' Sometimes other aspects of the criminal law, such as the enabling legal provisions for searches and other investigative checks, are sufficient as a tool to assert his authority over suspects he simply wants to 'shake up' and put in order (.e.g. proactive stops of 'pukers'). When the patrol officer does decide that criminal charges are in order, he can be reasonably assured that he will be backed up by the authority of the court through the way it is organized. He can use the charges either to get something else he wants or to have his earlier decisions affirmed by getting a conviction on something against somebody.

Police patrol officers are very rational actors operating within a very rational framework. Their work helps to reproduce this framework: what they do is influenced by what others have done before them and influences what others might do next. Our remaining task in this report is to use our research findings to make a concluding statement about what police patrol work is, in relation to where it has come from and where it might be going.

7

Conclusions and Implications: Some Comments on Constructive Policing

In this final chapter I 'raise' our findings to a different level in order to comment upon the role of policing in contemporary society. I initially document and consider the construction of organized police forces as a major force in Canadian society. I then review our findings, in conjunction with those of other researchers, to assess what is produced by this force. This in turn leads me to question the basis for the construction of policing and to suggest some constructive alternative strategies for an orderly existence.

Constructive Policing

As our research has shown, patrol officers are able to use strategically the resources of forums (police, legal/court, community) that make up their working environment. They use these resources skilfully to make the complex simple and to make the ambiguous definite in justifying a particular course of action. Indeed, they are so good at this that they help to make their own work routine, bringing on boredom and alienation. A situation with many possible interpretations, each with many possibilities for investigation, is transformed into one interpretation and one course of action that is routinely accepted by all parties concerned. The glass menagerie of social life remains intact; social order is reproduced.

The police organization is also accomplished in using the enabling features of the community to broaden its mandate and to secure the resources of power necessary to continue existing mandates. The move has been away from local control to a national and international standard of bureaucratic professionalism[1] in a general climate where the bureaucratic organization and professional imagery have become the standard for all large-scale operations. In short, police workers, and the bureaucracies they man, have constructed their spheres of operation in ways similar to other types of workers and organizations.

As we have argued, the patrol officer making his decisions on the street, and the police force on whose behalf he operates, are not reproducing their *own* order. Rather, they reproduce their own sense of order as it is filtered through to them via the organizational forums within which they operate. However, their key position as interpreters and translators of what is happening on the street, and of citizen-initiated troubles, gives them considerable influence over the constitution and reconstitution of what becomes generally accepted as 'order.' Whether routinely reacting to alarm calls and complaints of property crime or keeping 'pukers' and other marginal types in order, the patrol police are working on behalf of the 'higher orders' by keeping the 'lower orders' in their place. That is an essential aspect of what policing, and especially patrol policing, are about.

Police control in constituting what or who is a problem from among the wide range of offending and offensive behaviour at all levels of society is linked to police control over what gets known about their activities and the activities of those against whom they operate. The more generally accepted the police definition of the problem, the more easily the police can acquire power resources (legal, ideological, fiscal). The 'selling' job exploits the prevailing myths about the 'lower orders' to gain power resources, while concealing the basic conflicts and contradictions at the heart of the problems they dramatize. While not alone, the police force is instrumental in ensuring that currents of opinion about 'lawandorder' are stirred into tidal waves, and that their organization rides along at the crest of the waves to gain maximum advantage.

As mentioned in chapter 1 the public police in Canada have experienced a dramatic expansion of their resources.[2] In the period of 1971 to 1977 local governments increased their spending on police from approximately $337 million to $923 million (+174 per cent), provincial governments from approximately $159 million to $404 million (+154 per cent), and the federal government from approximately $199 million to $556 million (+179 per cent). Going back to 1961 and examining growth in spending up to the 1977–78 fiscal year, provincial spending increased almost twelvefold (approximately $34 million to $404 million), and federal spending increased more than elevenfold (approximately $49 million to $556 million).[3] The growth of spending on the police has far outstripped inflation.

The number of police officers in Canada has increased from about 28,000 in 1962 to more than 52,000 in 1977. This represents an increase in rate from 1.5 to 2.3 per 1,000 population. The total number of police personnel (including civilian employees) has increased from approximately 32,500 in 1962 to more than 65,000 in 1977, or from 1.7 to 2.8 per 1,000 population. In sum, the growth in police manpower is expanding much faster than the rise in the general population.

In face of this expansion of the police enterprise, one must consider what product is rendered. We have described and analysed this product in great detail in one police jurisdiction. We can use these findings, and relate them to other research, to make some comments on what is being constructed.

Evaluating Police

The arguments for expanding police resources are usually formulated in terms of the effect upon crime. Again borrowing from research reported in more detail elsewhere (Chan and Ericson, 1981: especially 51–3), we find that the number of reported crimes per police officer per annum in Canada has increased from 30 in 1962 to 45 in 1977, yet the number of persons charged per officer per annum has remained stable at approximately 14 throughout this period. The increase in the number of police has produced more crime-occurrence reports (cf McDonald, 1969). A levelling off of the crime – police ratio in the mid-1970s coincides with a levelling off of police strength.

There are a number of possible explanations for the relative stability in the ratio of the numbers of persons charged to the number of police during a period of increased crime reporting. Police officers may be diverting more suspects without charging. Most of the increase in reported crime is for property crimes, which have a relatively high probability of being recorded but a low potential for clearances. The police may be recording more petty occurrences. In turn, this may reflect the increasing bureaucratization of police forces with their specialized division of labour regarding investigation, whereby the patrol branch is encouraged to record matters rather than settle them informally or investigate them.

In any case, the 'crime problem' will not be alleviated by expanded police resources; indeed, fear of crime, given statistical information on reported crime, will likely lead to continued upward spirals of police expenditure and employment. The arguments will continue that each new force member, and each new technological aid, form the additional mortar needed to shore up the dyke that holds back the tidal waves of crime.[4] When crime remains 'high' or 'increases' in official terms, there is typically no search elsewhere for explanations. Rather, the fervour is renewed to the point where most people accept that it is better to be drowned by a flood of policing than by a wave of crime.

The 'crime problem' will also not be alleviated because the criminal law is used by the police as but one option in their more general mandate for reproducing order. The level of crime will vary by such things as legal changes which ease or hamper the use of criminal law as an option, as well as the existence of particular problems of 'order' the police decide to 'crack down' on by using the criminal law.[5] As we have argued, policing is concerned with the reproduction of order, and the criminal law is just one of the powerful resources available to police officers in the accomplishment of their tasks. The criminal law is always there as a background resource, part of the officer's 'office.' It contributes to the 'symbolic stick' of the office and helps to ensure that the officer's decisions will normally 'stick' whether or not the law is actually invoked. Its enabling provisions (e.g. regarding checks and searches after proactive stops on suspicion) provide an excuse to intervene in the lives of people who are deemed to be in need of a reminder of their place within the 'order of things.' This 'ordering' is the goal, although from the officer's perspective, in some circumstances, the product can be enriched by getting a charge against the offensive person. In *using* the law, patrol officers are very sensitive to the fact that it is no more than a tool, albeit an essential one, for producing other products from their labours.

As discussed in chapter 1, the research on 'police effectiveness' tends to disprove that the main effect of increasing police presence on the streets is crime prevention and law enforcement. As our research and other research show, the patrol police spend very little time on criminal-law enforcement. Moreover, the stress in our work is that the criminal law is only one *means* used to achieve the wider end of 'ordering' the population. In light of this, evaluating the build-up of police resources in terms of crime rates, arrest rates, and clearance rates is to assess one means, one tool of the police, but not how that tool fits in with many others in the production of a broader goal. It is like measuring a teacher by the number of essays and type of essays he assigns his students, rather than looking at what those essays are supposed to produce, or why the essay method was used instead of examinations, a dissertation, a series of tests, or nothing at all. In some instances researchers concerned with 'effectiveness' end up reproducing 'goal displacement' practices of the bureaucracies they are studying, i.e. the means are substituted as the goals, and consumers are 'blinkered' in relation to wider goals and the issues associated with them (cf Connidis, 1978).

In summary, the police sell themselves as crime fighters but do not spend much time on this activity per se. Rather, they spend their time ordering the population in ways which sometimes include the use of the criminal law. However, even when the criminal law might be usable it is often not used because the officer decides it is not relevant, possible, or necessary to do so. Moreover, when the criminal law is invoked the number and nature of charges are not clear-cut. Rather, charges are laid and cases constructed in a way that maximizes options, especially for securing a conviction on *some*thing.

We have found both quantitative and qualitative data useful. The former provide an overview of what patrol police produce in particular types of encounters with particular types of people, while the latter instruct us about the process of production. In evaluating patrol policing as we conceive it, it is especially important to have qualitative data because there is no other way of capturing the relevance of factors, including the criminal law, in any given situation, or of depicting organizational elements which affect this activity.

Furthermore, these qualitative data sharpen our understanding of the limitations of a quantitative approach. Researchers frequently spend hours in huge police and court dossiers selecting scores of factors to be related to decision-making or checkoff a multitude of factors they observe in transactions between citizens and the police. However, the police, along with other agents of crime control (and indeed decision-makers in all bureaucratic organizations), tend to look for a few situational cues to use in reaching an outcome they see as just and justifiable. For example, the defence lawyer, police officer, and crown attorney will spend a few seconds or a few minutes verbally working out a plea settlement, with perhaps casual reference to a tiny proportion of the court dossier. The dossier makes available a wide range of options and justifications for action, but the decision-making involves this availability only as a back-drop, and a back-up, to what is worked out verbally.

Beyond the narrow view of police work as crime work, one can see that the presence of police officers has become an end in itself, whether they merely are seen driving around the streets or proactively or reactively intervene in the lives of others. They *are* 'the law,' they represent order, they embody law and order.

This role may be a feature more of Canadian society than of most other Western industrialized countries. In the public's imagination, if not by official pronouncement, a police force (the 'Mounties') has been elevated to the status of a national symbol. 'The Mountie symbolizes not merely law and order, but Canada itself' (Peter Newman, quoted in Brown and Brown, 1973: 127). A postcard available to be sent far and wide to represent Canadian Life pictures two Mounties in the foreground flanking the Peace Tower of the federal Parliament Buildings in the background. The perspective is such that the Mounties are as tall as the Peace Tower, and broader. On the back we read: 'In the foreground, the scarlet uniforms of the legendary Royal Canadian Mounted Police, truly symbolise the strength and unity of Canada.'[6] Our predecessors long ago recognized the role of the police in terms of order first, and law second. We have inherited a tradition of order – then law if it is useful to the forces of order.[7] The RCMP has evolved into a centralized force with almost one-third of the total public police manpower in Canada. Moreover, as revealed by recent commissions of inquiry into their operations, members of the RCMP have taken seriously the mandate of order first, and law second – if at all (cf Mann and Lee, 1979). Similar to the police officers we have studied, and others have studied, they are 'practical' men first and foremost.

In mobilizing the police, citizens seek the use of police power. When citizens call the police, they very frequently regard police presence as an end in itself. They have defined a situation as 'out of order,' and they want the authority of the police officer as one powerful resource to assist them in putting things back in order. Just as the officer uses his symbolic authority as an implied threat, citizens can threaten or actually use the same authority by mobilizing the police to handle their troubles.

Regardless of how he is mobilized, once the patrol officer enters the encounter he effectively takes over. He is deferred to as the 'authority' in handling troubles, and his actions are rarely challenged.[8] He decides whether troubles will be made into police property (cf Christie, 1977; Ericson, 1981). He also can transform a conflict among private citizens into the property of the state by using the criminal law to define it as an offence against the state.

While he is searching for cues within the encounter, the officer is also bringing to the encounter the framework provided by the police organization. For example, as we learned in chapter 5, particular types of complaint (e.g. property) are likely to be dealt with through official channels (submission of occurrence reports), while other complaints (e.g. interpersonal) are likely to be dealt with by informal advice or various 'cooling out' strategies without official reporting. Particular types of people tend to make particular types of complaints (e.g. lower-status women in interpersonal complaints; middle-status men in property complaints), and official reporting differs, as do the chances that the complaint will receive further attention. The action taken is framed by the rules of the police and legal organizations. Even if a report is taken, it is formulated to serve particular police organizational needs as well as, and sometimes over, the needs of the complainant. Citizens' needs are very often met through actions by patrol officers (including actions that do not entail official reporting), because they coincide with the police organization's needs as articulated through the patrol officer.[9]

When reports are taken which designate something as a 'crime,' or when charges are laid which designate someone as a 'criminal,' it often reflects *on the surface* no more than the 'secretarial' function of patrol officers. A shoplifter is turned over by a store employee and is duly issued an appearance notice. An automobile accident is reported, and the damages to each car are duly noted on the accident report. A CPIC check reveals that a driver is disqualified from driving, and he is duly processed. However, *underlying* all of this is the control of information which is in the hands of the patrol officer. As I have shown in numerous case examples, acts of ommission and commission in the construction of reports are aimed at altering the course of a case, while the officer secures something else potentially useful to the police. In most of these cases, the officer's power lies in his control of information. However, this is not *his* power: most of the formulations he uses to justify his decisions, or to cover other realities of the case, are derived from a reservoir of legitimations within the police organization.

In some circumstances, the patrol officer may decide that formal action is needed to handle a situation or to punish summarily someone who is offensive. A report might be taken to 'cool out' disputants, giving the appearance that something is being (or will be) done. A charge might be made to remind an individual and others looking on about the *finality* of police authority. In these circumstances, the officer uses organizational resources to assert final control over a situation and to reproduce the authority of his office. In these circumstances, and in most others he confronts, he finds that his organizational environment is conducive to accomplishing his goals: it is 'made to order.'

If the goal of patrol policing were to record crime and to enforce the law against criminals, then one would expect more of both activities. In the force we studied, there are monthly production levels for occurrence reports and charging activities. Yet, there were very many occasions on which officers did not stop people when they could have, did not investigate alternative leads when they could have, did not record a complaint when they could have done so, recorded complaints with interpretations which excluded equally reasonable alternative interpretations, did not charge when they could have done so, charged for some offences and in some categories but not others, and so on. In light of these variations, it is extremely difficult to sustain the argument that patrol work has 'crime' and 'criminal' activity as its primary goal. The goal is much broader than this: it is 'ordering' the population in all of the senses we outlined in chapter 1 and documented in later chapters. Order is first, and law exists to be used selectively where it is strategically valuable to reproduce order. In this respect, campaigners for 'lawandorder' have got their ordering wrong: it should read 'order, and law.'

In our data, this 'ordering' function is particularly apparent vis-à-vis the many citizens stopped after a proactive mobilization. Many were 'marginal': young, male, of lower socio-economic status. Officers could predict fairly accurately the types most likely to be engaged in 'normal crimes.' In the lottery of investigative payoffs, officers know on whom to lay their bets. Even when there is no charge, the officer uses procedural laws (e.g. regarding searches) or other investigative procedures (e.g. CPIC checks; questioning) to remind the citizens involved that he is 'the Law.'

Constant proactive stops are a not-so-subtle way of reminding marginal people of the 'order of things.' Here, symbolic authority is paramount: for this reason, demeanour becomes a very important variable. The person deemed 'respectable-respectful' will nearly always avoid the full range of actions, while his opposite must endure personal and property searches, detention for CPIC checks, and the possibility of minor charges as an 'ordering' device. From the officers' perspective, it is a nice bonus to uncover a bit of 'grass' or an outstanding warrant. However, they are rarely disappointed when this does not happen because they know that their actions, while ostensibly geared to law enforcement, are of quite a different order.

Obviously, the targeted population of 'marginals' will vary according to the community concerned. In the urban core of Philadelphia as studied by

Rubinstein (1973), the target is lower-class individuals (many of whom are black) who engage in marginal vice activities (pimps, prostitutes, bootleggers, numbers dealers). In the rural prairie region of Canada, the target is lower-class people (many of whom are native Indians) who use and abuse liquor and other drugs. In the jurisdiction we studied, the target is lower-class young persons ('pukers') who may be involved occasionally in drug and property-related offences and who appear to some as offensive. Regardless of the community, some group will always be targeted.

If this sounds very Durkheimian (Durkheim [1964]; Erikson [1966]), that is precisely the view I wish to convey. When a relatively wealthy community is equipped with a healthy complement of police officers, its health will be defined in terms of very wide 'moral boundaries.' These broad definitions will allow its patrol officers to spend their time doing such things as flitting about from tree to tree in public parks trying to ferret out youths sipping a liquid which the same patrol officers, along with a wide range of the public, imbibe in great quantities at other times and places.

Obviously the police force, and the legal apparatus which supports it, are not concerned with equality among everyone. In some respects they may attempt to reproduce equality among equals, although even on this level there may be organizational elements, or situated elements in specific contexts, which lead to differential treatment.

Patrol officers are well aware of the structured inequality of systems of rules because of the system that is used to control their behaviour (see chapter 3; also Mann and Lee, 1979: especially chapter 9; Ericson, 1981a). Line officers can always be 'targeted' if a superior deems it 'in order' to do so. Patrol officers realize that when they 'blow the whistle' on a marginal suspect it is no different than when a superior officer 'blows the whistle' on them: it is a 'status-enforcing ritual' aimed at reproducing the 'order of things.' However, just as the suspect knows perhaps that he has committed many more acts than those made into 'crimes' by the police, and that there are many more people whose behaviour could be made into 'crimes' if they were caught, so the officer recognizes that enforcement against occupational misdeeds represents only the (rather arbitrary) tip of the iceberg. From the viewpoint of those at the bottom end, it could be far worse, although it might also be better. Enforcement can never do more than chip away at the surface; but it does produce a 'semblance of power' that in turn reproduces a sense of order.

Crime rates and clearance rates will inevitably vary among jurisdictions according to the organization of the community and the organization of the force. As we have learned, a single element in the police organization can greatly influence crime rates and clearance rates. If there is a strict division of labour between the patrol police and detectives in investigation, one can expect higher rates of recorded occurrences and lower rates of clearance. Multiple charging may arise to clear as many occurrences as possible by charge when the opportunity presents itself; it not only strengthens the prosecution's 'levering' position to secure a plea settlement, but also improves the productivity record of the officer and his force.

As the previous chapters testify, there are numerous organizational elements that can compound, and confound, the production of police business and how that business is concluded. From the 'controlological' (Ditton, 1979) position, the social construction of crime is seen as heavily influenced by the police force and its members as they interpret and use their organizational frameworks. It is they who make a crime a crime, a 'puker' a 'puker,' a domestic assault complaint a 'domestic.'

If we recall our definition of discretion as power for autonomy in decision-making, we must conclude that individual patrol officers, and the force on whose behalf they operate, have very substantial discretionary power. This power is located in legal rules, police administration rules, the occupational culture, and the organization of the court, which enable them to proceed against certain types of people and certain types of trouble. It is also located in the aura of the police office, which emits authoritative waves that are usually translated unquestionably into deference by the public. All of this is protected by the control of information; this is the core of police power, permitting the other elements we have identified to be even more 'enabling' than they might otherwise be.

Of course, we do not argue that when patrol officers are possessed of a free will, they can always exercise it in a free way. They are bounded organizationally in a series of hierarchical structures. In their efforts at reproducing order, they must negotiate, manipulate, and coerce that order (Strauss, 1978) against those who have other ideas and different interests. 'Society may be seen as a vast negotiated order constantly reproducing itself through a myriad of strategies and interpretive procedures ... [but this] negotiated order is a stratified one' (Plummer, 1979: 113–14). In terms of the operations of formal social control agencies, there are many levels within this hierarchy and a constant search for autonomy and control both among these agencies and within each agency. The controllers are in the business of controlling their officially designated clientele of citizens; they also seek control of each other.

In evaluating policing, this complex process of social control must be examined and understood. Included in this process are the citizens who become involved either willingly (e.g. as complainants) or unwillingly (e.g. as suspects). Who controls what these agencies and their agents are up to? What are the resources of control? Where do these resources come from? How are they used? How are they countered? The provision of adequate answers to these questions is a very difficult task indeed, but attempts must be made if one wishes to go on to ask: whose order is being reproduced?

In our research, we have examined one police force at one time to answer questions about social control, the controls that controllers place upon each other, and the role of these controls in the ordering of the population. The view that has emerged is that the police are a considerable force in shaping community order as well as the ordering of criminal cases through the criminal process. Equipped as they are with enormous organizational, legal, and community-support resources, one could hardly expect otherwise. What remains puzzling is why these resources, and the power they bring, have burgeoned on the scale documented earlier.

Justifying Policing

As we have emphasized repeatedly, the police seek to justify their resources by crime control. In arguments for more manpower, more equipment, and more enabling legislation, the formulation is always in terms of the 'war on crime.' Yet, the literature on 'effectiveness' suggests that more resources do not bring less recorded crime and better rates for the apprehension of suspects. More fundamentally, most of the patrol officer's time is not devoted to 'crime work', criminal designations are a means, not an end, of police work; and, as but a tool of police work, criminal designations are made according to influences upon, and within, the police force as a bureaucratic organization.

Given this, one can assume that the construction of policing involves much more than technical questions related to the production and control of crime. If it were simply a technical question, the weight of the evidence would suggest decreasing the size of police forces. However, we have experienced dramatic increases, so that in a community such as the one we studied police officers spend much of their time doing nothing – perhaps on the dubious assumption that crime is being prevented merely by their presence on the street – or 'hassling' marginal people who are offensive to those who want *their* streets clean (and perhaps their selves cleansed). In times of relative prosperity the populace is apparently content to leave the community's 'dirty work,' such as street 'cleaning,' to well-paid help. That way, both whoever is being cleaned up and those who do the job are kept at a distance. It appears as if few people even care to know what is, and is not, going on; indeed, the lack of questioning helps them to enjoy the *feeling* of security that comes from taking for granted that all is in order.

Beyond this, the construction of policing is only a part of wider social, moral, and political forces which perpetuate both crime and punitive reaction to it. The police, along with other forces of order, are merely beneficiaries of the politics of 'lawandorder.' Other areas of the punishment industry receive similar levels of resource support. For example, we have arrived at a state where the federal penitentiary service now looks after an equal number of employees and inmates (cf Friedenberg, 1980, 1980a; Chan and Ericson, 1981).

The police can easily justify additional resources, including the latest in protective headgear, because they have a solid populist constituency among the 'hard hats' of 'decent working people.' These people have a great stake in the status quo because they have invested their very lives in it. In relation to them, the politics of 'lawandorder' is part of 'the politics of resentment.' According to people who analyse this politics (e.g. Friedenberg, 1975, 1980, 1980a; Gaylin et al, 1978) these individuals are apparently frustrated by the imprisonment of conformity within the status quo. Conformity yields payouts which they judge to be meager; the payouts are assessed relatively and thus prove insatiable. These people take out their frustrations against those contained in the criminal prisons, and against all others who do things, however vaguely defined, which suggest that they are gaining pleasure outside conventional channels. For these conventionals, it is better to seek the painful channels of convention and to avoid pleasures. For this reason, they support the construction of an elaborate apparatus aimed at ensuring that those who seek to experience disreputable pleasures and to avoid pain will eventually, and often repeatedly, suffer pain that more than cancels out their pleasures. Moreover, it seems that people are willing to support the construction of this apparatus at all costs.

For the sake of a public sense of order, something must appear to be done even if nothing is actually done, or if what is done is not publicly known or even has identifiable negative consequences. Perhaps that is why the news media typically do nothing more than reproduce the popular myths about crime, its explanations, and control (cf Chibnall, 1977; Hall et al, 1978; Taylor, 1980). This mythology is so dominant that even when a major crisis erupts, and the media help to reveal systematic structural flaws in control agencies, public support for the police remains strong. This is clearly evident in the continuing revelations about the wide net of illegal practices cast by the RCMP (see Mann and Lee, 1979). In spite of repeated revelations about illegal practices against legitimate political groups, illegal opening of the mail, illegal trespasses and thefts in private premises, and the manufacturing of news stories to serve its own interests, the RCMP still maintains its popularity in public opinion polls (ibid). Indeed, some politicians have responded to this exposure by calling for legislation to legalize previously illegal practices and for a reassertion of authority within the administrative structure of the RCMP.

As Friedenberg (1980, 1980a) points out, this type of response is typical of the Canadian reaction to any crisis in authority: 'The solution for the failure of authority is more authority ... But authority is a powerful depressant and extremely addictive. Like other tranquilizers, authority is prescribed to solve problems that have been misstated initially, and whose real roots it cannot touch and serves, in fact, to obscure.' More power, including fiscal and legal resources, are placed in the hands of those working in the control organizations. In times of exposure, there are few if any calls for more procedural protections for citizens subject to police investigation. Changes are made to the procedural law and other structures of legitimation to lubricate further the control machinery. More fundamental questions about protection under legal due process (cf Hagan and Leon, 1977, 1980) and greater freedom of access to information are rarely asked, let alone answered. Crime is a matter of social, economic, cultural, and political forces beyond the control of any agency, or all governmental agencies combined.

While the construction of policing is justified in terms of crime control, the true role of the police is the ordering of the population. It is in this broader context that we have studied patrol policing and must question its fundamental assumptions.

Questioning Policing

In questioning the construction of policing, two points must be kept in mind. First, as I have previously stated, the police force is like other bureaucracies which have taken advantage of an enabling climate. One can point to many examples in the past two decades, including the expansion of community colleges and universities in the 1960s. The operation of prisons has many parallels with policing. The report of a parliamentary committee on the Canadian penitentiary service documents the fact that prison does not work in terms of various criteria of effectiveness, and then goes on to recommend the development of new prisons and new ways for controlling those they contain (MacGuigan, 1977). Modes of control have been formulated in terms of benefit to the individual and the community, but the real benefits accrue to those hired to implement the controls (Ellis, 1979; Friedenberg, 1980; see also Ericson, 1974, 1978; Burtch and Ericson, 1979; Chan and Ericson, 1981). The police are not alone in their constructive tendencies.

Second, we must keep in mind that the police can, and do, perform many valuable functions. We have enough evidence of what it was like in London before 1829 (Downes, 1979: 12–13), and of the extent to which the 'lower orders' prey on each other (Ennis, 1967), to know that substantial reduction in police power in the absence of other established sources of control can have very unfortunate consequences (Scull, 1977). Moreover, the history of alternative forms of power and changes in the structure of power (Foucault, 1977; Ignatieff, 1978) instructs us that what initially appears as a 'new' and 'deeper' understanding of social control, which will permit a more rational and just system, can be transformed into a base for exercising more power. This danger has been pointed to by critics of 'diversion' schemes and self-policing systems within selected communities (Ericson, 1977; Cohen, 1979a; Matthews, 1979; Chan and Ericson, 1981). Arguments made by both 'new conservative' (e.g. Wilson, 1975; Newman, 1974) and 'new left' (e.g. Taylor et al, 1973, 1975) criminologists can be criticized for perpetuating views and attendant policies not sufficiently sensitive to this danger (cf Cohen, 1979: especially 46).

With these two points in mind, we can question policing in terms of allocation of resources. We must ask if the patrol police are using their resources appropriately.

In our research, we found that the bulk of the patrol officer's time was spent doing nothing other than consuming the petrochemical energy required to run an automobile and the psychic energy required to deal with the boredom of it all. If he decided to initiate encounters, these were very often directed at the dirty work of 'street cleaning' 'pukers,' 'bikers,' and other 'marginal' types. While this work may serve to order the population, it hardly brings personal dignity to anyone involved. The question remains whether this work is worth doing with such intensity, if at all.

In recording 'crime,' we found that patrol officers were much more likely to record property complaints than, especially, interpersonal complaints. Most accused in cases under the Criminal Code and the Narcotics Control Act were essentially involved in property disputes (25), driving complaints (19), or 'public order' police-initiated charges (17); only 6 were in interpersonal complaints (mostly weapon offences and threatening telephone calls), and 6 in 'possession of marijuana' charges alone. Much of this work entailed recording and/or charging for petty crime, especially petty property crime,[10] often in situations that required no more than routine detailing of the 'facts' for administrative purposes. The great bulk of the work was not about serious threats to the person; indeed, when it was about such threats (e.g. 'domestics'), it most often received a 'non-criminal' disposition.

In sum, even in their 'crime work,' patrol officers are most often ordering petty disturbances, regulating driving, and sorting out property relations. Whether such large resources should be poured into these areas is a matter of debate. If we argue strictly in terms of harm done, it is doubtful whether the massive effort is worth it.

One can imagine many areas of far greater importance than most tasks performed by the patrol police. For example, any insurance agent knows that the value of claims for fire damage and loss is many times greater than the value of claims for property-crime damage and loss – and firemen stay in their stations until they are called for service. There is much greater potential for personal harm via industrial pollution, inadequate safety standards at work, and commercial fraud (e.g. misleading advertising, improperly labelled products, etc) than anything the patrol police routinely deal with.

If policing resources are to be maintained, they might be redirected into these areas. One major reason why they are not redirected is that the police force does not have the enabling structure of law, and the courts, to back up its efforts in these areas (cf Snider, 1978). As we have seen, the patrol police have ample resources to keep the 'lower orders' in order and to deal with the recording of selected types of mainstream criminal offences. As long as the legal, court, and police administrative structures seek these targets, patrol officers will continue to aim accordingly, and other areas will be ignored.

In keeping with their professional image, police forces, like other professions, have argued that they are the experts and that they should therefore have almost exclusive control over information about their operation. Unlike in some other professions, this control is further strengthened because the police can make it legitimate by referring to 'security needs' and 'the national interest.' However, it is essential to an open debate about policing, and ultimately to an open society, to have access for researchers to police operations. Only systematic access, such as we ourselves received, will permit an informed evaluation of police resources, how they are used, and how they might be used. We require continuing research, involving the many and varied police jurisdictions in Canada, in order that we can become confident that the construction of policing is in fact constructive.

Notes

1 For example, allegations of brutality and other wrongdoings by members of the Waterloo Regional Police Force (Ontario Police Commission, 1978) and by members of the Metropolitan Toronto Police Force (Morand, 1976), and allegations of various illegalities and wrongdoings by members of the Royal Canadian Mounted Police (Mann and Lee, 1979; McDonald Commission, 1981).

2 The figures on police personnel per 1,000 population include full-time employees other than sworn police officers. Police-officer strength in 1977 was 2.3 per 1,000 population. The vast majority are uniformed patrol officers. In the police force we studied as part of the research for this book, less than 20 per cent of police-officer personnel were assigned to detective units (Ericson, 1981). In a survey of American municipal and county police departments, Chaiken (1975: vii) discovered that on average 17.3 per cent of police-officer personnel are assigned to detective units.

3 This view is the dominant one in criminology and contributes more than anything else to making that subject less than respectable academically. As Hay (1975: 24n) notes, 'Historians have accepted the assumptions of reformers, which are also those of modern criminology: that the criminal law and the police are no more and no less than a set of instruments to manage something called crime. Effective detection, certain prosecution and enlightened rehabilitation will accomplish this practical task. Criminology has been disinfested of grand theory and class purpose. Much of it has thereby become ideology.'

4 Wilson and Boland categorized 'police activity' as 'aggressive' if a city had a high volume of traffic citations, on the assumption that those highly proactive in this area are also highly aggressive in making proactive stops on suspicion. This assumption may be correct to the extent that traffic stops are also used to check out suspicions about the vehicle's occupants (see chapters 4 and 6). However, the assumption requires confirmation from first-hand observation rather than solely from police records as employed by Wilson and Boland. A higher proactive-stop rate may be characteristic of police forces that have a lack of better things to do, including a lack of serious crime, which may be explained by factors independent of the police operation. For a critique of the work by Wilson and Boland, see Jacob and Rich (1980).

5 Of course, changing the status quo will not change the structural position of the police. As E.P. Thompson (1979: 325) remarks: 'The police, as defenders of "law and order," have a vested interest in the status quo, whether the *status* be capitalist or communist, and whether the *quo* be that of Somoza's Nicaragua or Rokosi's Hungary: that is, the

occupation is one which is supportive of statist and authoritarian ideologies. And, more simply, in whatever kind of society, the police will always have good reasons for pressing for more resources, more powers, and more pay. There is nothing sinister about this, in an alert and democractic society, since, once these things are understood, proper measures will be taken to ensure that the police have adequate resources for their legitimate functions, and to curtail in the strictest way those functions which are not. This is not a new problem. It is a problem we have lived with ... for centuries.'

6 'Shagwagon' is a slang term for a van or truck that has been customized with a finished interior and is used for driving adventures as well as amorous adventures. It was a term in currency among patrol officers and youths at the time the research for this book was undertaken.

7 This perspective is within the 'social action' tradition in sociology. 'Social action' theorists emphasize the 'situated,' 'negotiated,' 'tenuous,' 'shifting' nature of social order: 'Order is something at which members of any society, any organization, must work. For the shared agreements, the binding contracts—what constitute the grounds for an expectable, non-surprising, taken-for-granted, even ruled orderliness—are not binding and shared for all time ... In short, the bases of concerted action (social order) must be reconstituted continually' (Strauss et al, 1963: 129).

8 Mennel (1974: 116–17) counsels: 'Social order is the result of some people being able to coerce others into obedience; or it rests on general agreement among the members of society; or it stems from their striking bargains with each other which are to everyone's individual advantage as well as the collective advantage. But it is unhelpful to see these viewpoints as mutually exclusive. For the sociologist, social order must be a matter for empirical investigation.'

9 Friedenberg (1975: 90–1) suggests in a different context why social problems such as crime are perpetuated through mystification instead of being potentially subject to eradication: 'Public figures in quest of power have always found it useful to exploit prevailing myths, for it is the nature of myths both to dramatize conflict – psychic and social – and to conceal that conflict's real dynamism, thus ensuring that policies based on myth will not actually remedy the situation they dramatize. The day the boulder stays at the top of the hill, Sisyphus is out of office ... The very fact that politicians must accept and promote a formulation of social problems that so distorts the underlying dynamics as to make any real assessment of it impossible simply means that the popular conception itself becomes the problem, and usually a more serious problem than the one to which it refers.'

10 As Bittner (1970: 24) observes on the effect of established court rules upon police decision-making: 'The norms observable in open court reach down and govern even the process of its evasion. In the criminal process, like in chess, the game is rarely played to the end, but it is the rare chess player who concedes defeat merely to save time. Instead, he concedes because he knows or can reasonably guess what would happen if he persisted to play to the end. And thus the rules of the end-game are valid determinants of chess-playing even though they are relatively rarely seen in action.'

11 Manning (1977, 1977a, 1980) is the leading student of this link between rules and the sense of order used by the officer to place police work in context: 'The sense of order that emerges from and is displayed in organizationally bounded encounters is in part dependent upon the rules that are called upon or invoked by participants to order the interaction. Rules, although *tacitly* understood, make salient the set of assigned features of events that interactants take into account as members-in-role. Rules are thus resources to be used tacitly by participants, and by doing so participants negotiate the limits upon organizationally sanctionable activities' (1977a: 57).

12 This point has been repeatedly stressed by Bittner (1967, 1967a, 1970). Based on his observations of patrol policing in a skid-row area, Bittner (1967a: 710) concludes: 'Patrolmen do not really enforce the law, even when they do invoke it, but merely use it as a resource to solve certain pressing practical problems in keeping the peace ... The problem patrolmen confront is not which drunks, beggars or disturbers of the peace should be arrested and which can be let go as exceptions to the rule. Rather, the problem is whether, when someone 'needs' to be arrested, he should be charged with drunkenness, begging, or disturbing the peace.'

As Bittner (1970: 109) states elsewhere, the substantive law in these circumstances is simply employed as a convenient tool without regard to abstract principles such as legality: 'In discretionary law enforcement involving minor offences, policemen use existing law largely as a pretext for making arrests ... Because persons who in the judgment of the police should be detained must be charged with something the law recognizes as valid grounds for detention, many arrests have the outward aspects of adhering to principles of legality. In point of fact, however, the real reasons for invoking the law are wholly independent of the law that is being invoked. The point to be emphasized is not that this procedure is illegal, though it often enough is, but that it has nothing to do with considerations of illegality.'

13 For a detailed analysis of the procedural criminal law in Scotland and England as it supports police practices, see McBarnet (1976, 1979, 1981). For a similar analysis in the Canadian context, see Freedman and Stenning (1977) and Ericson (1981a). See also Ratushny (1979) and chapter 6 of this book.

14 The ideal of full enforcement and the rule of law has been particularly emphasized by some American legal scholars (e.g. Goldstein, 1960; Packer, 1968). Goldstein states that it is the duty of the police to carry out the dictates of the law by investigating every situation in which a criminal-law violation is suspected, to attempt to ascertain who violated the law, and to present the relevant information to the prosecutor for his further action. He documents that many American police acts specifically state this duty of full enforcement. The related ideal of the rule of law or principle of legality means that the police as agents of the criminal law should be restricted in their power to judge and punish by explicit rules which provide a justificatory framework for action or inaction. The aim is to reduce arbitrariness in police action, allowing assessment in review of the 'justice' of their action.

As stated earlier, in Canada there are no entrenched rights which might curtail a procedural law that is enabling for the police. Moreover, there is no provincial or federal statute explicitly imposing the duty of full enforcement, and the police officer's broad duties and responsibility for following directives from both police and political superiors are emphasized (Cameron, 1974: 40). There is some contradiction between the constable's constitutional position as having an original authority in law, and his organizational position as a subordinate who must follow orders on penalty of possible legal proceedings under the Police Act, but this has apparently caused little conflict (see Williams, 1974; Gillance and Khan, 1975; Oliver, 1975; Ericson, 1981a). In Canada, there is a recognition that ours is a government of both laws and men.

15 Reviews of this literature are provided by Box (1971) and Hagan (1979). Of course, the police are only one of many occupational groups employing moral judgments about status claims as a means of assessing what actions to take. For example, the medical profession makes moral judgments in discriminating among clients seeking the use of hospital emergency services (Roth, 1972).

16 The empirical record indicates that while citizens have these resources of resistance, manipulation, and coercion, they do not often use them. Citizens routinely turn over documents to the police and provide other information without question (Ericson, 1981),

and the channel of formal complaint is not often used, especially by the 'lower orders,' who have recurrent dealings with the police (Russell, 1976). This is particularly important regarding the previously mentioned 'low visibility' of the police. The patrol officer operates with 'high visibility' to those with whom he has regular contact, but these people typically have relatively little power. They therefore have no recourse or, except in an isolated and sporadic manner, cannot mobilize resources to take action if they do have recourse.

17 For example, Steer (1970: 10) reports that the development of juvenile liaison schemes in the United Kingdom resulted in more people reporting offences to the police because they believed the police would not prosecute and might even assist the offender. The net result was an overall increase in the number of offences known to the police. Skolnick and Woodworth (1967) report on differential enforcement of statutory rape by two police forces in California; the force which gained routine access to sources in welfare agencies for family support had a dramatically higher enforcement rate than the force which did not.

18 In the case of the police, this has been particularly well documented with respect to the law of confessions and the accused's right to silence (e.g. Wald et al, 1967; Medalie et al, 1968; Chambliss and Seidman, 1971; Greenawalt, 1974; Zander, 1978). It has also been shown to happen in relation to policies and attendant rules emanating from the police administration (e.g. Chatterton, 1979; James, 1979). Examples from other organizational settings include the way in which prison guards have dealt with apparent due-process protections for inmates (Harvard Center for Criminal Justice, 1972), and the way in which school principals have circumvented attempts to control their disciplinary actions against troublesome students (Gaylin et al, 1978: 136ff).

19 The arguement can be made that while not publicly visible in the courtroom, pre-trial 'plea bargaining' sessions between counsel for the defence, police, and prosecutor take on an adversarial character (e.g. Utz, 1978). In chapter 6 I consider this point in light of our empirical data.

20 Bittner (1970: 55) summarizes the matter: 'Because the real work of the policeman is not set forth in the regulations, it does not furnish his superior a basis for judging him. At the same time, there are no strongly compelling reasons for the policeman to do well in ways that do not count in terms of official occupational criteria of value. The greater the weight placed on compliance with internal departmental regulations, the less free is the superior in censoring unregulated work practices he disapproves of, and in rewarding those he admires, for fear that he might jeopardize the loyalty of officers who do well on all scores that officially count – that is, those who present a neat appearance, who conform punctually to bureaucratic routine, who are visibly on the place of their assignment, and so on. In short, those who make life easier for the superior, who in turn is restricted to supervising just those things. In fact, the practical economy of supervisory control requires that the proliferation of intradepartmental restriction be accompanied by increases in license in areas of behaviour in unregulated areas. Thus, one who is judged to be a good officer in terms of internal, military-bureaucratic codes will not even be questioned about his conduct outside of it.'

21 Some of the leading 'effectiveness' researchers have come to appreciate the limitations of their approach and the need to address more general issues with a theoretical focus. Kelling et al (1979) stress that the effectiveness research which they and others have engaged in 'focuses on where police officers are, how fast they get there, how many of them there are, and how they are organized. For all practical purposes, none deal with what police officers do in handling incidents and what effects their actions have. It is almost as if policing were an automated vending machine of service, with officer performance discounted as a "human factor," a mere electrical noise in an otherwise perfect system.'

CHAPTER THREE: The Occupational Environment

1 In commenting upon the manuscript for this book, an administrative representative of the force studied stated that this was a low rate of proactive stops. He explained what the administration perceives as a low proactive rate in terms of the fact that at the time of the research, patrol officers did not have personal radios and thus were constrained to stay near their cars in order to keep in touch with the communications centre. The representative assured that now the patrol officers have personal radios, they are more proactive than they were during the research period. The implications of this can be gleaned from our discussion and analysis of proactive work in chapters 4, 6, and 7.

2 Alarm calls are notoriously unproductive – they are usually judged to be unfounded (false alarms). Martin and Wilson (1969: 93–4) report that in 1965 in London, England, 897 of 39,767 were 'valid' alarms. Rubinstein (1973: 353) reports that in the December 1969 to July 1970 period in Philadelphia 705 of 18,879 alarm calls were 'valid.'

3 Rubinstein (1973: 11) cites other historians of the police (Reith, 1943; Cobb, 1957; Mather, 1959) in documenting that the early London police were characterized by internal disorder. In the initial years, more than one-third were discharged annually for various forms of misconduct. The first commissioner, an army colonel, responded with efforts to instil military-style discipline and suggestions that police recruitment should be direct from the élite military regiments. In the very first 'parade' of patrol officers 'It was quite a rainy day and many of the constables arrived bearing umbrellas. Quite a few were unable to stand at attention because they had been celebrating the historic occasion by getting drunk. Rowan's [the commissioner] first general regulation forbade any man to carry an umbrella with him on duty; the second forbade drinking. Umbrellas never again posed a serious problem.'

4 The patrol officers we observed were inexperienced in policing and specialized training. Almost 40 per cent had less than three years' experience in public policing of any kind, and 71 per cent had less than three years with the force and its prior municipal counterparts. Approximately 70 per cent had no specialized police experience apart from being on general patrol. However, 45 per cent of the patrol officers had experience on other public police forces before joining the force studied, including the Metropolitan Toronto Police Force (24 per cent), other Canadian police forces (10 per cent), and United Kingdom police forces (11 per cent).

5 'Now every occupation is not one but several activities; some of them are the dirty part of that trade. It may be dirty in one of several ways. It may be simply physically disgusting. It may be a symbol of degradation, something that wounds one's dignity. Finally, it may be dirty work in that it in some way goes counter to the more heroic of our moral conceptions' (Hughes, 1951: 401).

6 As Reynolds and Judge (1969: 25ff) inform us, using production systems as a form of bureaucratic control has an established history in policing. In London, England, at the turn of this century, divisional commanders were given a financial bonus for serious crime arrests which exceeded a quota. Not surprisingly, this system encouraged commanders to make false arrests and to add illegitimate charges.

7 According to a statement dated February 1981 and sent to the researchers by the chief of police of the force studied: '[The] Force has never had a policy of setting production quotas for officers to fulfill within certain time frames. It has, in fact, been an explicit policy of this Force that no such quota system shall operate. Officers' misconceptions about the policy may have arisen at the time of the research because of the diverse training practices and policies under which officers operated in Forces prior to amalgamation and which continued to be manifested after the inception of the Regional Force. Intensive efforts by senior administrators during those early years, including the research

period, were directed towards clarifying Force policy and eliminating the predispositions of officers resultant from earlier training in other Forces. Concomitantly, officers or researchers may have misconceived the purpose of "monthly activity sheets" and *may* have, given the predisposed attitudes just noted, made erroneous assumptions that the sheets were designed as a quota register. The monthly activity sheets are, in fact, designed to record the workload and nature of the duties of uniform patrol officers including calls for service, citizen contacts of all types, man hours devoted to investigation, patrol, court, report writing, and special duties such as community relations, crime prevention, training, public lectures and escorts. It is equally as important to record traffic cautions as it is traffic charges. A "quota system", then, is contrary to the very nature of the activity sheets, with supervisors utilizing them in a way which gives the officer credit for quality policing. The number of "tics" on the sheet has never been of importance to administration. Rather, the variety and quality of activities of the officers, together with other information derived from effective supervision techniques, provide the basis for evaluation.'

As is evident from our data, patrol officers perceived a quota and believed that the monthly activity sheets were used in their personal evaluation and in platoon evaluation. Their actions reflected their perception.

8 In cross-tabulating police experience and the patrol officer's stated preference for shift activity, we found that officers with less than one year of police experience (i.e. those on probation) were more than twice as likely as more experienced officers to express a preference for traffic enforcement.

9 The Police Act RSO 1970 lists a long schedule of offences and attendant punishments and reads like a set of rules comparable to those existing in prisons and other forms of total institution (compare, for example, the Auburn rules of 1836 in Kingston Penitentiary as cited by Beattie, 1977).

Most offences have a very broad definition, allowing interpretive latitude to those who have the power to use these rules. For example, a police officer is guilty of 'discreditable conduct' if he 'acts in a disorderly manner, or in a manner prejudicial to discipline or likely to bring discredit upon the reputation of the police force' or if he 'uses profane, abusive or insulting language to any other member of a police force,' among other things. Further-more, he is guilty of 'discreditable conduct' by virtue of being found guilty under any other offence of the Police Act. He is guilty of 'insubordination' if he 'is insubordinate by word, act or demeanor.'

An officer is guilty of 'neglect of duty' if he 'without lawful excuse, neglects or omits promptly and diligently to perform a duty as a member of the police force'; 'idles or gossips while on duty'; 'fails to work in accordance with orders, or leaves an area, detachment detail or other place of duty, without due permission or sufficient cause'; 'fails to report a matter that it is his duty to report'; 'fails to report anything that he knows concerning a criminal or other charge, or fails to disclose any evidence that he, or any person within his knowledge, can give for or against any prisoner or defendant'; 'omits to make any neces-sary entry in any official document or book'; 'feigns or exaggerates sickness or injury to evade duty'; 'is improperly dressed, dirty or untidy in person, clothing or equipment while on duty', among others.

An officer is guilty of 'deceit' if he 'without proper authority communicates to the public press or to any unauthorized person any matter connected with the police force,' among others. He is guilty of 'corrupt practice' if he 'directly or indirectly solicits or receives a gratuity, present, pass, subscription or testimonial without the consent of the Chief of Police'; 'improperly uses his character and position as a member of the police force for private advantage'; 'in his capacity as a member of the police force writes, signs or gives, without the consent of the Chief of Police, a reference or recommendation to a member or former member of the police force, or any other police force', among others. He is guilty of 'Unlawful or Unncessary Exercise of Authority' if he 'is uncivil to a member of the public,' among others.

A police officer is guilty of 'Consuming Intoxicating Liquor in a Manner Prejudicial to Duty' if he '(a) while on duty is unfit for duty through drinking intoxicating liquour; or (b) reports for duty and is unfit for duty through drinking intoxicating liquour; or (c) except with the consent of a superior officer or in the discharge of duty, drinks or receives from any other person intoxicating liquor on duty; or (d) demands, persuades or attempts to persuade another person to give or purchase or obtain for a member of the police force any intoxicating liquor, while on duty.' No mention is made of other drugs.

10 In the case of the RCMP, see Mann and Lee (1979). Prisoner disturbances are handled in the same way. A few prisoners are selected out, and have their obvious biographical credentials (criminal record) used as evidence that they are capable of further disruption, thereby justifying further banishment. Alternatively, prison guards may be 'scapegoated' (e.g. MacGuigan, 1977; Ellis, 1979).

11 When asked in the abstract, patrol officers have difficulty conceiving of a segmented public. During the course of each patrol shift, the officer was asked an open-ended survey question concerning whom he felt the force was serving. 39.6 per cent of the respondents did not identify any particular group, and a further 18.4 per cent put forward the consensus notion that the police serve 'everyone' in the community. Many had a problem with this question and were unable to conceive abstractly of a segmented community served in different ways by the police. Among those who did identify particular groups, the 'middle class' was most frequently mentioned as the segment served by police efforts (23.3 per cent of the total sample). A further 10.1 per cent said they serve that segment of the community who routinely call upon their services, and 8.6 per cent said the force is self-serving, operating largely in its own self-interest rather than for the benefit of the community.

In contrast, when actually engaged in particular types of work officers do differentiate among segments of the public. For example, many complain about spending an inordinate amount of time and effort doing property checks. These checks are seen as a privileged service to the more wealthy, and in this context many officers see themselves as serving the interests of the propertied. Thus, an officer complained about property checks and alarm calls during an afternoon shift, and suggested that this task should be undertaken by private security companies or that the police should charge these businesses for the special service.

12 At the time of the research most female officers were inexperienced, many having been hired the previous year. Thus, their perceived inability to handle some aspects of patrol work may have been partly related to their inexperience.

13 The significance of this categorization for encounters with citizens is considered in detail in chapters 4, 5, and 6.

14 As outlined in chapter 1, the same observation has been made by academic researchers (e.g. Wilson, 1968: 52; Reiss, 1971: 135).

15 Rubinstein (1973: 67) observes that 'Patrolmen who refuse to sleep often speak contemptuously of their colleagues who do, but every policeman understands the desire to do it, and the obligation to work last out [midnight shift] is an important source of the feelings of solidarity that policemen share.' Rubinstein notes that sleeping on the midnight shift is also practised in industry (Dalton, 1959: 80) and in public service jobs such as hospital work (Goffman, 1961: 204).

16 For an example of this in the environment of detectives, see Ericson (1981: chapter 3). Rubinstein (1973: 119) observes, 'The collusions the men employ provide them with all the necessary cover to protect themselves from unknown ears. Revelations of laxness are almost always the consequence of some incompetence. The punishments that follow are as

much payments for failures to maintain cover as they are for violations of department regulations.'

CHAPTER FOUR: Mobilization

1 During a workshop on our research on 5 March 1980, Reiss agreed that his sampling techniques probably artificially depressed the relative amount of proactive policing. He agreed that if he had sampled as we have done, taking into account all patrol areas, days of the week, and shift periods, the rate would have been similar to ours.

2 Black (1968: 163) discusses the greater potential for conflict in proactive encounters.

3 As documented in chapters 5 and 6, the vast majority of citizens confronted by patrol officers after proactive mobilization are defined as 'suspects' rather than as 'victim-complainants.' After proactive mobilization 632 suspects were encountered, and only 40 victim-complainants. In chapter 6 we examine the investigative actions taken against these suspects (CPIC checks and searches) and consider proactive patrol work as a means of ordering the streets and keeping certain types of people in place.

4 Rubinstein (1973: 253) makes a similar point: 'Policemen also use excuses about faulty lights to get unwary owners to open their trunks. While the unwitting person is checking his wiring, the policemen can look inside and check the contents.' The issues involved in using excuses under one type of legislation (e.g. Highway Traffic Act) to justify stops and investigation for other matters (e.g. possible 'impaired' under the Criminal Code) have been addressed in a recent Ontario case *R.* v *Dedman* (1980 – Ontario Supreme Court, Maloney, J. – unreported).

5 For theoretical discussion and empirical data on the 'making' of deviance see Ditton (1977, 1979). In the case of how detectives work at 'making crime,' see Sanders (1977) and Ericson (1981).

6 According to a statement dated February 1981 and sent to the researchers by the chief of the force studied: 'The promotional policy within the Force is published in the form of a routine procedure so that all officers will understand the system and how they can compete for promotion. This system encompasses promotion from Constable to Sergeant or Detective, from Sergeant or Detective to Staff Sergeant or Detective Sergeant, and from Staff Sergeant or Detective Sergeant to Inspector. The system consists of credits being awarded in categories during the competition for a particular promotion. It is based on a maximum of 100 credits which are allocated as follows for the promotion of Constable to Sergeant or Detective: 1) Performance in the field – maximum 35 credits; 2) Meritorious service and/or self-improvement – maximum 5 credits; 3) Seniority – maximum 5 credits; 4) Experience- – maximum 5 credits; 5) Written examinations – maximum 25 credits; 6) Oral examination of the candidate – maximum 25 credits. Officer eligibility is clearly stated. The procedure then outlines how credits are earned in each category.'

   According to a force general order dated 20 September 1974 concerning the promotional system, 'performance in the field' is 'based on the performance rating that has been evaluated by the Candidate's Sergeant and the Divisional Commander's appraisal ... Notwithstanding any of the provisions of this Promotional System, the Chief of Police, may select candidates for promotion if, in the opinion of the Chief of Police it is necessary to do so, keeping in mind the exigencies of the Police Force.'

7 As noted by the two fieldworkers present, there was not a smile in the whole parade at the apparent humour of a group lined up with the left and the right at the same time.

8 As Rubinstein (1973: 249) notes, the specific cues are bound by time periods and local variations in fashion. What is suspect in one place may not be in another; what was once suspect may now be fashion. An administrative directive within the Los Angeles police department in 1959 'urged its men to be suspicious of persons wearing sneakers at night.'

9 As Taylor (1980) states, one of the 'moral panics' (Cohen, 1972) in Canada pertains to motorcycle gangs. The police help to fuel the panic by supporting claims in the media that 'bikers' are connected with organized crime. For example, Peter Moon writes in an article entitled 'The Outlaw Bikers: War Looms to Control the New Organized Crime' (*Toronto Globe and Mail*, 23 June 1979) that 'bikers' are a 'burgeoning criminal network that police rank next in power to the Mafia.' The panic is also carried into action and amplified by the everyday actions of patrol officers. They have been known to use every technique possible – including extreme forms of physical violence – to keep 'bikers' in their place, a most recent example being the case of the Waterloo Regional Police (see Ontario Police Commission, 1978).

10 Rubinstein (1973: 20) cites a 'little classic of bureaucratic optimism' expressed by August Vollmer, an American police reformer in the 1920s and 1930s: 'With the advent of the radio equipped car a new era has come ... Districts of many square miles ... are now covered by roving patrol car, fast, efficient, stealthy, having no regular beat to patrol, just as liable to be within 60 feet as 3 miles of the crook plying his trade – the very enigma of this specialized fellow who is coming to realize now that a few moments may bring them down about him like a swarm of bees – this lightening swift "angel of death." '

11 At the time of the research, damage under $200 was assessed to be unreportable under the Highway Traffic Act 1970 RSO c 202 sec 139(1). This figure was amended to $400 under the Highway Traffic Act RSO c 54 sec 17, in force 1 January 1978.

12 As recorded earlier, 66.4 per cent of 'automobile' related incidents were reactive. Both the citizen and the police are influenced by the structure of insurance arrangements that require official police reports to settle property claims.

13 Manning (1979: 7) notes that 'from dispatch studies, it is known that somewhere between 30% and 70% of all calls are handled by the dispatcher [communications officer] without sending a vehicle.' In a study of the communication officer and the dispatch process within the force studied, Jorgensen (1979) found that in a 16-hour period 210 of 313 citizen calls to communication officers resulted in a dispatch to patrol officers.

14 At the time of the research the police force studied did not use a vehicle-locator system.

15 It is possible the patrol officer did not respond to this call because of the presence of the researcher. On another occasion a dispatcher advised a patrol officer not to proceed to the scene of a reported homicide because of the presence of a researcher; there was probably a wish to avoid having the researcher placed in the position of being a witness who might be subpoenaed for a *voir dire* hearing.

16 For this and other reasons – e.g. dispatched calls to a single officer, dispatched back-up calls, and reactive calls to other officers in which an officer informs the dispatcher that he is responding also – over one-third of all reactive encounters in our sample took place outside the patrol area of the officer being observed.

17 According to the Highway Traffic Act 1970 RSO c 202 sec 82(a), 'The speed limits prescribed under this Act or the regulations of any by-law passed under this Act do not apply to a motor vehicle of a municipal fire department while proceeding to a fire or answering a fire alarm or to a motor vehicle operated by a person in the lawful performance of his duty as a police officer.' This was repealed and substituted in 1980 RSO c 87 sec 14 (in force 1 September, 1980): 'The speed limits prescribed under this section or any regulation or by-law passed under this section do not apply to ... (b) a motor vehicle while used by a person in the lawful performance of his duties as a police officer.'

18 Holzner's (1972: 167) definition of trust coincides with our usage here: '[Trust involves] the acceptance of a social relation or state of affairs as unproblematic and therefore a reliable context for action. Trust consists in the naive and unreflected acceptance of states of affairs as straight-forward and valid on the terms on which they present themselves, excluding noxious consequences ... Trust ... reduces social complexity.' Rubinstein (1973: 81, 229) discusses trust between the dispatcher and the patrol officer.

CHAPTER FIVE: Dealing with Victim-Complainants

1 In this and all subsequent discriminant analyses, cases with missing information on any variable have been excluded. In this section, the age variable has been divided into 1) those under 17 and over 24 years of age and 2) those aged 17 to 24, and the socio-economic status variable has been split into 1) middle-class and 2) lower-or working-class. Here and later the other decisions of the patrol officer are included to determine how much they contribute in the prediction and classification of the decision. We are not simply viewing them as both 'independent' and 'dependent' variables, rather, we simply wish to consider how they contribute to the classification of groups of citizens who did or did not receive given responses.

2 Sparks et al (1977: 120) report that personal injury increases the chances a victim will make a complaint to the police; also, the greater the degree of property loss, the greater the chance the victim will complain.

3 While we did consider separately victim-complainant 'special requests' of patrol officers (see Tables 5.11 and 5.12), we did not include this as an independent variable for the cross-tabulation and discriminant analyses. These requests vary greatly and cannot be reduced to two or three categories. We might have taken the requests to 'arrest a suspect' and related this variable to actions against suspects, but these requests were few (38), and we would have had to analyse separately situations in which 1) suspects were present, 2) suspects were apprehendable, 3) suspects were not apprehendable and would have been pursued, if at all, by detectives. Also, as we argue in our qualitative analysis, preferences of victims could be interpreted and transformed by officers.

4 Here and later, the dispute-type variable has been divided into 1) 'interpersonal' disputes and 2) all 'other' types of disputes (combined automobile, property, other). The age variable is split into those 1) under 16 and over 24 and 2) 16 to 24. The SES variable is divided into 1) the 'middle' and 2) the 'working/lower' group.

5 McCabe and Sutcliffe (1978: 58n) cite a Greater London (England) police force order: 'In minor cases, where the identity of the offender is known, particularly when the Police have no knowledge of the matter and it arises from a dispute between relations, neighbors etc., the Police should leave the complainant to apply for a summons and should only arrest the offender if he refuses to desist, or a breach of the peace may otherwise occur.'

6 This differs radically from much of the 'policy talk' in Canada about 'diversion' and 'violence' (e.g. Law Reform Commission of Canada, 1974, 1975). The official approach is to divert minor property complaints from the criminal process and to concentrate law enforcement and correctional attention on violence. Our data indicate that the police are much more likely to make property disputes official and 'criminal,' while dealing informally with most complaints of violence and leaving them unofficial.

7 Wiley and Hudik (1974) suggest that a citizen's co-operation depends upon the value he places on police actions and the formulations of the police officer. If the citizen is co-operative, the officer is likely to respond in kind. Sheley and Harris (1976) suggest that citizens co-operate not because of the reward for co-operation, but because they know the probable costs of not co-operating with the police.

8 Rubinstein (1973: 145) observes, 'Unfounding calls is one of the ways policemen have of reducing the amount of paper work they are obliged to do and also curbing the rate of reported crime. When a patrolman tells his dispatcher that a job is unfounded, he is claiming that his investigation has not substantiated the initial claim of the person who called for a police officer. Frequently this is the case, but often enough it is not.'

9 Several copies of official reports are made for various purposes within the police force, but a copy is not made for the complainant. The complainant may not know even whether or not a report is filed and is unlikely to know how a report is labelled or what account is constructed by the officer to justify his designations and decisions.

10 ' "Necessary paper" is defined by external pressures as much as by features of the incident. In other words, paper that is written is written at such time that one needs to show paper work. Sometimes, this action of generating the proper paper is called "covering your ass". Thus, the remarkable discretion of the officer is constantly in working tandem with the complex web of internal rules and guidelines' (Manning, 1979a: 54–5).

11 This production of accounts can be viewed as part of the micro-politics of defining deviance. Similar processes also occur on the macro- level of conflict among different interest groups (Schur, 1980: especially chapter 3).

12 According to a statement dated February 1981 and sent to the researchers by the chief of police of the force studied: 'In order to give direction to the uniform patrol officer as to the manner in which an occurrence report is labelled, he is given instruction during his recruit orientation classes as to the categories of incidents and the necessity for labelling the occurrence with the most serious offence.'

13 In other cases we observed, entries into open garages were recorded as 'break and enter' offences according to Criminal Code sec 306.

14 For example, McCabe and Sutcliffe (1978: 20n) observe: 'In Oxford and Salford ... most [written note] entries concerning domestic complaints ended with the expression "advice given". What the advice was and how it was given was not specified. The question, "What is the advice?" addressed to a number of policemen from many parts of the country who were attending a conference on police matters, seemed to require no answer since it was well understood to be a placebo if not for the complainant at least for supervisory officers.'

15 'The reaction is *constitutive* of the criminal (or deviant) act. In fact, the reaction *is* the "commission" of the act. Accordingly, the *idea* of a "dark figure" of offences committed without a reaction is an unnecessary absurdity ... So what, in *all* cases, makes an act a crime? *Control.* In sum, it is not the offend*er* who "commits" the crime: it is the offend*ed* ... "Crime" is ... *not* an activity engaged in by an offender, it is one formulated ... by others. Similarly, "criminal activity" is the activity of calling activities crimes' Ditton (1979: 20–3).

16 For detailed discussion of original and published data on the process of discovery, reporting, and recording, see Bottomley and Coleman (1979, 1980).

17 Sparks et al (1977: 155) point out in relation to their findings: 'In the case of burglary and thefts in dwelling houses ... only about one offence in five is recorded. Thus, a 5 per cent increase in the *proportion* recorded would by itself result in over a 20 per cent increase in the *numbers* recorded, which is more than enough to give the impression of a "crime wave". In the case of assaults and other thefts, the effect would be even more drastic: on our findings, a 5 per cent increase in the proportion of such offences recorded would at least treble their numbers in the police statistics, even if the total volume of offences actually committed remained unchanged.'

CHAPTER SIX: Dealing with Suspects and Accused Persons

1 Those citizens encountered reactively tended to be involved in minor traffic accidents or minor public disturbances.

2 As Rubinstein (1973: 249–50) observes, 'Most stops are made for violations of traffic regulations or to point out some fault in the car, and all of them are made under the umbrella of the patrolman's writ to check licensing, but often these reasons are incidental to his real interest ... While these stops frequently reveal infractions of the codes regulating the ownership and use of cars, these violations are incidental to the officer's interest in finding stolen cars, cars carrying contraband, illegally armed people, and persons sought by the police.' A recent legal opinion concerning stops justified for one purpose being used to investigate for other purposes is provided in *R.* v *Dedman* (1980 – Ontario Supreme Court, Maloney, J. – unreported).

3 In the vast majority of cases, the patrol officer's only knowledge about the suspect's criminal record came from a CPIC check. The fact that the majority of suspects were not checked on CPIC indicates that patrol officers most frequently decided such information was not relevant to their inquiries. In the subsequent analyses, the CPIC check is viewed as both following from particular elements (e.g. the matter in dispute and characteristics of the suspect) as well as a possible spur to other action (e.g. a source of additional information which may lead to other actions such as a search, execution of a warrant, etc). This is another example of why we have included 'other police officer actions' in examining each decision by a patrol officer (see chapter 5, note 1).

4 For *all* primary citizens encountered in both contacts and incidents, 443 CPIC checks were undertaken. For 82.4 per cent there was no information on the citizen, for 10.4 per cent criminal-record information only, and in 7.2 per cent there was a 'hit,' i.e. an outstanding warrant or indication that the person was wanted for police investigation.

5 The relatively fewer checks in the other category were in part because it includes juveniles, whose criminal records are not supposed to be listed on the CPIC system. However, the CPIC system does list outstanding bench warrants and missing-person information on juveniles.

6 The enabling aspect of the 'obstruct police' charge under the Criminal Code has been indicated in the case of *Moore* v *R.* (1979) 5 CR (3d) 289. More generally, it has been argued that procedural law as written and interpreted is so enabling for the police that the suspect is well advised to comply (cf Freedman and Stenning, 1977; McBarnet, 1981; Ericson, 1981).

7 See *The Queen* v *Wray* (1970) 4 CCC 1; Law Reform Commission of Canada (1973: 6–8); Kaufman (1974: especially 180–1).

8 These data were produced by Helder (1978: 18).

9 It is for this reason that we employ the term 'further processing' rather than 'arrest.' For a discussion of police powers of arrest, see Freedman and Stenning (1977).

10 We have included traffic charges along with other charges as 'formal actions' because

1/In some cases traffic charges are chosen by the patrol officer as a means of 'ordering' the suspect whom he judges to be 'unco-operative' or 'out of place.' This is equivalent to the use of sections of the Liquor Licence Act, the Narcotics Control Act, and the Criminal Code (e.g. 'breach of peace'; 'cause disturbance') in similar circumstances.

2/Traffic offences can have very serious consequences in terms of personal injury and property damage. Many of the Highway Traffic Act charges in incidents arose from personal injury accidents and/or accidents involving over $200 in property damage.

3/While one might argue that most traffic violations arise from negligence rather than intent, one could say the same about some Criminal Code offences, e.g. the 'shoplifter' who forgets to pay for an item. See generally Cressey (1974) for a discussion on the seriousness of traffic offences compared with criminal offences.

11 If the search did not turn up stolen property, it might still have been legitimated on the grounds of being under the authority of Criminal Code sec 103(1), which provides for search without warrant of persons, vehicles, or premises other than a dwelling house regarding prohibited or restricted weapons. Moreover, the law covers arrest and attendant investigative actions (including searches) by policemen by allowing them to take immediate action on a complaint, even if the substance of the complaint is later deemed to be unfounded, e.g. *Kennedy* v *Tomlinson et al* (1959) 126 CCC 175 Ont).

12 Fontana (1974: 169): 'The test which is common to most sections or statutes authorizing entry and search without a warrant ... is that the officers must find someone actively committing an offence. The difficulty in applying this test lies in the fact that offences are committed in a variety of ways appropriate to their nature: some offences, such as breaking and entering, or theft, may constitute a single, individual act. Other offences, such as possession of stolen goods or possession of burglary tools might constitute lengthy, continuing acts ... The problem is: How may the officer determine when he has found someone "committing" an offfence in order to exercise his right to arrest or to seize without either a search warrant or arrest?'

13 The detention of anyone for simple possession of marijuana was not usual. The typical practice was to release the suspect on an appearance notice (summons to appear in court) under the provisions of the Bail Reform Act, although in this case an additional reason that could be given for detaining the suspect was his inability to provide identification. The fact that the crown attorney subsequently agreed to withdraw the charge against this suspect may be a further indication that the police were mainly interested in detention for investigation regarding property offences.

14 Ericson (1981: chapter 6) documents that suspects in the custody of detectives rarely ask for access to a third party, and when they do they are more likely to ask for a non-lawyer (usually a friend or relative) than for a lawyer. The legal position on access to a third party is outlined by Kaufman (1974). There is no requirement for police officers to inform the suspect of the apparent right of access to a third party under the Canadian Bill of Rights, and refusal to grant access after the suspect requests it is only one factor taken into account by the courts in assessing the admissibility of any statement by the accused.

15 Based on interviews with accused persons, Ericson and Baranek (1982) record that the vast majority (38 of 39) of 'bargains' for information in exchange for apparent police leniency are initiated by the police and not the accused. This supports our observations. Other researchers have documented 'levering' practices against criminal informants, e.g. Rubinstein (1973: especially 182); Mann and Lee (1979: chapter 11). The position of the accused- (or accusable) turned-police-informant is very similar to that of the debt defaulter in relation to the bailiff (see McMullan, 1980).

16 In a separate analysis of 46 encounters in 'domestic' circumstances involving allegations of assault, Kokis (1977) finds only five resulted in police-initiated arrests and/or charges against a suspect, and that all were 'substitute charges,' i.e. not based upon the initial allegation and not dependent on testimony by a complainant.

17 In particular, I examined and used data collected by James Wilkins (mainly tape-recorded transcripts of conversations in the crown attorneys' offices), Dianne Macfarlane (tape-recorded open-focused interviews with defence lawyers), and Pat Baranek (tape-recorded open-focused interviews with accused persons). I am extremely grateful to these researchers for allowing me to use these data.

18 The power of the crown attorney to withdraw charges is discussed from a legal perspective by Gautier (1980). Lawyers' views on multiple charging and the legitimacy of withdrawn charges are discussed by Ericson and Baranek (1982) and by Macfarlane (1982).

19 Ferguson's (1972: 29) definition of 'plea bargaining' correctly adds that the accused might not have a say in the agreement. Plea bargaining is 'the process whereby the accused or someone else on his behalf makes an agreement or "deal" with the police, Crown, or judge to plead guilty to a charge in exchange for some benefit.' Ferguson sees 'withdrawal or reeduction of charges [as]... simply different forms of sentence leniency.'

Ericson and Baranek (1982) see three types of plea discussions (characterized respectively by manipulation, coercion, or negotiation), possibly resulting in plea agreements which may or may not be viewed as a 'bargain' by the accused and/or his lawyer. Interviews with lawyers indicate that most withdrawn charges represent no 'bargain' because they are part of questionable or illegitimate overcharging or are insignificant extra charges in light of the main charges. Some accused do view withdrawn charges as a 'bargain' because they were initially willing to plead guilty on all charges before their lawyers arranged some withdrawals for them, or because they believed they could have been convicted on the charges that were withdrawn if it were not for the generosity of the crown and/or the skill of their lawyers.

20 For an American counter-example which suggests friction between police and prosecutor resulting from prosecutors asserting control over police charges and negotiation of outcomes, see Neubauer (1974: especially 60ff).

21 Laskin, in *Kienapple*, stated: 'When both charges have been laid, they must be treated as alternative counts, and if an accused is convicted of rape he cannot also be convicted of unlawful sexual intercourse. There cannot be multiple convictions from the same delict against the same girl, either by virtue of the plea of *autrefois convict* in *S*.537 (1) (a) of the *Criminal Code*, or by the broader common law defence of *res judicata* preserved by *S*.7(2) of the *Criminal Code*. The latter best expresses the theory of precluding such multiple convictions where the matter is the basis of separate offences. Section II of the *Criminal Code*, barring multiple punishments arising under two or more Acts of Parliament for the same act or ommission, does not modify the scope of *res judicata* or the special pleas of *autrefois*. The relevant inquiry, therefore, so far as *res judicata* is concerned, is whether the same cause or matter (rather than the same offence) is comprehended by two or more offences. This applies equally to several counts in an indictment and to successive indictments. This usage of *res judicata* as a complete defence applies the *bis vexari* principle grounded on the court's power to protect an individual from an undue exercise by the crown of its power to prosecute.'

22 See Ericson (1981: chapter 6). In her analysis of interviews with lawyers who represented the accused in our study, Macfarlane (1979) supports the view that uniformed officers are less often than detectives involved in pre-trial discussions with lawyers. One of her lawyers explains: 'I won't say these are less important officers. These are uniform street officers [whom] I really don't know that well or deal with. And they'd be somewhat hesitant [to discuss the case]. And I wouldn't really gain any meaningful information from them. They wouldn't give me *true* discovery so to speak.'

23 Macfarlane (1979) interviewed lawyers for 75 people charged in cases generated by studies of our patrol officers and of police detectives. Lawyers for 71 per cent reported pre-trial discussions with police officers. Two-thirds of these discussions were said to have occurred prior to the proceed date and one-third on the proceed date. 85 per cent were said to be initiated by the lawyer. In 20 per cent of the discussions the lawyers believed a police officer was instrumental in producing an acceptable plea agreement. Quotations from lawyers reveal their reliance upon the police; one observed: 'The Crown attorneys change so often that they don't even know who's going to be on what case until the morning of the trial so they don't have the time to assess it, and they won't make any decision without the investigating officers.' Another said: 'As a matter of fact, there are several counsel, some senior counsel, who probably get most of it [disclosure] from the officer and never touch the crown because by the time they [counsel] get there [the crown's office] the deal is already made and the officer just rather tries to go to bat for the defence and get the deal made.'

24 See Giddens (1976: 109): 'The production of a normative order exists in close relation to the production of meaning; what the transgression *is* is potentially negotiable, and the manner in which it is characterized or identified affects the sanctions to which it may be subject. This is familiar, and formalized, in courts of law, but also pervades the whole arena of moral constitution as it operates in day-to-day life.'

25 Similar relationships, with similar ends, exist in other areas of law. For example, McMullan (1980) reports that in Montreal 'an informal network of close and regular contacts between creditors, collectors, lawyers, bailiffs, and judge exists. There are two basic reasons why this informal network is operative among collection specialists. First, it permits the debt collection agents to work out in advance economical rates of payment ... [Second, there is] increased production output. Legal proceedings may be ignored or obtained post facto.' In the case of insurance-claim settlements out of court (80 to 90 per cent of all settlements), see Ross (1970). In the case of 'negotiations' in non-legal arenas of organizational life, see generally Strauss (1978).

26 Accused 3 was unrepresented and had a later separate trial at which he was found not guilty on one charge after the other charge was dismissed. The written statement of

confession he had given to the police was ruled by the judge to be inadmissible on the grounds that it was given under the threat of prolonged detention.

27 Here the lawyer is indicating that a plea to the 'possession of stolen property' charge implies an 'automatic' withdrawal of the theft charge. As discussed earlier, it is legally possible to gain a conviction on both. However, the 'implicit bargain' in this jurisdiction is to withdraw one in exchange for a guilty plea to the other.

28 In this case the accused was charged with two counts of 'obstruct police' after having alledgely obstructed two different police officers during the same incident. The crown attorney attempted to proceed to trial on both counts, but the judge ordered one charge dropped because they both came from the same set of circumstances.

CHAPTER SEVEN: Conclusions and Implications

1 See Fogelson (1977), Cain (1979). As documented in chapter 1, centralization has been the trend in Canada.

2 This growth is documented in greater detail by Chan and Ericson (1981: especially 45–54, 82–7); they also develop a model to explain the increasing numbers subject to criminal control and the attendant expansion of the crime-control industry. The rapid expansion of policing in the private sector is documented and discussed by Shearing, Farnell, and Stenning (1980), and by Shearing and Stenning (forthcoming).

Some theorizing about this expansion of crime control (especially in Britain with the election of the Conservative party in 1979) suggests that it reflects the role of the state in keeping people in 'working order' during a time of fiscal crisis. While the public sector cuts back in health, education, and welfare in the hope of stimulating the private sector, it requires a greater regulatory and coercive role from the crime-control apparatus (e.g. Matthews, 1979; Taylor, 1980).

Contrary to the tendency toward expansion in Britain and Canada, the city of Detroit announced in the summer of 1980 that 690 officers (18 per cent of its patrol force) were being laid off for fiscal reasons (*New York Times*, 7 September 1980). Perhaps massive unemployment in the automobile and related industries could not be met by extensive cuts in health and welfare in a city so dependent upon this industry. The health and welfare systems may be the most convenient means of ordering the population.

3 Because local governments did not subdivide police, court, and correctional spending until 1971, data for earlier periods are not available.

4 For an example of this form of argument, see the leading editorial 'More Metro Police Needed' in the *Toronto Star*, 21 January 1981. This editorial followed a series of articles describing the 'crime problem' and the difficulties of police in face of it.

5 For example, one night's worth of raids on four Toronto bathhouses netted more than 250 accused charged as 'found-ins' in 'common bawdy houses', 20 accused charged with keeping a 'common bawdy house,' 14 drug charges, and 11 further accused arrested during a public demonstration held the following night to protest the raids. See Toronto *Globe and Mail*, 7 February 1981.

6 'Mounties at the Peace Tower, Parliament Buildings, Ottawa, Ontario, Canada,' printed and published by John Hinde Ltd, County Dublin, Republic of Ireland!

7 For example, Penner (1979: 113) cites a debate in Parliament in 1922 in which J.S. Woodsworth moved that the RCMP should not police the provinces because, according to the constitution, the administration of justice is a provincial matter. In response, the Liberal minister of militia and defence stated in parliament: 'Speaking technically, on absolutely legal or constitutional grounds, my honourable friend is right that the provinces ought to look after the maintaining of order within their several territories ... I agree that constitutionally my honourable friend is absolutely right, but in working out the affairs particularly

of a new country, we are not always safe in adhering to the letter of the constitution. Sometimes we even have to violate almost the letter of the law, to be practical.'

8 Complainants are undoutedly aware of the weakened position they face if they object to the way in which the agent they mobilize is exercising power on their behalf. A challenge is likely to lead to a further loss of support from the patrol officer, or even an alteration in the complainant's status to that of 'suspect.' The police force can be as ominous for the complainant seeking redress as it is for the suspect who feels that all is not in order with the way he has been treated. In a recent English case, a high court jury awarded £100 damages and costs against a citizen who had lodged an official complaint of harassment against a Chesire constable, had his complaint 'unfounded' by the complaints-investigation team of the Chesire police, and then was subject to a civil-libel action taken out by the constable. The chairman of the Police Federation is quoted as saying, 'We are very pleased with the decision and we will be looking to this case for guidance for what to do in the future in similar cases' (*Guardian*, 6 January 1979).

9 Police officers are skilful at producing satisfaction among victim-complainants, even if the latter know little or nothing about how their complaints are dealt with. Several studies have discussed the public-relations function of interviews with victim-complainants and how police officers produce satisfaction with their actions among the citizenry (e.g. Greenwood et al, 1975; Sanders, 1977). Other studies have documented the degree of satisfaction achieved. Knudten et al (1976) report that approximately 80 per cent of victims interviewed in their Milwaukee survey 'who had contact with the police indicated that they were generally either "satisfied" or "very satisfied" with the handling of their cases by the police.' Hagan (1980) reports on a survey of victim-complainants in the same jurisdiction as our research: 'Before court, 89.0 per cent of the victims felt the police did a good job; after court, 85.0 per cent continued to rank the job done by the police as good.' How this favorable attitude is accomplished in the work of patrol officers is evident from our discussion in chapter 5. (In the case of detectives, see Ericson [1981: chapter 5]).

10 The emphasis on property crime is reflected in the reports of Statistics Canada for the entire country. Each year, approximately three-quarters of all persons charged, convicted, and incarcerated in Canada have been so dealt with for offences against property. Less than 11 per cent are charged, convicted, and incarcerated for offences against the person. A Toronto survey by Waller and Okihiro (1978) found the average amount taken in residential 'break, entry and theft' to be under $300.

Bibliography

Alschuler, A. 1968 'The Prosecutor's Role in Plea Bargaining,' *University of Chicago Law Review* 36: 50–112

Arnold, T. 1962 *The Symbols of Government*. New York: Harcourt, Brace and World

Asworth, A. 1976 'Some Blueprints for Criminal Investigation,' *Criminal Law Review* 594–609

Ayres, R. 1970 'Confessions and the Court,' in A. Niederhoffer and A. Blumberg, ed *The Ambivalent Force*. Waltham, Mass.: Ginn, pp 274–8

Balbus, I. 1973 *The Dialectics of Legal Repression*. New York: Sage

Baldwin, J. and McConville, M. 1977 *Negotiated Justice: Pressures to Plead Guilty*. London: Martin Robertson

Banton, M. 1964 *The Policeman in the Community*. London: Tavistock

Bayley, D. and Mendelsohn, H. 1969 *Minorities and the Police: Confrontation in America*. New York: Free Press

Beattie, J. 1977 *Attitudes towards Crime and Punishment in Upper Canada, 1830–1850: A Documentary Study* Toronto: Centre of Criminology, University of Toronto

– 1981 'Administering Justice without Police: Criminal Trial Procedure in Eighteenth Century England,' in *Proceedings of A Symposium on the Maintenance of Order in Society*. Ottawa: Canadian Police College

Bensman, J. and Gerver, I. 1963 'Crime and Punishment in the Factory: The Function of Deviancy in Maintaining the Social System,' *American Sociological Review* 28: 588–98

Berger, P. and Luckmann, T. 1966 *The Social Construction of Reality: A Treatise in the Sociology of Knowledge*. Harmondsworth: Penguin

Biderman, A. et al. 1967 *Report on a Pilot Study in the District of Columbia on Victimization and Attitudes Toward Law Enforcement and Administration of Justice: Field Surveys I*. Washington, DC: United States Government Printing Office

Bittner, E. 1967 'Police Discretion in Emergency Apprehension of Mentally Ill Persons,' *Social Problems* 14: 278–92

- 1967a 'The Police on Skid Row: A Study of Peace Keeping,' *American Socio-logical Review* 32: 699–715
- 1970 *The Functions of the Police in Modern Society*. Rockville, Md.: NIMH
- 1974 'A Theory of the Police,' in H. Jacob ed *The Potential for Reform of Criminal Justice*. London: Sage, pp 17–44

Black, D. 1968 'Police Encounters and Social Organization: An Observation Study,' PhD dissertation, University of Michigan
- 1970 'Production of Crime Rates,' *American Sociological Review* 35: 733–48
- 1971 'The Social Organization of Arrest,' *Stanford Law Review* 23: 1087–1111
- 1972 'The Boundaries of Legal Sociology,' *Yale Law Journal* 81(6): 1086–1110
- 1976 *The Behavior of Law*. New York: Academic Press

Blumberg, A. 1970 'The Practice of Law as a Confidence Game: Organizational Cooptation of a Profession,' in A. Niederhoffer and A. Blumberg, ed *The Ambivalent Force*. Waltham, Mass.: Ginn, pp 279–92

Blumer, H. 1969 *Symbolic Interactionism*. Englewood Cliffs, NJ: Prentice-Hall

Bordua, D. 1968 'The Police,' in D. Sills ed *International Encyclopedia of Social Science*. New York: Free Press, pp 174–81

Bottomley, A. 1973 *Decisions in the Penal Process*. London: Martin Robertson

Bottomley, A. and Coleman, C. 1979 'Police Effectiveness and the Public: The Limitations of Official Crime Rates.' Paper presented to the Cambridge Conference on Police Effectiveness, Cambridge, England, 11–13 July
- 1980 *Understanding Crime Rates*. Farnborough: Saxon House

Bottoms, A. and McClean, J. 1976 *Defendants in the Criminal Process*. London: Routledge and Kegan Paul

Box, S. 1971 *Deviance, Reality and Society*. New York: Holt, Rinehart and Winston

Breck, W. 1977 'Response Time Analysis: Executive Summary.' Kansas City, Missouri, Police Department

Brogden, M. 1977 'A Police Authority – the Denial of Conflict,' *Sociological Review* 25: 325–49

Brown, L. and Brown, C. 1973 *An Unauthorized History of the R.C.M.P.* Toronto: James Lewis and Samuel

Bruyn, S. 1966 *The Human Perspective in Sociology*. Englewood Cliffs, NJ: Prentice Hall

Bryant, D. 1974 *Deviant Behavior: Occupational and Organizational Bases*. Chicago: Rand McNally

Buckner, H. 1970 'Transformations of Reality in the Legal Process,' *Social Research* 37: 88–101

Bunyan, T. 1976 *The Political Police in Britain*. London: Julian Friedman

Burtch, B. and Ericson, R. 1979 'The Control of Treatment: Issues in the Use of Prison Clinical Services,' *University of Toronto Law Journal* 29: 51–73

Cain, M. 1973 *Society and the Policeman's Role*. London: Routledge and Kegan Paul
- 1979 'Trends in the Sociology of Police Work,' *International Journal of the Sociology of Law* 7: 143–67

Cameron, N. 1974 'The Control of Police Discretion,' Draft manuscript, Centre of Criminology, University of Toronto. 91 pp

Carlen, P. 1976 *Magistrates' Justice*. London: Martin Robertson

Chaiken, J. 1975 *The Criminal Investigation Process. Vol. II: Survey of Municipal and County Police Departments*. Santa Monica: Rand Corp.

Chambliss, W. and Seidman, R. 1971 *Law, Order and Power*. Reading, Mass.: Addison-Wesley

Chan, J. and Doob, A. 1977 *The Exercise of Discretion with Juveniles*. Toronto: Centre of Criminology, University of Toronto

Chan, J. and Ericson, R. 1981 *Decarceration and the Economy of Penal Reform*. Toronto: Centre of Criminology, University of Toronto

Chappell, D. et al. 1977 'A Comparative Study of Forcible Rape Offenses Known to the Police in Boston and Los Angeles,' in D. Chappell et al *Forcible Rape*. New York: Columbia University Press, pp 227-44

Chatterton, M. 1973 'A Working Paper on the Use of Resources – Charges and Practical Decision-Making in Peace-Keeping.' Paper presented to seminar on the sociology of police, Bristol University

– 1976 'Police in Social Control,' in *Control without Custody*. Cropwood Papers, Institute of Criminology, University of Cambridge

– 1979 'The Supervision of Patrol Work under the Fixed Points System,' in S. Holdaway (ed) *The British Police*. London: Edward Arnold

Chevigny, P. 1969 *Police Power*. New York: Vintage

Chibnall, S. 1977 *Law and Order News*. London: Tavistock

Christie, N. 1977 'Conflicts as Property,' *British Journal of Criminology* 17: 1-15

Clark, J. and Sykes, R. 1974 'Some Determinants of Police Organization and Practice in Modern Industrial Democracy,' in D. Glaser *Handbook of Criminology*. Chicago: Rand-McNally, pp 455-94

Clarke, R. and Heal, K. 1979 'Police Effectiveness in Dealing with Crime: Some Current British Research,' *The Police Journal* 52(1): 24-41

Cobb, B. 1957 *The First Detectives*. London: Faber and Faber

Cohen, P. 1979 'Policing the Working-Class City,' in B. Fine et al *Capitalism and the Rule of Law*. London: Hutchinson

Cohen, S. 1972 *Folk Devils and Moral Panics*. London: MacGibbon and Kee

– 1979 'Guilt, Justice and Tolerance: Some Old Concepts for a New Criminology,' in D. Downes and P. Rock ed *Deviant Interpretations*. Oxford: Martin Robertson

– 1979a 'The Punitive City: Notes on the Dispersal of Social Control,' *Contemporary Crises* 3: 339-63

Coleman, J. 1973 'Loss of Power,' *American Sociological Review* 38: 1-17

Comrie, M.D. and Kings, E.J. 1975 'Study of Urban Workloads: Final Report.' Home Office Police Research Services Unit (unpublished)

Connidis, I. 1978 'A Theoretical Development of Social Systems Analysis and an Examination of its Applicability to the Criminal Justice System.' PhD dissertation, Department of Sociology, University of Toronto

Cook, K. 1977 'Exchange and Power in Networks of Interorganizational Relations,' *The Sociological Quarterly* 18: 62-82

Cordner, G. 1979 'Police Patrol Work Load Studies: A Review and Critique.' Unpublished paper, Michigan State University

Cox, S. et al. 1977 *The Fall of Scotland Yard*. Harmondsworth: Penguin

Cressey, D. 1974 'Law, Order and the Motorist,' in R. Hood ed *Crime, Criminology and Public Policy*. London: Heinemann, pp 213–34

Cumming, E. et al. 1970 'Policeman as Philosopher, Guide and Friend,' in A. Niederhoffer and A. Blumberg ed *The Ambivalent Force*. Waltham, Mass.: Ginn, pp 184–92

Dalton, M. 1959 *Men Who Manage*. New York: Wiley

Davis, K. 1969 *Discretionary Justice*. Baton Rouge: Louisiana State University Press

Ditton, J. 1977 *Part-Time Crime*. London: Macmillan

– 1979 *Controlology: Beyond the New Criminology*. London: Macmillan

Douglas, J. 1971 *American Social Order*. New York: Free Press

Downes, D. 1979 'Praxis Makes Perfect: A Critique of Critical Criminology,' in D. Downes and P. Rock ed *Deviant Interpretations*. Oxford: Martin Robertson, pp 1–16

Durkheim, E. 1964 *Rules of Sociological Method*. Trans S.A. Solovay and John H. Mueller. New York: Free Press

Ellis, D. 1979 'The Prison Guard as Carceral Luddite: A Critical Review of the MacGuigan Report on the Penitentiary System in Canada,' *Canadian Journal of Sociology* 4: 43–64

Ennis, P. 1967 *Criminal Victimization in the United States: A Report of a National Survey*. Washington DC: United States Government Printing Office

Ericson, R. 1974 'Psychiatrists in Prison: On Admitting Professional Tinkers into a Tinkers' Paradise,' *Chitty's Law Journal* 22(1): 29–33

– 1975 *Criminal Reactions: The Labelling Perspective*. Farnborough: Saxon House

– 1977 'From Social Theory to Penal Practice: The Liberal Demise of Criminological Causes' *Canadian Journal of Criminology and Corrections* 19: 170–91

– 1978 'Penal Psychiatry in Canada,' in W. Greenaway and S. Brickey ed *Law and Social Control in Canada*. Scarborough: Prentice-Hall, pp 105–17

– 1981 *Making Crime: A Study of Detective Work*. Toronto: Butterworths

– 1981a 'Rules *for* Police Deviance,' in C. Shearing ed *Organizational Police Deviance*. Toronto: Butterworths

Ericson, R. and Baranek, P. 1982 *The Ordering of Justice: A Study of Accused Persons as Dependants in the Criminal Process*. Toronto: University of Toronto Press

Erikson, K.T. 1966 *Wayward Puritans*. New York: Wiley

Etzioni, A. 1961 *A Comparative Analysis of Complex Organizations*. New York: Free Press

Evans, P. 1974 *The Police Revolution*. London: Allen and Unwin

Ferguson, G. 1972 'The Role of the Judge in Plea Bargaining,' *Criminal Law Quarterly* 15: 26–51

Fishman, M. 1978 'Crime Waves as Ideology,' *Social Problems* 25: 531–43

– 1980 *Manufacturing the News*. Austin: University of Texas Press

Fisk, J. 1974 *The Police Officer's Exercise of Discretion in the Decision to Arrest: Relationship to Organizational Goals and Societal Values*. Los Angeles: UCLA Institute of Government and Public Affairs

Fogelson, R. 1977 *Big City Police*. Cambridge, Mass.: Harvard University Press

Fontana, J. 1974 *The Law of Search Warrants in Canada*. Toronto: Butterworths

Foucault, M. 1977 *Discipline and Punish: The Birth of the Prison*. Trans Alan Sheridan. New York: Pantheon

Freedman, D. and Stenning, P. 1977 *Private Security, Police and the Law in Canada*. Toronto: Centre of Criminology, University of Toronto

Friedenberg, E. 1975 *The Disposal of Liberty and Other Industrial Wastes*. New York: Doubleday

– 1980 'The Punishment Industry in Canada,' *Canadian Journal of Sociology* 5: 273–83

– 1980a *Deference to Authority: The Case of Canada*. New York: Sharpe

Gardiner, J. 1969 *Traffic and the Police: Variations in Law Enforcement Policy*. Cambridge, Mass.: Harvard University Press

Gautier, U. 1980 'The Power of the Crown to Reinstitute Proceedings after the Withdrawal or Dismissal of Charges,' *Criminal Law Quarterly* 22: 463–83

Gaylin, W. et al. 1978 *Doing Good: The Limits of Benevolence*. New York: Pantheon

Giddens, A. 1976 *New Rules of Sociological Method*. London: Hutchinson

Gilliance, K. and Khan, A. 1975 'The Constitutional Independence of a Police Constable in the Exercise of the Powers of His Office,' *Police Journal* 48(1): 55–62

Glaser, B. and Strauss, A. 1967 *The Discovery of Grounded Theory: Strategies for Qualitative Research*. Chicago: Aldine

Goffman, E. 1961 *Asylums*. New York: Doubleday

Goldstein, H. 1970 'Police Discretion: The Ideal versus the Real,' in A. Niederhoffer and A. Blumberg, ed *The Ambivalent Force*. Waltham, Mass.: Ginn, pp 148–56

Goldstein, J. 1960 'Police Discretion Not to Invoke the Criminal Process: Low Visibility Decisions in the Administration of Justice,' *Yale Law Journal* 69: 543–94

Green, B. 1970 'Race, Social Status and Criminal Arrest,' *American Sociological Review* 35: 476–90

Greenawalt, K. 1974 'Perspectives on the Right to Silence,' in R. Hood ed *Crime, Criminology and Public Policy*. London: Heinemann

Greenberg, D. 1979 *Mathematical Criminology*. New Brunswick, NJ: Rutgers University Press

Greenwood, P. et al. 1975 *The Criminal Investigation Process. Volume III: Observations and Analysis*. Santa Monica: Rand Corp.

Grosman, B. 1969 *The Prosecutor*. Toronto: University of Toronto Press

– 1975 *Police Command: Decisions and Discretion*. Toronto: MacMillan

Hagan, J. 1979 'The Police Response to Delinquency: Some Observations on a Labelling Process,' in E. Vaz and A. Lodhi ed *Crime and Delinquency in Canada*. Scarborough: Prentice-Hall

– 1980 *The Organizational Domination of Criminal Law: A Study of Victim Involvement in the Criminal Justice System*. Unpublished manuscript, Centre of Criminology, University of Toronto. 359 pp

Hagan, J. and Leon, J. 1977 'The Philosophy and Sociology of Crime Control: Canadian-American Comparisons,' *Sociological Inquiry* 47: 181–208

- 1980 'The Rehabilitation of Law: A Social-Historical Comparison of Probation in Canada and the United States,' *Canadian Journal of Sociology* 5: 235–51
Hagan, J. and Meyers, M. 1979 'Private and Public Trouble: Prosecutors and the Allocation of Court Resources,' *Social Problems* 27: 439–451
Hall, S. et al. 1978 *Policing the Crisis*. London: Macmillan
Halpern, S. 1974 *Police Association and Department Leaders: The Politics of Co-Optation*. Lexington, Mass.: Lexington Books
Harvard Center for Criminal Justice 1972 'Judicial Intervention in Prison Discipline,' *Journal of Criminal Law and Criminology* 63: 200–28
Hay, D. 1975 'Property, Authority and the Criminal Law,' in D. Hay et al *Albion's Fatal Tree*. Harmondsworth: Penguin
Helder, H. 1978 'Power Relationships and Proactive Police Searches,' Unpublished paper, Centre of Criminology, University of Toronto
Hydebrand, W. 1977 'Organizational Contradictions in Public Bureaucracies: Toward a Marxian Theory of Organizations,' *Sociological Quarterly* 18: 83–107
Hogarth, J. 1971 *Sentencing as a Human Process*. Toronto: University of Toronto Press
Holdaway, S. 1979 'Introduction,' in S. Holdaway ed *The British Police*. London: Edward Arnold
Holzner, B. 1972 *Reality Construction in Society*. Cambridge, Mass.: Schenkman
Hudson, J. 1970 'Police-Citizen Encounters that Lead to Citizen Complaints,' *Social Problems* 18: 179–93
Hughes, E. 1951 'Work and Self,' in J. Rohrer and M. Sherif ed *Social Psychology at the Crossroads*. New York: Harpers
Ignatieff, M. 1978 *A Just Measure of Pain*. London: Macmillan
- 1979 'Police and People: The Birth of Mr. Peel's "Blue Locusts," ' *New Society* (30 August): 443–5
Inbau, F. and Reid, J. 1967 *Criminal Interrogation and Confessions*. Baltimore: Williams and Wilkins
Jacob, H. and Rich, M. 1980 'The Effects of the Police on Crime: A Second Look' *Law and Society Review* 15: 109–22
James, D. 1979 'Police–Black Relations: The Professional Solution,' in S. Holdaway ed *The British Police*. London: Edward Arnold, pp 66–82
Jermier, J. and Berkes, L. 1979 'Leader Behavior in a Police Command Bureaucracy: A Closer Look at the Quasi-military Model,' *Administrative Science Quarterly* 24: 1–23
Johnson, C. 1978 'Police Discretion as Rule Governed Action.' MA dissertation, Centre of Criminology, University of Toronto
Jorgensen, B. 1979 *Transferring Trouble: The Initiation of Reactive Policing*. Unpublished research report, Centre of Criminology, University of Toronto
Juris, H. and Feuille, P. 1973 *Police Unionism*. Lexington, Mass.: Lexington Books
Kadish, M. and Kadish, S. 1973 *Discretion to Disobey: A Study of Lawful Departures from Legal Rules*. Stanford: Stanford University Press
Kaufman, F. 1974 *The Admissibility of Confessions*. Toronto: Carswell
Kelling, G. et al. 1974 *The Kansas City Preventive Patrol Experiment*. Washington, DC: Police Foundation

– 'Policing: A Research Agenda for Rational Policy Making,' Paper presented to the Cambridge Conference on Police Effectiveness, Cambridge, England, 11–13 July

Klein, J. 1976 *Let's Make a Deal*. Lexington, Mass.: Lexington Books

Knudten, R. et al. 1976 'The Victim in the Administration of Criminal Justice: Problems and Perceptions,' in W. McDonald ed *Criminal Justice and the Victim*. Beverley Hills: Sage, pp 115–46

Kokis, R. 1977 'Domestic Violence: A Study of Police Non-Enforcement.' MA dissertation, Centre of Criminology, University of Toronto

LaFave, W. 1965 *Arrest: The Decision to Take a Suspect into Custody*. Boston: Little, Brown

Lambert, J. 1970 *Crime, Police and Race Relations*. London: Oxford University Press

Larson, R. et al. 1978 'Evaluation of Phase I Implementation of an Automatic Vehicle Monitoring (AVM) System in St. Louis,' in K. Colton ed *Police Computer Technology*. Lexington, Mass.: Lexington Books

Laurie, P. 1970 *Scotland Yard*. London: Bodley Head

Law Reform Commission of Canada. 1973 *Evidence: Compellability of the Accused and the Admissibility of His Statements*. Study Paper. 42 pp

– 1974 *The Principles of Sentencing and Dispositions*. Ottawa: Information Canada

– 1975 *Diversion*. Ottawa: Information Canada

– 1976 *Criminal Procedure: Control of the Process*. Ottawa: Information Canada

Lofland, J. 1971 *Analyzing Social Settings*. Belmont, Calif.: Wadsworth

McBarnet, D. 1976 'Pre-Trial Procedures and the Construction of Conviction,' in P. Carlen ed *The Sociology of Law*. Keele: Department of Sociology, University of Keele

– 1979 'Arrest: The Legal Context of Policing,' in S. Holdaway ed *The British Police*. London: Edward Arnold

– 1981 *Conviction: Law, the State and the Construction of Justice*. London: MacMillan

McCabe, S. and Sutcliffe, F. 1978 *Defining Crime: A Study of Police Decisions*. Oxford: Basil Blackwell

McDonald Commission. 1981 *Final Report*. Ottawa: Ministry of Supply and Services

McDonald, L. 1969 'Crime and Punishment in Canada: A Statistical Test of the "Conventional Wisdom" ' *Canadian Review of Sociology and Anthropology* 6: 212–36

– 1976 *The Sociology of Law and Order*. London: Faber and Faber

Macfarlane, P.D. 1979 *Lawyering in the Lower Courts: Making the Best of Bad Cases*. Unpublished research report, Centre of Criminology, University of Toronto

– 1982 *Lawyering in the Lower Criminal Courts*. Forthcoming

MacGuigan, M. 1977 *The Report of the Sub-Committee on the Penitentiary System in Canada*. Ottawa: Information Canada

McMullan, J. 1980 'Maudit Voleurs: Racketeering and the Collection of Private Debts in Montreal,' *Canadian Journal of Sociology* 5: 121–43

MacNaughton-Smith, P. 1968 'The Second Code: Toward (or away from) an Empiric Theory of Crime and Delinquency," *Journal of Research in Crime and Delinquency* 5: 189–97

Mann, E. and Lee, J. 1979 *R.C.M.P. vs. The People*. Don Mills: General Publishing

Manning, P. 1971 'The Police: Mandate, Strategy and Appearances" in J. Douglas ed *Crime and Justice in American Society*. Indianapolis: Bobbs-Merrill, pp. 149–94

– 1972 'Observing the Police: Deviants, Respectables and the Law,' in J. Douglas ed *Research on Deviance*. New York: Random House, pp 213–68

– 1977 *Police Work*. Cambridge, Mass.: MIT Press

– 1977a 'Rules in Organizational Context: Narcotics Law Enforcement in Two Settings,' *Sociological Quarterly* 18: 44–61

– 1979 'Organization and Environment: Influences on Police Work.' Paper presented to the Cambridge Conference on Police Effectiveness, Cambridge, England, 11–13 July

– 1979a 'The Social Control of Police Work,' in S. Holdaway ed *The British Police*. London: Edward Arnold

– 1980 *The Narcs' Game: Organizational and Informational Limits on Drug Law Enforcement*. Cambridge, Mass: MIT Press

Martin, J. and Wilson, G. 1969 *The Police: A Study in Manpower*. London: Heinemann

Mather, F. 1959 *Public Order in the Age of the Chartists*. Manchester: Manchester University Press

Matthews, R. 1979 ' "Decarceration" and the Fiscal Crisis,' in B. Fine et al ed *Capitalism and the Rule of Law*. London: Hutchinson

Medalie, R. et al. 1968 'Custodial Police Interrogation in Our Nation's Capital: The Attempt to Implement Miranda,' *Michigan Law Review* 66: 1347–1422

Mennel, S. 1974 *Sociological Theory*. New York: Praeger

Meyer, J. 1974 'Patterns of Reporting Non-Criminal Incidents to the Police,' *Criminology* 12: 70–83

Miller, W. 1977 *Cops and Bobbies*. Chicago: University of Chicago Press

– 1979 'London's Police Tradition in a Changing Society,' in S. Holdaway ed *The British Police*. London: Edward Arnold

Morand, Mr Justice. 1976 *Royal Commission into Metropolitan Toronto Police Practices*. Toronto: Queen's Printer

Morris P. 1978 'Police Interrogation in England and Wales.' A critical review of the literature prepared for the UK Royal Commission on Criminal Procedure

Morrison, D. 1969 'On the Interpretation of Discriminant Analysis,' *Journal of Marketing Research* 6: 156–63

Moylan, J.F. 1929 *Scotland Yard*. London: Putnam

Muir, W. 1977 *Police: Street Corner Politicians*. Chicago: University of Chicago Press

Murphy, C. 1981 'Community and Organizational Influences on Small Town Policing.' Forthcoming PhD dissertation, Department of Sociology, University of Toronto

Neubauer, D. 1974 *Criminal Justice in Middle America*. Morristown, NJ: General Learning Press

Newman, D. 1966 *Conviction: The Determination of Guilt or Innocence Without Trial*. Boston: Little, Brown

Newman, O. 1974 *Defensible Space*. London: Architectural Press

Niederhoffer, A. 1969 *Behind the Shield: The Police in Urban Society*. New York: Doubleday

Norris, D. 1973 *Police Community Relations*. Lexington, Mass.: Lexington Books

Oliver, I. 1975 'The Office of Constable – 1975' *Criminal Law Review* 313–22

Ontario Ministry of the Attorney-General. 1975 *Annual Report*. Toronto: Queen's Printer

Ontario Ministry of the Solicitor-General. 1978 *Annual Report*. Toronto: Queen's Printer

Ontario Police Commission. 1978 *Inquiry into Police Practices in the Waterloo Regional Police Force*. Toronto: Ontario Police Commission

Packer, H. 1968 *The Limits of the Criminal Sanction*. London: Oxford University Press

Pate, T. et al. 1976 *Police Response Time: Its Determinants and Effects*. Washington, DC: Police Foundation

Payne, C. 1973 'A Study of Rural Beats,' *Police Research Services Bulletin* 12: 23–9

Penner, N. 1979 'How the RCMP Got Where It Is,' in E. Mann and J. Lee *R.C.M.P. vs. the People*. Don Mills: General Publishing, pp 107–21

Pepinsky, H. 1975 'Police Decision-Making,' in D. Gottfredson ed *Decision-Making in the Criminal Justice System: Reviews and Essays*. Rockville, Md.: NIMH, pp 21–52

– 1976 'Police Patrolmen's Offense-Reporting Behavior,' *Journal of Research in Crime and Delinquency* 13(1): 33–47

Plummer, K. 1979 'Misunderstanding Labelling Perspectives,' in D. Downes and P. Rock (ed) *Deviant Interpretations*. Oxford: Martin Robertson, pp 85–121

Pound, R. 1960 'Discretion, Dispensation and Mitigation: The Problem of the Individual Special Case,' *New York University Law Review* 35: 925

Punch, M. 1979 *Policing the Inner City*. London: Macmillan

Punch, M. and Naylor, T. 1973 'The Police: A Social Service,' *New Society* 24(554): 358–61

Quebec Police Commission. 1977 *The Fight Against Organized Crime in Quebec*. Quebec City

Ramsay, J. 1972 'My Case Against the R.C.M.P.,' *MacLean's* (July): 19

Ranson, S. et al. 1980 'The Structuring of Organizational Structures.' *Administrative Science Quarterly* 25: 1–17

Ratushny, E. 1979 *Self-Incrimination in the Criminal Process*. Toronto: Carswell

Reed, M. et al. 1977 'Wayward Cops: The Functions of Deviance in Groups Reconsidered,' *Social Problems* 24: 565–75

Reiss, A. 1968 'Police Brutality – Answers to Key Questions,' *Trans-Action* (July – August): 10–19

– 1968a 'Stuff and Nonsense about Social Surveys and Observation,' in H. Becker et al *Institutions and the Person*. Chicago: Aldine, pp 351-67

- 1971 *The Police and the Public*. New Haven: Yale University Press
- 1971a 'Systematic Observation of Natural Social Phenomena,' in H. Costner ed *Sociological Methodology*. San Francisco: Jossey-Bass
- 1974 'Discretionary Justice,' in D. Glaser ed, *Handbook of Criminology*. Chicago: Rand McNally, pp 679–99

Reith, C. 1943 *The Police and the Democratic Ideal*. London: Oxford University Press

Reynolds, G. and Judge, A. 1969 *The Night the Police Went on Strike*. London: Weidenfield-Nicholson

Rock, P. 1979 'The Sociology of Crime, Symbolic Interactionism and Some Problematic Qualities of Radical Criminology,' in D. Downes and P. Rock ed *Deviant Interpretations*. Oxford: Martin Robertson, pp 52–84
- 1979a *The Making of Symbolic Interactionism*. London: Macmillan

Ross, H. 1970 *Settled Out of Court*. Chicago: Aldine

Roth, J. 1972 'Some Contingencies of the Moral Evaluation and Control of Clientele: The Case of the Hospital Emergency Service,' *American Journal of Sociology* 77: 839–56

Royal Commission on Criminal Procedure (United Kingdom) 1980 *Police Interrogation: Research Studies 1 and 2*. London: HMSO
- 1980a *Police Interrogation: Research Studies 3 and 4*. London: HMSO

Royal Commission on the Police (United Kingdom). 1962 *Final Report*. London: HMSO

Rubinstein, J. 1973 *City Police*. New York: Farrer, Strauss and Giroux

Russell, K. 1976 *Complaints Against the Police: A Sociological View*. Leicester, UK: Milltak Ltd

Sanders, W. 1977 *Detective Work*. New York: Free Press

Schur, E. 1971 *Labeling Deviant Behavior*. New York: Harper and Row
- 1980 *The Politics of Deviance: Stigma Contests and the Uses of Power*. Englewood Cliffs, NJ: Prentice-Hall

Scull, A. 1977 *Decarceration*. Englewood Cliffs, NJ: Prentice-Hall

Shearing, C., Farnell, M., and Stenning, P. 1980 *Contract Security in Ontario*. Toronto: Centre of Criminology. University of Toronto

Shearing, C. and Leon, J. 1978 'Reconsidering the Police Role: A Challenge to a Challenge of a Popular Conception,' *Canadian Journal of Criminology and Corrections* 19: 331–45

Shearing, C. and Stenning, P. (Forthcoming) *Policing for Profit*

Sheley, J. and Harris, A. 1976 'Communication: On Police-Citizen Encounters,' *Social Problems* 23: 630–31

Silver, A. 1967 'The Demand for Order in Civil Society: A Review of Some Themes in the History of Urban Crime, Police, and Riot,' in D. Bordua ed *The Police: Six Sociological Essays*. New York: Wiley, pp 1–24

Silverman, D. 1970 *The Theory of Organizations*. London: Heinemann

Skogan, W. 1975 'Public Policy and Public Evaluations of Criminal Justice System Performance,' in J. Gardiner and M. Mulkey ed *Crime and Criminal Justice: Issues in Public Policy Analysis*. Lexington, Mass.: Lexington Books
- 1976 'Crime and Crime Rates,' in W. Skogan ed *Sample Surveys of Victims of Crimes*. Cambridge, Mass.: Ballinger Press

Skolnick, J. 1966 *Justice without Trial*. New York: Wiley

Skolnick, J. and Woodworth, J. 1967 'Bureaucracy, Information and Social Control: A Study of a Morals Detail,' in D. Bordua ed *The Police: Six Sociological Essays*. New York: Wiley, pp 99–136

Snider, L. 1978 'Does the Legal System Reflect the Power Structure? A Test of Conflict Theory.' PhD dissertation, Department of Sociology, University of Toronto

Solicitor General of Canada. 1979 *Selected Trends in Canadian Criminal Justice*. Ottawa: Communication Division, Ministry of the Solicitor General of Canada

Sparks, R. et al. 1977 *Surveying Victims: A Study of the Measurement of Criminal Victimization, Perceptions of Crime, and Attitudes to Criminal Justice*. London: Wiley

Steer, D. 1970 *Police Cautions – A Study in the Exercise of Police Discretion*. Oxford: Basil Blackwell

Stinchcombe, A. 1963 'Institutions of Privacy in the Determination of Police Administrative Practice,' *American Journal of Sociology* 69: 150–60

Strauss, A. 1978 *Negotiations*. San Francisco: Jossey-Bass

Strauss, A. et al. 1963 'The Hospital and Its Negotiated Order,' in E. Friedson ed *The Hospital in Modern Society*. New York: Free Press

Sullivan, D. and Siegel, L. 1974 'How Police Use Information to Make Decisions,' *Crime and Delinquency* 18: 253–62

Sykes, R. and Clark, J. 1975 'A Theory of Deference Exchange in Police Civilian Encounters,' *American Journal of Sociology* 81(3): 584–600

Tatsuaka, M. 1971 *Multivariate Analysis: Techniques for Educational and Psychological Research*. New York: Wiley

Taylor, I. 1980 'The Law and Order Issue in the British and Canadian General Elections of 1979: Crime, Populism and State,' *Canadian Journal of Sociology* 5: 285–311

Taylor, I. and Walton, P. 1971 'Industrial Sabotage: Motives and Meanings,' in S. Cohen ed *Images of Deviance*. Harmondsworth: Penguin, pp 219–45

Taylor, I. et al 1973 *The New Criminology*. London: Routledge and Kegan Paul

Taylor, I. et al eds 1975 *Critical Criminology*. London: Routledge and Kegan Paul

Thomas, D. 1974 'The Control of Discretion in the Administration of Criminal Justice,' in R. Hood ed *Crime, Criminology and Public Policy*. London: Heinemann, pp 139–55

Thompson, E.P. 1979 'On the New Issue of Postal Stamps,' *New Society* 50: 324–26

Turk, A. 1976 'Law as a Weapon in Social Conflict,' *Social Problems* 23: 276–92

United States National Crime Commission. 1967 *The Challenge of Crime in a Free Society*. Washington, DC: US Government Printing Office

Utz, P. 1978 *Settling the Facts: Discretion and Negotiation in the Criminal Courts*. Lexington, Mass.: Lexington Books

Van Maanen, J. 1978 'On Watching the Watchers,' in P. Manning and J. Van Maanen ed *Policing: A View from the Street*. Santa Monica, Calif.: Goodyear Publishing, pp 309–49

– 1978a 'The Asshole,' in P. Manning and J. Van Maanen ed *Policing: A View from the Street*. Santa Monica, Calif.: Goodyear Publishing, pp 221–38

Vera Institute. 1977 *Felony Arrests: Their Prosecution and Disposition in New York City's Courts*. New York: Vera Institute

Vincent, C. 1979 *Policeman*. Toronto: Gage

Wald, M. et al. 1967 'Interrogations in New Haven: The Impact of Miranda,' *Yale Law Journal* 76: 1521–1648

Waller, I. and Okihiro, N. 1978 *Burglary and the Public*. Toronto: University of Toronto Press

Washnis, G. 1976 *Citizen Involvement in Crime Prevention*. Lexington, Mass.: Lexington Books

Webster, J. 1970 'Police Task and Time Study,' *Journal of Criminal Law, Criminology, and Police Science* 61: 94–100

Weick, K. 1969 *The Social Psychology of Organizing*. Reading, Mass.: Addison-Wesley

Werthman, C. and Piliavin, I. 1967 'Gang Members and the Police,' in D. Bordua ed *The Police: Six Sociological Essays*. New York: Wiley, pp 56–98

Whitaker, B. 1964 *The Police*. Harmondsworth: Penguin

Wiley, M. and Hudik, T. 1974 'Police-Citizen encounters: A Field Test of Exchange Theory,' *Social Problems* 22: 119–27

Wilkins, L. 1964 *Social Deviance*. London: Tavistock

Willett, T. 1964 *Criminal on the Road*. London: Tavistock

Williams, D. 1974 'Prosecution, Discretion and the Accountability of the Police,' in R. Hood ed *Crime, Criminology and Public Policy*. London: Heinemann, pp 161–95

Wilson, J. 1968 *Varieties of Police Behavior*. Cambridge, Mass.: Harvard University Press

– 1975 *Thinking about Crime*. New York: Basic Books

Wilson, J. and Boland, B. 1979 'The Effect of the Police on Crime,' *Law and Society Review* 12: 367–90

Wilson, O.W. 1962 *Police Administration*. New York: McGraw-Hill

Zander, M. 1978 'The Right of Silence in the Police Station and the Caution' in P. Glazebrook ed *Reshaping the Criminal Law*. London: Stevens, pp 108–19

Index